The Complete Guide to Spotting Accounting Fraud & Cover-Ups:

Everything You Need to Know Explained Simply

By Martha Maeda

With Foreword By Thomas M. Neches, CPA

THE COMPLETE GUIDE TO SPOTTING ACCOUNTING FRAUD & COVER-UPS: EVERYTHING YOU NEED TO KNOW EXPLAINED SIMPLY

Library of Congress Cataloging-in-Publication Data

Maeda, Martha, 1953-
  The complete guide to spotting accounting fraud & cover-ups : everything you need to know explained simply / by Martha Maeda.
     p. cm.
  Includes bibliographical references and index.
  ISBN-13: 978-1-60138-212-2 (alk. paper)
  ISBN-10: 1-60138-212-X (alk. paper)
  1. Accounting fraud. 2. Corporations--Accounting--Corrupt practices. I. Title. II. Title: Complete guide to spotting accounting fraud and cover-ups.
  HF5636.M34 2010
  364.16'3--dc22
                              2009050823

Printed in the United States

PROJECT MANAGER: Melissa Peterson • mpeterson@atlantic-pub.com
PEER REVIEWER: Marilee Griffin • mgriffin@atlantic-pub.com
ASSISTANT EDITOR: Angela Pham • apham@atlantic-pub.com
INTERIOR DESIGN: Samantha Martin • smartin@atlantic-pub.com
FRONT & BACK COVER DESIGNER: Jackie Miller • millerjackiej@gmail.com

Printed on Recycled Paper

We recently lost our beloved pet "Bear," who was not only our best and dearest friend but also the "Vice President of Sunshine" here at Atlantic Publishing. He did not receive a salary but worked tirelessly 24 hours a day to please his parents. Bear was a rescue dog that turned around and showered myself, my wife, Sherri, his grandparents Jean, Bob, and Nancy, and every person and animal he met (maybe not rabbits) with friendship and love. He made a lot of people smile every day.

We wanted you to know that a portion of the profits of this book will be donated to The Humane Society of the United States. *–Douglas & Sherri Brown*

The human-animal bond is as old as human history. We cherish our animal companions for their unconditional affection and acceptance. We feel a thrill when we glimpse wild creatures in their natural habitat or in our own backyard.

Unfortunately, the human-animal bond has at times been weakened. Humans have exploited some animal species to the point of extinction.

The Humane Society of the United States makes a difference in the lives of animals here at home and worldwide. The HSUS is dedicated to creating a world where our relationship with animals is guided by compassion. We seek a truly humane society in which animals are respected for their intrinsic value, and where the human-animal bond is strong.

Want to help animals? We have plenty of suggestions. Adopt a pet from a local shelter, join The Humane Society and be a part of our work to help companion animals and wildlife. You will be funding our educational, legislative, investigative and outreach projects in the U.S. and across the globe.

Or perhaps you'd like to make a memorial donation in honor of a pet, friend or relative? You can through our Kindred Spirits program. And if you'd like to contribute in a more structured way, our Planned Giving Office has suggestions about estate planning, annuities, and even gifts of stock that avoid capital gains taxes.

Maybe you have land that you would like to preserve as a lasting habitat for wildlife. Our Wildlife Land Trust can help you. Perhaps the land you want to share is a backyard— that's enough. Our Urban Wildlife Sanctuary Program will show you how to create a habitat for your wild neighbors.

So you see, it's easy to help animals. And The HSUS is here to help.

2100 L Street NW • Washington, DC 20037 • 202-452-1100
www.hsus.org

TABLE OF CONTENTS

Chapter 8: Financial Statement Fraud   171

Chapter 9: Detecting Accounting Fraud Within an Organization   205

Chapter 10: For Investors: Detecting Financial Statement Fraud in Public Financial Statements   229

Chapter 11: Detecting Seven Types of Financial Statement Manipulations   251

 # FOREWORD

Accounting fraud is everywhere.

According to the *2008 Report to the Nation on Occupational Fraud & Abuse*, prepared by the Association of Certified Fraud Examiners, organizations in the United States lose 7 percent of their annual revenues to fraud. Applied to the projected 2008 U.S. gross domestic product, this 7 percent figure translates to approximately $994 billion in fraud losses annually.

As a certified public accountant and certified fraud examiner specializing in financial litigation, I encounter fraud on a daily basis. I got into the fraud investigation business 23 years ago when I was asked to help the receiver appointed by the Securities & Exchange Commission figure out how to return what was left of $70 million stolen from 5,000 investors, mostly elderly, retired couples. The fraudsters operated a "Ponzi" scheme using the facade of a bank. Typical of Ponzi schemes, fictional investments were offered to investors, in this case phony commodities, arbitrage trading, and gold mines. In fact, investors were paid "profits" using money collected from new participants because there were no profits from actual investments. In this case, the duped investors fared far better than most victims of such scams: On average, we were able to return $.30 for every dollar the victim invested.

Of course, most frauds do not involve millions of dollars. Small businesses are especially vulnerable to accounting fraud. I have lost track of the number of times I have heard the defrauded small business owner say, "I can't believe they the money. They worked for me as my (bookkeeper, office manager, secretary, assistant, or controller) for (5, 10, 15, or 20) years. I trusted them completely."

Who commits accounting fraud? How much do they steal? How do they do it? How are they caught? Here are some fascinating statistics:

- The median loss caused by a financial statement fraud* is $2,000,000.
- The median loss caused by an occupational fraud† is $175,000.
- Occupational fraud is most often committed by the accounting department (29 percent) or upper management (18 percent).
- The most common occupational fraud scheme in small businesses is the submission of invoices for phony goods or services, or for personal expenses (29 percent).
- Nearly all perpetrators are first-time offenders (93 percent).
- Most frauds are detected by tips (42 percent) or by accident (30 percent).
- The typical fraud lasts two years from inception to detection.

---

* Financial statement fraud involves the intentional misstatement or omission of material information from an organization's financial reports.

† Occupational fraud involves the use of one's occupation for personal enrichment through the deliberate misuse or misapplication of the employing organization's resources or assets.

What can an employee, business owner, or investor do to prevent or uncover accounting fraud? It can be hard to find out; most books about fraud are written by experts for experts. In *The Complete Guide to Spotting Accounting Fraud & Cover-Ups*, Martha Maeda provides simple and clear explanations of important accounting fraud issues using terms easily understood by the novice. She also supplies numerous case studies, data sources, and results of surveys valuable to the professional fraud investigator.

Directed primarily at the layperson, this book provides a comprehensive overview of accounting fraud both in large corporations and in small businesses. You will learn who perpetrates accounting frauds, the different types of frauds committed, and how these frauds are accomplished. You also will learn basic steps you can take to detect fraud after it has occurred (for example, simply noticing that an employee previously in financial difficulty now appears to be living beyond his or her means) and to avoid fraud in the first place (for example, requiring that the person who signs the checks not be the person who reconciles the bank statements).

One of the most important messages of *The Complete Guide to Spotting Accounting Fraud & Cover-Ups* is that while accounting fraud is rampant, if you are armed with the knowledge found in this book, you can protect yourself and your investments against fraud and maximize your chances of success in the dangerous world of business.

—*Thomas Neches*

About Thomas Neches:

Thomas Neches, managing partner of Thomas Neches & Company LLP, provides accounting, financial, business valuation, and statistical analyses to assist attorneys involved in litigation. Neches has testified as an expert in state and federal courts in Arizona, California, Florida, Missouri, Nevada, New York, and Oregon. He is a certified public accountant, accredited in business valuation, a certified valuation analyst, and a certified fraud examiner. He received his bachelor's degree in mathematics from University of California, San Diego, and his master's degree in operations research from UCLA.

Thomas Neches, CPA, CFE

Managing Partner

Thomas Neches & Company LLP

609 South Grand Avenue, Suite 1106

Los Angeles, California 90017-3848

E-mail: tmn@thomasneches.com

Web site: **www.thomasneches.com**

Telephone: 213-624-8150

Facsimile: 213-624-8152

Mobile: 213-448-7750

INTRODUCTION

Fraud — the theft of assets from a company or individual through the manipulation and abuse of legitimate processes — exacts a heavy price every year. The cost of fraud cannot be measured simply in dollars; the damage it causes extends far beyond victims' bank accounts. No one can measure lost opportunity, the effect of negative publicity on a company's reputation, the human toll of anguish and stress, the decline in employee morale when a fraud is discovered, and the effect on our economy when investors lose confidence in the stock market. In 2009, high-profile fraud cases like the Ponzi schemes of Bernard Madoff and Arthur Nadel vividly illustrated the harm done to investors who placed their trust in these apparently successful money managers — and then discovered that their money had never been invested at all. News stories featured 90-year-olds being forced by necessity to work in supermarkets, elderly people losing their homes because their life savings were gone, and wealthy retirees suddenly finding themselves unable to pay their electricity bills. Charities were forced to curtail their services, lay off staff, and even close their doors forever as their funds evaporated. Almost every day, there are stories in the media about dishonest employees who have robbed their organizations of hundreds of thousands of dollars. Not so well-publicized are the count-less smaller thefts occurring every day from cash registers, warehouses, and business bank accounts. Sadly, the organizations that have the most to lose — small businesses, family-run companies, churches, and charities — are often the most vulnerable because of their size and inexperience.

Ponzi scheme

A Ponzi scheme is an investment scam in which money from new investors is used to pay off earlier investors and hide the fact that no investment is being made at all. Although Ponzi schemes have existed in some form for centuries, they are named after Charles Ponzi, an Italian immigrant who perpetrated a notorious scheme that duped 40,000 investors from 1919 to 1920. A Ponzi scheme requires a constant stream of new investors and is destined to collapse when payouts exceed available funds. A pyramid scheme is a more complex form of Ponzi scheme in which the perpetrator employs "feeders" who recruit increasing numbers of new investors.

Fraud has existed since commerce began and will continue to occur as long as there is something to be gained by it. Financial fraud is often referred to as "occupational fraud" because it involves abuse of the responsibilities associated with a job or occupation. Professional fraud examiners responding to a survey conducted by the Association of Certified Fraud Examiners (ACFE) estimated that in 2007, U.S. businesses and organizations lost 7 percent of their annual revenues because of occupational fraud. Seven percent of the projected U.S. Gross Domestic Product (GDP) for 2008 would amount to approximately $994 billion in losses. Fraud could be taking place anywhere, in any organization, at any time. It is in the interest of all businesses to discourage would-be perpetrators from committing fraud and to detect fraud quickly when it does occur.

Fraud weakens the economy. Government regulators are increasingly concerned with preventing and detecting fraud in publicly traded companies because the proper functioning of the U.S. capital markets depends on the reliability of financial statements. Corporate executives are concerned with fraud prevention not only because fraud causes immediate financial losses, but because it can result in costly litigation and penalties. Public exposure of fraud within an organization destroys investor confidence and drops the value of company stock. Business owners must control and prevent fraud to avoid loss of revenue and ensure the business remains viable. When a business loses money because of fraud, its investors lose not only their dividends, but the profit they could have earned if that stolen money had instead been invested in improving and expanding the business.

When deciding whether to invest in a company, investors rely on financial statements to evaluate the financial stability of a company and its potential for future growth. Fraudulent financial statements rob investors by artificially inflating the prices at which they buy shares of company stock and by misleading them into investing in a failing business. Though government regulations mandate honesty in the financial statements of publicly traded companies, individual investors bear the responsibility of protecting themselves by carefully examining these statements for signs of fraud or deception.

Many business managers are under the mistaken impression that fraud can be prevented by implementing a strict system of financial controls, inventory checks, and regular audits. But fraud, by nature, is difficult to detect because it often involves exploitation of just such a system by those who know best how to circumvent it. Even when strict controls are in place, company employees are so thoroughly familiar with any weaknesses in company procedures that they are able to disguise their illegal activities, at least for a period of time. Dishonest employees will always seek new ways to take advantage of their positions for personal gain. The detection and prevention of fraud is much more than a mathematical exercise; it incorporates elements of psychology, common sense, and intuition.

Though no scientific evidence is available yet, many experts believe that recent developments in technology have increased the likelihood and occurrence of fraud. The introduction of computerized supply-chain programs, Internet banking, and computerized financial and inventory systems has provided new opportunities for cyber-theft and increased the incidence of credit card fraud. In addition, easy access to online gambling and pornography has strengthened the possibility that a company employee will be embroiled in financial difficulties and become motivated to commit fraud. The ability to buy and sell stocks online has greatly increased the number of individuals who manage their own investments and are therefore vulnerable to manipulations of stock prices. At the same time, some of these technological developments have made it easier to investigate fraud by creating electronic trails of bank transactions, and to detect it by automatically monitoring large quantities of data for irregular activity.

The first chapters of this book explore occupational fraud, the circumstances under which it occurs, and the ways in which it is detected. The second part discusses various types of fraud including asset misappropriation, fraudulent disbursements, and corruption, and how each one can be detected and prevented. The chapters that follow will help both senior management and investors detect financial statement fraud. The last chapters in the book discuss fraud prevention: how to conduct a fraud risk assessment, establish a code of ethics for an organization, and create a corporate "culture" that discourages illegal activity. Learn how to establish strong internal controls, conduct a fraud investigation when irregularities have been discovered, and decide when you need the services of a professional fraud investigator. You will also learn how technology is being used to monitor accounting systems and detect fraud. Throughout the book, you will find "Straight from the Headlines" sections, which recall real-life examples of fraud cases. Case studies by professionals highlight some of the current concerns in the rapidly-developing field of fraud detection and prevention.

This book is intended to familiarize you with all aspects of fraud detection and prevention and give you basic knowledge to help protect your financial assets. If you are dealing with a large-scale fraud case or one that might have serious legal implications, and need to seek professional assistance, this book will prepare you to communicate effectively with fraud investigators, auditors, and lawyers. At the end of the book, you will find a list of resources for further research.

CHAPTER 1

Defining and Measuring Fraud

The legal definition of fraud contains four elements: It is intentional, involves falsification of records or information regarding some material point, misrepresents the truth, and causes harm to its victim(s). Fraud can harm a victim materially by causing financial losses, or in other ways, such as rigging the results of an election, damaging a person's reputation, or misleading a person into making a bad decision based on erroneous information. Accounting fraud encompasses a variety of activities that cause economic harm to customers, businesses, and business owners (including investors). It includes theft and embezzlement, corruption, use of company resources for personal benefit, and the willful misrepresentation of a company's financial status.

Fraud prevention is an element of every organization's accounting procedures and business policies. In order to use their resources effectively in implementing fraud prevention measures, managers and executives need to be able to assess risk, identify weaknesses, and set priorities. Fraud is difficult to measure and quantify because it occurs in such a variety of forms, and because it is largely hidden. No one knows how many cases of fraud remain undiscovered. When a fraud is detected, many companies choose not to prosecute the perpetrator, preferring to settle out of court or impose their own disciplinary measures, rather than attract negative attention in the media. Various academics and professional associations have conducted studies of fraud, but often this research is not updated on a regular basis. In 1995, the Association of Certified Fraud Examiners (ACFE) began collecting data from its members and presenting it at regular intervals in a *Report to the Nation on Occupational Fraud and Abuse*. These reports can be found online at **www.acfe.com/resources/publications.asp?copy=rttn**. Though this report includes only a representative number of cases, it provides a valuable snapshot of the incidence of fraud by industry, company size, and occupation. It also reveals how fraud is detected, how organizations respond to fraud, and the effect of internal controls on the detection and on the length of time that frauds continue before being discovered.

Association of Certified Fraud Examiners

In his book, *Corporate Fraud Handbook: Prevention and Detection*, Joseph T. Wells, an accountant and criminologist, describes how discussions with sociologists and criminologists Donald R. Cressey, Dr. Stephen Albrecht, and other colleagues during the 1970s and 1980s gave rise to the concept of a certified fraud examiner — a person trained in accounting, law, investigation, and criminology, who would be prepared to deal with complex financial crimes. In 1988, Wells founded the ACFE to provide anti-fraud education and training. Today, the ACFE has almost 50,000 members worldwide and offers seminars, conferences, and educational materials. It administers the Certified Fraud Examiner (CFE) program and has established the Anti-Fraud Education Partnership to promote anti-fraud education in universities and colleges.

In 1993, the ACFE began to gather detailed information on occupational fraud and, in 1996, produced its first *Report to the Nation*. To compile the report, members of the ACFE were asked to fill out a survey detailing any one of the cases they had investigated during a particular time frame. Later studies were published in 2002, 2004, 2006, and 2008. Starting with the 2006 study, participants were asked to report on the largest fraud case they had investigated. They were also asked to estimate the extent of occupational fraud based on their personal experiences. Their reports provide a representative snapshot of occupational fraud. The number of cases analyzed for each report ranges between 500 and 1200. These detailed studies provide valuable information about the characteristics of fraud perpetrators, the types and sizes of the frauds they commit, how the frauds were discovered, how employers responded to the instances of fraud, and the effectiveness of various types of fraud controls.

Insights from the 2008 ACFE *Report to the Nation* are presented throughout this book. The 2008 *Report* analyzes data from 959 occupational fraud cases investigated between January 2006 and February 2008.

Occupational Fraud

Occupational fraud is the use of one's occupation to conduct illegal activities for direct or indirect personal gain. The ACFE's 1996 *Report to the Nation* identified four elements characterizing occupational fraud:

Occupational fraud violates an employee's fiduciary duties to an organization

Every employee in an organization, from the lowest position to the highest, has a responsibility to contribute materially to the business or purpose of the organization. A cashier is responsible for protecting the cash drawer, counting out change accurately, and submitting all the proceeds at the end of the day. A sales representative with an expense account is expected to use company funds only for legitimate expenses incurred while representing the company, and to provide receipts and an accurate expense report.

A chief financial officer (CFO) should monitor the accounting systems at a company, implement sound financial policies, and ensure the company is in compliance with accepted accounting practices. A buyer is employed to negotiate the best possible prices and purchase materials of an acceptable standard and quality. Whenever an employee deviates from his or her job responsibilities and acts for personal gain in a way that causes financial losses to the organization, this is fraud.

Occupational fraud is concealed and clandestine

Any employee can make an honest mistake, and that mistake will soon become apparent when accounts do not reconcile or money is found to be missing. A dishonest employee manipulates company accounts in some way to cover up the fact that money is being stolen. The theft may go undetected for long periods because the employee knows how to circumvent the company's policies and procedures.

Occupational fraud directly or indirectly benefits the perpetrator

An employee may benefit directly by stealing cash from an employer, using company funds for personal expenses, or deliberately inflating sales figures in order to receive a higher bonus or commission. The perpetrator of a fraud may also benefit indirectly through activities such as granting favors to a vendor in exchange for a promise of future employment or altering a company's financial statements to artificially inflate the price of the company's stock and increase the value of his or her stock options.

Occupational fraud costs the employer or investor assets, revenues, or reserves

The defining characteristic of occupational fraud is that it causes a financial loss to the business or to its stakeholders. In cases of fraud, profit that should have been reinvested in the business or paid out as dividends to investors goes into the pockets of one or more dishonest individuals; inventory may be stolen, or investors might be duped into throwing their money away on a business venture that cannot earn the promised returns.

The ACFE classifies the hundreds of types of occupational fraud into three basic categories: corruption, asset misappropriation (theft), and fraudulent financial statements. Corruption is the abuse of the authority associated with a position in an organization for direct or indirect personal benefit. It includes paying or accepting bribes, price fixing, corporate espionage, kickback schemes, and receiving illegal gifts from customers or vendors. Asset misappropriation covers every kind of theft, from stealing money out of a cash register to diverting company funds into a private bank account, and non-cash theft, such as stealing goods and supplies or using company property for private purposes. Financial statement fraud is the presentation of fraudulent information in a company's financial statements and takes place on many levels. Within an organization, it may cover up an individual's misappropriation of funds or misrepresent a department's true financial condition to higher management. Publicly, financial statement fraud may mislead lenders, potential buyers of a business, and investors who rely on these statements by indicating that a company is in good financial condition when it is not.

The following diagram shows 82 types of occupational fraud and how they fit into the three basic categories:

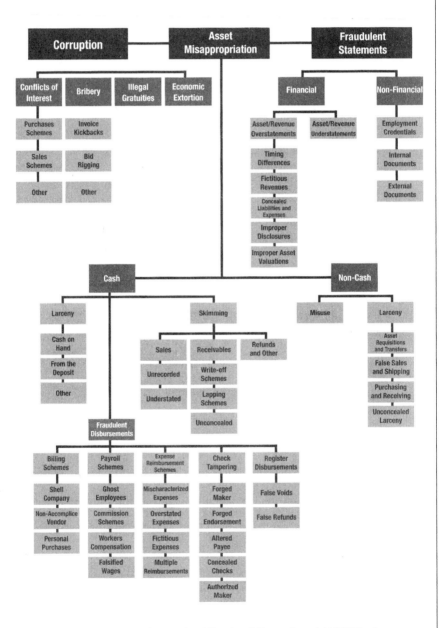

Occupational Fraud and Abuse Classification System

2008 Report to the Nation on Occupational Fraud and Abuse. Copyright 2008 by the Association of Certified Fraud Examiners, Inc.

CHAPTER 2

The Scope of the Problem

It is almost impossible to scientifically measure or quantify fraud. In many cases, fraud is ongoing for months and years before it is finally discovered. By then, records and supporting documents can no longer be retraced. Most fraud perpetrators do not keep accurate records of their activities and are only able to estimate how much they might have stolen. Fraudulent transactions are often hidden or disguised in company accounts, making it difficult to determine exactly how much has been lost. Some types of fraud, such as bribes paid to secure contracts and illegal gratuities given to purchasing agents by vendors, result in a company paying more than it should for goods and services or suffering other losses that are difficult to measure. The estimated 7 percent of 2007 revenues lost by U.S. companies because of occupational fraud, noted in the introduction of this book, does not take into account the money lost by investors as a result of Ponzi schemes and investments based on deceptive financial statements, or opportunity loss when fraud victims are not able to earn interest on the money that has been stolen instead of being reinvested in a business.

Who is Hurt by Fraud?

Everyone is hurt by fraud — the business itself, customers, investors, and taxpayers. Company executives make decisions based on the estimated costs of operating their businesses. When these costs are unexpectedly or artificially inflated because of fraud, the assumptions on which business decisions are based are no longer accurate, and the business may fail. The dishonesty, corruption, and greed of company employees are paid for by its customers when prices are raised to cover the company's losses.

When an employee engages in fraud, his or her company suffers financial setbacks due to lost revenue. In the survey conducted for the ACFE's 2008 *Report to the Nation*, the median loss to private companies due to fraud was $278,000. Small companies with fewer than 100 employees suffered a median loss of $200,000 and were victims of fraud more frequently than larger organizations. The business's reduced cash flow may make it difficult for the company to buy enough raw materials or sell enough products to make up the loss. Money that should have gone into marketing, research and development, or the purchase of new equipment evaporates, slowing the growth of the business. A fraud perpetrator's fellow employees also become victims when their company suffers financial losses. The company may no longer be able to offer benefits or bonuses and may implement more restrictive employee policies. Company morale is lowered when employees learn they have been betrayed by a trusted coworker.

A healthy economy depends on the efficiency and stability of its capital markets. Fraud, corruption, and deceptive accounting practices introduce an element of instability and uncertainty, magnifying the declines in ordinary business cycles. Highly publicized fraud weakens the confidence of investors and consumers, making them less willing to invest their money in the stock market or make large purchases, and slowing the economy. After several large-scale corporate frauds came to light in 2000 – 2002, the U.S. economy slowed. Congress passed the Sarbanes-Oxley Act, mandating new standards for the financial reporting of publicly traded companies, in an effort to restore global confidence in the U.S. stock markets. Investors in an unstable environment require compensation for the greater risk they are taking in the form of higher interest rates on bonds and more collateral for loans, making it more difficult and more costly for companies to get capital to finance their business operations. This discourages expansion and causes the job market to stagnate, further weakening the economy.

Investors are victimized by fraud in several ways. Financial losses caused by fraud may force a company to declare lower profits, reducing the value of its shares on the stock market. The amount a company pays out in dividends may decrease when its profits fall. Financial statement fraud may completely misrepresent a company's true financial status and artificially inflate the price of its shares, or portray the company as a sound investment opportunity when it is really a poor one. When the fraud is eventually discovered, share prices plummet. Fraudulent financial statements also cost investors millions of dollars when they overstate a company's assets during a merger or takeover and the buyer pays more than the company is worth.

The government depends on revenue from taxes. All income is taxed, whether it is personal income or profits from business operations. Stolen money is taxable as personal income, even though it is obtained illegally. For example, money skimmed from a company's cash receipts will not be recorded as revenue in company accounts, so it will not be taxed as business income. Instead, that money becomes personal income for the person who stole it, and that person is required to pay income tax on it. Many embezzlers conceal stolen money or simply do not file personal tax returns because they are afraid of being discovered. Federal, state, and local governments are robbed of millions of dollars in tax revenues when money is stolen and concealed. When fraud perpetrators are prosecuted, they are often charged with income tax evasion in addition to their other crimes, and they must pay fines to the IRS along with restitution.

Why Fight Fraud?

Fraud prevention costs money. It may be necessary to bring in consultants or outside accountants, hire additional personnel, and purchase sophisticated security devices or computer software. Small organizations in particular may not have the resources to implement complex fraud prevention measures. Money spent on fraud prevention does not bring a direct return on investment, but studies have shown that implementing fraud prevention measures reduces losses from fraud and shortens the length of time that fraud goes undetected. Fraud prevention benefits an organization in several ways.

Fraud is extremely costly. For the 959 cases of occupational fraud studied for the ACFE's *2008 Report to the Nation*, the median loss was $175,000, and in more than 25 percent of the cases, the loss was more than $1 million. Financial statement fraud caused the greatest damage, with a median loss of $2 million. The largest median losses occurred in the manufacturing, banking, and insurance industries. The cost of implementing or strengthening fraud controls in a business is only a fraction of the amount the business could potentially lose if fraud occurs.

Fraud can never be completely eliminated, because no matter how many deterrents and controls are in place, there will always be dishonest employees who find a way to beat the system. There is solid evidence, however, that companies implementing policies to detect and control fraud suffer fewer losses. Among the fraud cases surveyed for the ACFE's *2008 Report to the Nation*, the median loss for companies that had anti-fraud controls in place was 30 to 60 percent less than the median loss for companies that did not have anti-fraud controls. Anti-fraud controls not only act as a deterrent, but reduce losses by uncovering fraud earlier. Strong controls also discourage minor thefts that might never be discovered but collectively whittle away at a company's profits.

Companies are always striving to increase their profit margins through drastic cost-cutting measures, staff reductions, outsourcing, improved efficiency, and use of cheaper materials. Implementing simple policies to monitor employees and prevent fraud could improve the bottom line faster than any of these efforts by protecting the company from the loss of its assets. Many companies react after a fraud has been committed and money has already been lost, rather than putting strategies in place to prevent it in the first place. Very little of the money lost to fraud is ever recovered. Awareness of the possibility that fraud might be occurring and the ways in which it might be perpetrated should be part of any company's management program.

Studies have shown that small lapses in personal or professional conduct often lead to larger offenses. Most of the employees involved in embezzlement or theft also exhibited other signs of disregard for company policies, such as regularly coming to work late, taking undocumented personal leave, or charging personal expenses to a company expense account. Many fraud schemes begin with a single incident and escalate when the employee realizes that he or she is able to repeat it without being discovered. Department managers who start by fudging a few sales figures or re-characterizing losses as expenses may eventually progress to a complex scheme of money laundering to make themselves appear more successful than they really are. If a company discovers regulators are overlooking questionable accounting practices, it may take this as a license to commit further offenses. Penalizing perpetrators for small offenses is an effective way of preventing larger ones. Enforcing controls and policies lets potential offenders know that fraud will not be tolerated.

The announcement that a company has had to "make an adjustment" to its financial statement due to "accounting errors" inevitably incites negative media publicity and damages the company's reputation. Even if the fraud has been uncovered and remedied, the resulting loss of investor confidence may lower the price of the company's shares and make it difficult for that company to borrow the money needed to continue doing business.

Though the widespread use of technology and electronic data systems makes fraud detection easier, it has also increased the opportunities for employees to commit fraud and magnified its consequences. Large amounts of sensitive information can be quickly and easily transmitted. Stolen customer data can be used for identity theft even before the security breach has been discovered. Negative publicity about a fraud incident spreads like wildfire over the Internet, on blogs, and in commentaries, making it difficult for a company to protect its reputation. It makes sense, in the face of such risk, to do everything possible to prevent and detect fraud.

CHAPTER 3

Who Commits Fraud?

There are some criminals who make a career out of defrauding their victims, but most fraud is committed by seemingly ordinary individuals who, for one reason or another, betray the trust placed in them by their employers. In surveys of close to 1,000 fraud cases conducted by the ACFE for the *2004, 2006,* and *2008 Report to the Nation,* only 7 percent of fraud perpetrators had a prior criminal conviction, and only 12 percent had been fired by a previous employer because they committed fraud.

In order to operate a business, an employer must place a certain amount of trust in its employees. A trusted employee is expected to act in the best interests of the company and to carry out his or her fiduciary responsibilities with honesty and integrity. As an employee demonstrates that he or she is capable and trustworthy, he or she is given increased authority and access to company assets. Along with these privileges comes increased opportunity to commit fraud. The more an employee is trusted, the longer he or she can carry on a fraud without being discovered. Often when a fraud is discovered, the perpetrator's superiors and coworkers feel shocked and betrayed because they trusted this person not only in business, but in shared aspects of their personal lives.

Company executives, regulators, and administrators who are interested in identifying employees who have the potential to commit fraud are faced with a daunting challenge, because the personal profile of a fraud perpetrator is complex and made up of many elements. No single personality trait is a solid indication that fraud is taking place, but when an employee exhibits a combination of several traits, or when there are other suspicious circumstances — such as accounting irregularities, unexplained wealth, or unusual relationships with vendors or other employees — an initial investigation is warranted. Knowledge of the characteristics of a typical fraud perpetrator can be helpful in detecting fraud.

Scientific Study of White-Collar Crime

The term "white-collar crime" was coined by the sociologist and criminologist Edwin H. Sutherland (1883–1950), who pioneered the modern study of occupational fraud. In his book *White Collar Crime*, published in 1949, he defined white-collar crime as "a crime committed by a person of respectability and high social status in the course of his occupation." Today, the term "white-collar crime" refers to any type of financial and economic crime. Sutherland also advanced the concept of "differential association," asserting that criminal behavior, motivation, and techniques were learned from a person's associates and environment and did not arise from inherent personality traits.

Cressey triangle

During the early 1950s, one of Sutherland's students, Donald R. Cressey (1919–1987), conducted a groundbreaking study of occupational fraud in which he visited prisons in the Midwest and interviewed 200 convicted embezzlers. His research, published in 1953 as *Other People's Money; a Study in the Social Psychology of Embezzlement*, established the classic profile of an employee who commits occupational fraud.

Cressey's final hypothesis was that an ordinary person can become dishonest when three factors converge: a compelling personal motivation, the opportunity to commit fraud, and a means of rationalizing the criminal behavior as somehow justified. This hypothesis is often expressed as the Cressey triangle, or more commonly, the fraud triangle. Though society and business culture have changed in the 60 years

since the fraud triangle was developed, the concept is still widely used in the study of fraud.

Pressure

Pressure is the most significant of the three elements. From his interviews, Cressey observed that fraud occurred when the perpetrator believed that a perceived financial difficulty could be resolved in secret. In every case, the fraud perpetrator felt pressured by a financial problem which he or she felt could not be shared with other people who could probably have helped to solve it. Cressey identified six types of these "nonsharable" problems: violation of ascribed obligations, personal failure, business reversals, physical isolation, status gaining, and relationship between employer and employee. These six problems are discussed in depth in the following sections.

Violation of ascribed obligations

Someone who holds a position of trust and financial responsibility in a company is naturally expected to manage his or her personal finances responsibly and not to engage in financially risky behavior, such as gambling, dissipation, or living beyond his or her means. When a person in such a position is not able to pay his or her debts, it may seem necessary to keep this secret from employers, family, and friends. Admitting to the mismanagement of personal finances seems a direct contradiction of that person's perceived role in the organization.

Personal failure

Someone who is in financial trouble because of poor investment choices, mistakes, or simply unfavorable economic conditions may fear a loss of status if the situation becomes public. Instead of confessing the problem to a superior who might be able to help resolve it, the perpetrator's pride motivates him or her to disguise the losses in hopes of making enough money from further transactions to compensate.

STRAIGHT FROM THE HEADLINES

Nick Leeson, Rogue Trader

Nick Leeson is the former derivatives broker who infamously brought about the collapse of Barings Bank, the oldest investment bank in the United Kingdom, with his unsupervised and unauthorized speculative currency trading. In 1992, at the age of 25 and with no formal training, Leeson was appointed general manager of Barings' new operation in futures markets on the Singapore International Monetary Exchange (SIMEX). When Leeson applied for his broker's license in Singapore, neither Leeson nor Barings disclosed that he had been denied a license in the U.K. because of a fraudulent application.

At first, he was wildly successful. His unauthorized, speculative trades produced a profit of £10 million (about $16 million U.S.), 10 percent of Barings' income for 1992. Leeson was rewarded with a bonus of £130,000 ($207,000 U.S.) in addition to his salary of £50,000 ($80,000 U.S.). His luck soon changed, however, and he hid losses from several bad trades using one of Barings' error accounts. Barings Bank allowed Leeson, as chief trader, to settle his own trades — a job that is normally done by a second person. This freedom made it easy for Leeson to hide his losses from his superiors. A deficit of more than £2 million ($3 million U.S.) at the end of 1992 grew to £208 million ($332.5 million U.S.) by the end of 1994, while Leeson continued to speculate in hopes of recouping his losses.

On January 16, 1995, Leeson placed an authorized short straddle in the Singapore and Tokyo stock exchanges, expecting that the Japanese stock market would not move significantly overnight. Early in the morning of January 17, the Kobe earthquake sent Asian markets into a tailspin, and Leeson suffered extensive losses, from which he attempted to recover by making a series of increasingly risky new trades that only incurred further losses. Leeson fled Singapore on February 23, and Barings' losses eventually amounted to £827 million ($1.4 billion U.S.), two times the bank's available trading capital. On February 26, 1995, Barings was declared insolvent after a failed bailout attempt.

Barings Bank was strongly criticized for deficiencies in its internal auditing and risk management policies, and for allowing Leeson to operate with so little supervision. Released after four and a half years in Singapore's Tanah Merah prison, Leeson is now a guest speaker at economic forums, where he explains how he — and Barings — went wrong. He admits to having an addictive personality, and that his desire to retain his status among his colleagues prevented him from revealing his losses to his superiors at Barings while the situation still could have been salvaged.

Business reversals

The owner or manager of a business may not want to admit publicly that a business is failing. Even if the business is no longer profitable because of circumstances beyond his or her control, such as inflation, a rise in interest rates, difficulty in raising capital, or a slump in sales due to new competition or an economic recession, the owner or manager will go to great lengths to keep the business operating. A department manager may tamper with sales figures to make his or her superiors think the department is still successful, or a business owner may misrepresent the company's true situation in order to receive a loan from a bank.

Physical isolation

An employee struggling with financial problems may be unable to share them with someone who could help because there is no opportunity for communication. The employee might be working with little supervision in a branch office or overseas or may be telecommuting. Physical isolation can also occur when an office is structured so that employees have little contact with their superiors.

Status gaining

Competitive American social culture places great emphasis on financial success. An employee may strongly desire to possess symbols of status and prestige — such as a luxury car, brand-name clothes, expensive computers, and a large home — or to associate with a social group whose lifestyle is beyond his or her means. Many perpetrators commit fraud because they do not have the means to acquire the status symbols that they consider essential to their self-image.

Relations between employer and employee

A common motivation for fraud is an employee's resentment toward an employer and the feeling of being underpaid and unappreciated. The employee believes nothing can be accomplished by expressing these feelings to a superior and that doing so might jeopardize his or her job. Instead, the employee attempts to "get even" with the employer or steals as a compensation for the perceived injustice.

Employers who impose unrealistic sales targets or employ aggressive motivational tactics may be creating a situation in which employees feel reluctant to report poor results. Unable to produce the desired sales figures, an employee may commit fraud in order to receive commissions and bonuses, or to make it appear as though he or she is performing as expected.

Strained interpersonal relationships in a work setting may make communication between employees and their managers difficult so that employees are unable to report their failures and difficulties or ask for assistance.

Opportunity

Cressey determined that a person needs both general information and the requisite technical skills to commit fraud. Any employee in a position of trust has access to information that could be used dishonestly. If that person also has the accounting skills to mask questionable transactions or the ability to forge necessary documentation, the opportunity to commit fraud exists. Today, when so much information is stored and processed electronically, opportunity exists for anyone who has the computer skills to access and manipulate that information. Even teenagers have enough knowledge of computers to bypass simple security controls and alter electronic data stored in a computer system.

Rationalization

Cressey found that his subjects rationalized their crimes in one of three ways: as a noncriminal act, as somehow justified, or as part of a situation beyond the control of the offender. He categorized the offenders into three groups, each of which had its own type of rationalization. This rationalization frequently existed in the mind of the offender for some time before the crime was first committed and evaporated when the person became desensitized after repeated offenses.

Independent businesspeople either viewed their stealing as "only borrowing" until the money could be paid back at a later date, or regarded the funds entrusted to them as their own property. Frequently, they believed their actions to be standard business practices, and almost all of them considered their crimes to be a response to some "unusual situation," which was in fact a financial problem they felt unable to share with others.

Long-term violators also favored the "borrowing" rationalization. In addition, they justified themselves by believing they were acting to preserve their families from shame, disgrace, and poverty; that it was necessary to embezzle because their employers were cheating them financially; or that their employers were dishonest and deserved to be robbed. Most of these offenders eventually began to feel nervous, tense, and unhappy.

The third group, absconders, typically consisted of isolated loners who fled with money or goods that had been entrusted to them. They recognized their behavior as criminal, but blamed it on a personal defect of character or on circumstances beyond their control.

The fraud scale

In the early 1980s, another pioneer in the study of occupational fraud, Dr. Stephen Albrecht, with his colleagues Keith Howe and Marshall Romney, used extensive questionnaires to survey the internal auditors of 212 companies that had experienced cases of fraud. Their study, published in 1984 as "Deterring Fraud: The Internal Auditor's Perspective," characterized nine types of "motivators" for committing fraud:

1. Living beyond one's means
2. An overwhelming desire for personal gain
3. High personal debt
4. A close association with customers
5. The feeling of being underpaid
6. A wheeler-dealer attitude — a person who is always looking for a chance to make money from a business deal
7. A strong challenge to "beat the system"
8. Excessive gambling habits
9. Undue pressure from family or peers

Albrecht and his colleagues also uncovered interesting correlations between perpetrators and the frauds they committed. For example, perpetrators of large frauds used the money to support lavish lifestyles, extramarital relationships, and speculative investments, while perpetrators of small frauds did not. Large frauds were usually associated with deficient accounting procedures, lack of sound organizational procedures, and unrealistic goals and expectations imposed by management. Employees who felt they were underpaid committed small frauds, and those motivated by a desire to "beat the system" committed larger frauds.

Like Cressey's, Albrecht's study concluded that fraud occurs when three factors converge: situational pressure, a perceived opportunity to commit and conceal fraud, and a means of justifying or rationalizing the act as somehow inconsistent with one's personal level of integrity. Albrecht developed a "fraud scale" to demonstrate how these factors, present in varying degrees, indicated a higher or lower probability of fraud. Albrecht and his colleagues agreed that fraud is difficult to predict and compiled a list of 82 "red flags" that might point to fraud or occupational abuse. These red flags were present in many of the cases they studied, but because no research has been done to see how these characteristics manifest in non-offenders, it is impossible to pinpoint any of them as conclusive indicators of fraud.

STRAIGHT FROM THE HEADLINES

Priest Calls Theft from Collection Basket His "401(k)"

In February 2004, a Roman Catholic priest, the Rev. John F. Johnston, 64, pleaded guilty to grand larceny in the third degree, a class D felony. He told investigators that from 1998 until October 2003, he skimmed $100 per week from the collection basket at St. Martin of Tours in Bethpage, New York, where he had said mass for 30 years, as his "401(k) plan."

The theft was discovered while police were investigating another crime. They searched Johnson's apartment and found a bag full of stolen cash, along with Nazi memorabilia and pornography. The Rev. James Vlaun, a spokesman for the Diocese of Rockville Centre, said the diocese did not know how much Father Johnston had stolen. "We have no reason to believe it was more than he admitted," Father Vlaun said. "He has been very forthright. He was good enough to admit it and seek help, for which I give him credit." Father Johnston agreed to return $50,000 to St. Martin of Tours.

Hollinger-Clark study

In 1983, Richard C. Hollinger and John P. Clark published *Theft by Employees*, the result of a federally funded survey of almost 10,000 employees. Their conclusion was that employees steal primarily because workplace conditions allow it, and that the primary motivation for employee theft was job dissatisfaction. Hollinger and Clark did not find a correlation between household income and employee theft, but they did find a statistical relationship between the level of a person's concern over his or her personal financial situation and the level of employee theft.

They also found that younger workers have a greater tendency to steal and engage in counterproductive activity, perhaps because they are less committed to their organizations and experience less job satisfaction. They found the highest level of theft among those who had the greatest access to company assets and cash. Senior company officials with financial authority stole less often — but in greater amounts — than employees in lower positions, such as those who operated retail cash registers.

The Hollinger and Clark study concluded that organizational controls — such as electronic inventory systems, security procedures, and internal audits — and social controls — such as employee education, development of a corporate culture, and the hiring of employees who were likely to conform to expectations — were effective in deterring theft when executed with sensitivity and fairness. They believed the problem of employee theft had been vastly understated and such controls were inadequately applied.

Hollinger and Clark found substantial evidence that employees who engage in other types of occupational abuse, such as calling in sick when they are not, arriving late and leaving early, taking extended breaks, and showing sloppy workmanship, are the same employees who commit theft and occupational fraud.

STRAIGHT FROM THE HEADLINES

One Fraud Leads to Another

In September 2009, according to a news release from the U.S. Attorney's Office, Mary R. Storer, 40, of Wood River, Illinois, pleaded guilty to tax evasion, willful failure to file federal income tax returns, embezzlement from an employee benefit plan, and failure to pay employment taxes.

Storer began to embezzle as soon as she was hired as an office manager by Elk Heating and Sheet Metal, Inc. in February 2006. Her duties included payroll, filing, paying the company's payroll taxes, and handling accounts receivable and accounts payable. When Storer presented her superiors with stacks of checks to sign for bills, she requested blank checks to purchase office supplies. She then made the blank checks out to herself and cashed them. In May 2006, when Storer refused to allow the vice president of the company to see the bank statements, he checked with the bank and discovered that Storer was embezzling. Storer agreed to return the money she had stolen and was allowed to keep her job.

Storer then began telling customers they could get a discount on their bills if they paid in cash; she then stole the cash payments. Storer also took the payroll taxes instead of filing and paying the Form 941 Employer's Quarterly Payroll Tax Returns for the second, third, and fourth quarters of 2006 and the first quarter of 2007. In August 2007, Storer embezzled from employees' weekly paycheck deductions, including withholdings for 401(k) retirement and vacation pay accounts.

Storer embezzled an estimated $266,056 from the company. The news release from the U.S. Attorney's Office stated, "Storer is a heavy gambler and lost over $103,000 at the Alton Belle Casino during 2006."

ACFE *Report to the Nation*

The ACFE's *Report to the Nation on Occupational Fraud and Abuse* represents the first ongoing study of occupational fraud. The report uses detailed evaluations of fraud cases by professional experts to document the extent to which the various factors identified above influence fraud perpetrators and also the effect of accounting controls and other deterrents in reducing fraud. Conducted over a period of 13 years, these studies also help to identify trends and changes in the way frauds are committed and detected.

Employee red flags

Red flags are signs something may be amiss — signals that trigger suspicion and indicate that a situation should be watched or investigated. The work of Hollinger and Clark, Cressey, Albrecht, and the ACFE has helped to pinpoint a number of indicators that an employee might be involved in fraud or embezzlement. Among the frauds studied for the ACFE's *2008 Report to the Nation*, the most common red flags associated with a fraud were an employee living beyond his or her apparent means and those who were experiencing severe personal financial difficulties.

Training managers to be aware of these warning signs will make them more alert to the possibility of fraud. Remember that none of these indicators are conclusive evidence of fraud, but when combined with other factors, such as easy access to cash, accounting irregularities, loose organizational controls, a chaotic working environment, or unexplained deficits, they are signs that fraud could be taking place:

- Significant personal debt and credit problems
- Borrowing money from coworkers
- Creditors calling or appearing at the workplace
- Lifestyle changes, such as the purchase of an expensive car or new home, or a lifestyle beyond the employee's apparent means
- Bragging about new purchases of large or expensive items
- Carrying unusually large amounts of cash
- Refusal to take vacation or sick leave, or refusal to relinquish responsibilities when out of the office
- Refusal to accept a promotion
- Strong desire to retain control, or unwillingness to delegate responsibilities to coworkers

- Behavioral changes that might indicate an addiction to alcohol, drugs, or gambling, or stress over the possibility of losing the job
- Excessive drinking, gambling, or other addictive behavior
- Dishonesty on expense reports, or use of company property for personal benefit
- Irritability, suspicion, or defensiveness when asked reasonable questions
- Inability to produce documents and reports when questioned
- Marital infidelity
- Personal difficulties such as divorce, problems with children or parents, foreclosure, instability, or family illness
- Unusual relationships with coworkers, vendors, suppliers, or customers
- Consistently comes to work unusually early or stays unusually late
- Has authority over one or more accounting processes
- Has unsupervised access to cash, supplies, or assets
- Resentful attitude toward employer
- Comes in late, leaves work early, takes excessive breaks, or falsely calls in sick
- Physical isolation, both in the office and in personal life
- Difficulty communicating with superiors
- Open disregard for company policies and procedures
- Complains about lack of authority
- Wheeler-dealer attitude
- Close association with other employees who have demonstrated resentful or disrespectful attitudes
- Is under unreasonable pressure to perform from within the organization
- Is under pressure from family or peers
- Previous criminal record for theft or embezzlement
- Past legal problems
- Past employment-related problems

Gender, Age, Education, and Tenure

Among the fraud cases studied for the ACFE's *Report to the Nation* for both 2006 and 2008, approximately 60 percent were committed by men and 40 percent by women. The median loss in frauds committed by males ($250,000 in 2008) was twice that in frauds committed by female perpetrators ($110,000 in 2008). The report suggested this disparity might reflect the fact that more men than women occupy high-level management positions. Employees in management and executive positions have the opportunity to steal much larger amounts than those in lower positions.

Many criminologists and sociologists expect an increase in the number of women involved in white-collar crime, as well as an increase in the average amount they steal. As the number of educated women and women occupying positions in upper-level management rises, more women will have the opportunity to commit large-scale fraud. According to the U.S. Census Bureau's *Families and Living Arrangements: 2006*, there were 10.4 million single-mother families in the United States that year. Single mothers are likely to experience heavy financial pressures and the temptation to commit fraud as they deal with the responsibilities of raising children alone.

Over half of the fraud cases studied for the *2008 Report to the Nation* were perpetrated by employees older than 40, and approximately 35 percent of the perpetrators were between the ages of 41 and 50. The highest median loss ($500,000) was incurred by fraudsters in the 51–60 age group. The number of reported violent crimes has been steadily dropping over the past decade; violent theft is more frequently committed by young people, while older people favor white-collar crime as a means of obtaining money illegitimately. Criminologists predict that as baby-boomers age, and there are more people in their 50s and 60s in the workforce, the incidence of white-collar crime will increase.

The amount of time an employee had worked for a company seemed to have little correlation with fraud, but employees who had been with a company for five years or more committed much larger frauds than those who had only been there a short while. This is probably related to the position of trust they had achieved and increased access to company assets.

Collusion

Fraud perpetrators acted alone in more than 60 percent of the cases studied for the 2006 and 2008 ACFE's *Report to the Nation*. When two or more individuals collaborated in a fraud scheme, the damage was much greater. The median loss for frauds involving two or more perpetrators ($500,000 in 2008) was four times greater than the median loss for crimes committed by individuals ($115,000 in 2008). Two or more people can help each other circumvent accounting and inventory controls, and hide their activities from detection. For example, someone in the accounting department can alter statements or records to cover up theft on the sales floor.

Corruption, bribery, and extortion schemes by nature involve two or more individuals, but one or more of them is typically a vendor, customer, or other outsider. Often, the first indication of fraud is an unusually close relationship between an employee and an outside vendor or customer.

Conditions Under Which Fraud Occurs

The fraud theories discussed earlier in this chapter emphasized that fraud occurs when opportunity converges with motivation and rationalization. Most perpetrators do not seek employment with the intent of committing fraud. When someone under the pressure of financial or personal difficulties sees an easy way out through committing fraud and finds a way to justify his or her actions, he or she begins to act dishonestly.

If the opportunity did not exist, that person would not commit fraud. Just as there are red flags that suggest an employee might be acting dishonestly, there are also red flags that point out workplace situations in which fraud could easily occur. Signs of high risk include:

- An organization that is always operating in "crisis mode" instead of following established procedures
- Unrealistic expectations of employees, such as unreasonably high sales targets, overly heavy workloads, or excessive production goals
- Strained relationships between employees and their superiors
- Lack of separation between cash-handling and accounting responsibilities
- Too much responsibility and authority in the hands of one person
- Poor internal controls
- Lack of security for electronic data and computer networks
- Employees working in isolation without supervision
- An organizational culture that appears to overlook small lapses

Fraud Appears to be Addictive

Fraud perpetrators typically do not stop at one fraudulent transaction. When the first attempt is successful, there is a tendency to repeat the fraud again and again, and even to branch out into other types of fraud and deception. The perpetrator becomes dependent on the extra income and begins to desire more. The deceptions become bolder until finally the perpetrator makes a mistake and the fraud is discovered. If the fraud is not discovered early, the perpetrator can cause a great deal of damage.

STRAIGHT FROM THE HEADLINES

CFO Embezzles $10 Million from Florida Tree Farm

On November 30, 2009, U.S. District Judge Patricia C. Fawsett sentenced Gary Ernest Williams to eight years in federal prison for mail fraud and income tax evasion and forfeiture of homes in Pennsylvania and North Carolina, a 2007 Lexus automobile, and cash payments that had been used to purchase property in the Bahamas. Williams was ordered to pay more than $14 million in restitution to the United States and to his former employer, Marian Gardens Tree Farm. According to court documents, Williams had used his position as CFO of Marian Gardens Tree Farm in Groveland, Florida, to embezzle $10.5 million from the company by falsifying checks, taking out a business credit card in the company's name, and making large cash withdrawals that bank officials were told would be used to pay "employee bonuses." Instead, Williams deposited the stolen funds into his personal accounts and funded a lavish lifestyle that included homes, luxury cars, jewelry, drugs, and elaborate vacations with private jet transportation. Williams had worked for Marian Garden Tree Farm for approximately 20 years and had begun embezzling in 2000 when he was appointed CFO.

Fraud is Associative

Sutherland's theory of "differential association," the concept that criminal behavior is learned from associates and environment, clearly applies to occupational fraud. Employees who see their superiors or coworkers committing fraud and getting away with it are more likely to engage in similar behavior. If they perceive that management is not closely monitoring their activities, or that accounting controls are loose, employees are more inclined to become involved in theft. In some cases, workers regard the appropriation of supplies or unreported cash as a sort of informal compensation for their job. The example set by executives and managers in a company is strongly influential. Employees who are aware that a manager is cheating on expense reports may feel it is acceptable to do the same. In some companies, management creates a "culture of noncompliance" by openly disobeying company policies and procedures.

Fraud Schemes Are Not Seamless

Though a fraud perpetrator may engage in complicated tactics to cover up theft or accounting irregularities, most frauds are not carefully planned in advance. A typical fraud begins with one or two transgressions and gradually expands into larger transactions and different types of activities. Sooner or later, the perpetrator will make a mistake and get caught, or the fraudulent activities will become extensive enough to catch attention.

Psychopathic Behavior

Details revealed in the media about the behavior of blatant fraudsters, executives responsible for massive cases of financial statement fraud, and perpetrators of Ponzi schemes — apparent lack of conscience, complete self-absorption, greed, ability to lie, and unconcern for harm they are doing to others — seem to fit the clinical profile of a psychopath.

CASE STUDY: EXCERPT FROM "KEEP PSYCHOPATHS OUT OF YOUR ACCOUNTING FIRM"

May 21, 2009
by Mitchell Langbert, Ph.D.
AICPA Career Insider

Dr. Mitchell Langbert is a published author and experienced expert on employee benefit programs, ERISA litigation, and human resource management. He is an associate professor of business and economics with tenure at Brooklyn College-CUNY.

"Traditional human resource management models do not consider the issue of psychopathy, which may be defined as an employee's lack of empathy, conscience, or guilt with respect to unethical or even criminal acts. In his sociological study of embezzlement, *Other Peoples' Money,*

Donald R. Cressey suggests a model of embezzlement according to which an honest employee who never intended to embezzle and who occupies a fiduciary role is motivated to embezzle by a lapse in expected conduct (such as gambling) that cannot be shared with others and results in financial need. Cressey's model does not contemplate crimes by those who take a job *intending* to do wrong."

"Psychopaths represent about 1 percent of the general population, but comprise about 3.5 percent of high-potential corporate employees. The percentage of upper management with psychopathic traits is probably higher still. Although they are responsible for 3.5 percent of high potential employees, they may be responsible for more than four times that percentage of firms' ethical lapses."

"In recent years, psychologists have begun to study the role of psychopaths in ethical misconduct. One important book is Paul Babiak's and Robert D. Hare's *Snakes in Suits.* The well-known corporate ethical lapses earlier this decade can be interpreted to have been a function of psychopathy that had been unleashed by elimination of traditional bureaucratic and accounting controls."

"Not only do many HR departments overlook psychopathy in staffing, performance appraisal, and promotion, but some view some psychopathic characteristics as desirable. For example, in an article titled 'From Darkness Into the Light: Psychopathy in Industrial and Organizational Psychology,' Paul Babiak notes that psychopathic charm and charisma can often be mistaken for leadership; psychopathic talk of imaginary goals can be mistaken for visionary leadership; and psychopathic lack of emotion can be mistaken for being in control."

"It is true that ordinary impression management, managerial skills, and corporate gamesmanship can at times look like psychopathic behavior. The difference is that psychopaths do not feel remorse at lying and will lie unrestrainedly. They take pleasure in manipulating and causing harm to others. They delight in bullying. They do not wince at committing fraud or other crimes. Harming others does not trouble them. They often feel that they are the ones who have been wronged, and are charming enough to convince others of their case."

"Frequently, psychopaths are expert at grasping others' psychological needs. This psychological competence enables the psychopath to engage in manipulation, intimidation, and harassment, in which they take pleasure. Because the psychopath seems charming to higher-ups and to many coworkers, he can undermine accusations that begin to develop. Thus, it is common for psychopaths to be surrounded by conflict. One sign of psychopathy is the inability to work in teams."

"No one knows the degree to which ethical lapses in business are attributable to psychopaths, but it seems likely that if 3 to 10 percent of top managers are psychopaths, their firms will be among the worst offenders. Moreover, psychopathic employees cause disruption, conflict, and turnover of capable employees. Hence, HR might consider the role it can play in identification of psychopaths before they are hired, and assist the firm in identifying psychopathic behavior when it occurs."

"Unfortunately, there is no magic bullet or psychological test that can screen out psychopaths...Babiak and Hare recommend a structured interview process in which résumés are checked against factual evidence; for instance, calling every former employer and college on the résumé before inviting a candidate in for an interview."

"A good tool … is the structured behavioral interview in which the interviewer asks the interviewee to describe actual responses to past problems. The answers can be reviewed for evidence of dishonesty and inconsistency as well as quality. Multiple interviewers from different departments should conduct interviews and then compare notes. A candidate who says one thing to one interviewer and a very different thing to a different interviewer should be suspect."

"Rigorous reference-checking is advisable. An outright lie (as opposed to exaggerations about things like salary) on a résumé should be a sufficient tip-off to reject a candidate. In addition, work samples are one of the best selection tools."

CHAPTER 4

How Fraud is Detected

Fraud prevention professionals are concerned that, in spite of improvements in internal financial controls and increasingly sophisticated methods of fraud detection, fraud schemes often go undiscovered for months and even years. Among the 959 fraud cases surveyed by the ACFE for the *2008 Report to the Nation*, one-fifth were initially detected by accident, and nearly one half through tips from employees, vendors, and customers. If the ACFE survey is taken as a representative example of all fraud schemes, these statistics indicate that even rigorous internal controls have little more than a one-in-five chance of detecting a fraud scheme. These statistics also point to the importance of establishing anonymous hotlines for tipsters, creating an atmosphere that motivates employees and outside associates to report dishonest activities, and making it easy for them to do so.

The chart below shows how fraud was initially discovered in the cases surveyed for the ACFE's *2006* and *2008 Report to the Nation*. In some cases, a fraud was discovered by more than one method, so the percentages add up to more than 100 percent. It is interesting to note the percentage of frauds uncovered because of tips increased significantly in two years, and the percentage discovered by accident decreased slightly. This is a hopeful sign that organizations are implementing fraud detection strategies more effectively.

Ways in Which Fraud Was Discovered from the ACFE's *2006* and *2008* Report to the Nation on Occupational Fraud and Abuse

	2006	2008
Number of cases studied	1,134	959
Tips	34.2%	46.2%
By accident	25.4%	20.0%
Internal audit	20.2%	19.4%
Internal control	19.2%	23.3%
External audit	9.1%	9.1%
Notification by police	3.8%	3.2%

The ACFE's *2008 Report to the Nation* turned up some other meaningful statistics. More than half of the frauds perpetrated by owners and senior executives were discovered through tips. Internal controls were much less effective in uncovering these types of fraud because owners and executives are often in a position to override internal controls without being questioned. External audits were more effective in uncovering fraud by owners and executives than in detecting fraud by lower-level employees. External audits were also more effective in discovering frauds in which the loss was greater than $1 million and in discovering fraud in small businesses. Frauds in small businesses were more likely to be discovered by accident or by tips than frauds in larger businesses, most likely because they tend to have weaker internal controls.

The *2008 Report to the Nation* also showed that frauds in general went undetected for a median period of 24 months. Check-tampering frauds and financial fraud schemes had a median duration of 30 months. This indicates it is typically approximately two years from the time employees first steal from an organization until their activities escalate to the point that a mistake is made or a coworker or associate turns them in. Some frauds are carried on for several years before being detected. During this time, management is not aware the organization is being short-changed and revenue is being lost.

Tips

Even the most devious fraud perpetrator cannot conceal his or her illegal activities forever. Sooner or later, close associates will become suspicious and sense something is wrong, or they may come across evidence of the fraud. Colleagues might notice an employee is behaving strangely or spending extravagantly. Fellow workers may even be aware of the fraud taking place but refrain from speaking out because they fear losing their jobs or because they feel more loyalty to the fraud perpetrator than to their employer. Some fraud schemes require the cooperation of fellow employees or of outside accomplices; the fraudster may pay these people a cut of the proceeds so they are motivated to continue participating, or try to enforce their silence through threats and intimidation. The more people involved in a fraud scheme, the greater the likelihood one of them will become disgruntled and betray the others, or a third party — such as a family member or friend — will learn about the scheme and report it.

Because tips from employees, vendors, and customers are the most common way fraud is discovered, it makes sense to do everything possible to encourage people to report their suspicions. Two factors influence the likelihood employees and associates will report fraud: a belief there is some kind of physical or moral reward for turning in a tip, and the existence of available channels for easily reporting information. A simple example of a tip mechanism is a sign outside a fast food drive-through window asking customers to call an 800 number if their receipts do not match the amounts they were charged.

If people who know about a fraud believe they will be directly or indirectly rewarded for turning the fraud perpetrator in, or if they have ethical concerns, they will be motivated to report their suspicions to someone of authority. Many companies are now investing considerable effort to create an "ethical culture" in the workplace by establishing and enforcing clear policies and standards. This kind of education tells employees what is expected of them and what kind of behavior is not acceptable. When policies are clear, employees are more likely to report violations. *See Chapter 12 for more information on how to develop an ethical culture in an organization.*

Sometimes illicit activities go unreported because there is no clear hierarchy of responsibility. Employees do not know how to report illicit activities or who is responsible for receiving and investigating reports of fraud. An employee cannot report to a supervisor if the supervisor is the one committing fraud. Small companies and family businesses sometimes have a loose power-sharing arrangement among several partners. Employees may believe that their report will simply be ignored, or that the person to whom they are reporting has no authority to do anything about the situation. An employee who feels isolated or has a difficult relationship with his or her supervisor may not feel able to communicate such a serious accusation against another employee. Organizations that have a clear chain of command, along with alternative reporting mechanisms such as an employee hotline or direct access to a human resources officer, are more likely to receive tips about suspicious activities.

The Sarbanes-Oxley Act mandates that publicly traded companies set up employee hotlines that report directly to company audit committees and provide legal protection for employee "whistleblowers." A hotline is a confidential and anonymous way for employees to submit a tip. Many private companies and organizations also operate employee hotlines. The ACFE's *2008 Report to the Nation* reported that among the 217 organizations in its study who had a formal hotline in place when fraud was discovered through a tip, the hotline was used in little more than half of the cases. This suggests remaining anonymous is not a concern for many tipsters, or they find it easier to report directly to someone in authority than to use a hotline. Anonymity is important when the fraud is being perpetrated by a senior executive or manager. *See Chapter 12 for more information on setting up a hotline.*

The *2008 Report to the Nation* also revealed that among the cases discovered through tips, approximately 30 percent of the tips were from external sources such as a customer, vendor, or competitor. All of this evidence suggests every organization should have a formal complaint mechanism, and all employees should be educated to recognize fraud and to report suspicious activities. Customers and vendors can also be coached to report discrepancies in their accounts or unfair practices to someone of authority.

Accident

The second most common way fraud is discovered — after tips from fellow employees, customers, and vendors — is by accident. A telephone call might be routed to the wrong person, a returned letter opened by mistake, or a supervisor might notice irregularities on checks and invoices during an employee's unexpected absence. Most fraud schemes are not carefully thought-out in advance; the perpetrator gets away with one deception and begins to expand the fraud by bypassing internal controls and taking advantage of any weakness or opportunity that arises. Sooner or later he or she will go a little too far, or lose control of some aspect of the scheme, and the scheme will be discovered.

Anything disrupting a perpetrator's routine is conducive to the "accidental" discovery of fraud. One of the most effective controls in reducing loss by fraud is a mandatory vacation policy requiring every employee to be absent from the office for two weeks every year. During those two weeks, the people who assume that employee's responsibilities are likely to come across evidence of any fraud taking place. Another effective control leading to early accidental discovery of fraud is mandatory job rotation for employees who have access to cash or accounts. Every two or three years, the employee is moved to a different position, and someone else takes over his or her responsibilities. In the ACFE's *2008 Report to the Nation*, the median loss to fraud for companies following these two practices was $64,000, compared to $164,000 for companies that did not.

Other practices that enhance the accidental discovery of fraud are surprise audits and surprise inventory counts. Because they are unannounced, they catch the fraud perpetrator unprepared and without time to conceal discrepancies by making alterations to the accounts or forging documents.

Internal and external audits

An internal audit is an ongoing or frequent evaluation of a company's financial and business processes, carried out by a company's own employees, typically accountants or other finance professionals. It includes a verification of accounts and supporting documents and can extend to evaluating the efficiency of purchasing and manufacturing procedures and compliance with generally accepted accounting principles (GAAP), laws, and regulations. Internal auditors for publicly traded companies are expected to conduct a fraud risk assessment for the organization and incorporate it into their reviews by looking for specific signs of fraud.

External audits are conducted by independent professional auditors or auditing firms who are not associated with the organization. Publicly traded companies are required to perform external audits every year. Private companies, charities, and government entities may conduct an external audit for a specific purpose or at regular intervals. An external audit confirms that the organization's accounts are accurate and complete, and that its financial statements reflect the true financial status of the organization.

Financial statement fraud is sometimes discovered when external audits detect unexplained discrepancies or improper accounting practices.

Although senior executives and management regard internal audits as an effective means of detecting and controlling fraud, audits are not as effective as the first two methods described previously: tips and accidental discovery. An internal audit verifies that an organization's accounts reconcile, but it may miss fraudulent entries and adjustments made to those accounts and their supporting documents if everything appears accurate on the surface. Fraud occurs when the perpetrator finds a way to circumvent controls and manipulate accounts so the fraud is not easily detected. In many cases, the perpetrator is someone in the accounting department who can manipulate an internal audit, or a senior manager with the authority to sign off on an audit.

Law enforcement

Occasionally, fraud is uncovered by a police or FBI investigation into another crime, such as the sale of pornography, drug dealing, or identity theft. Large-scale fraud is often associated with other crimes, such as the sale of stolen goods. Stolen inventory discovered in a warehouse may be the first indication a fraud has taken place. In the example in Chapter 3, the priest was not suspected until police, investigating a complaint that he had made threatening phone calls to a high school, searched his house and found a bag of cash stolen from the collection plate at his church.

Training management to be aware of fraud risk

Professional fraud investigators say they are often guided by intuition in uncovering exactly how a fraud has taken place. As they examine a company's accounts and interview its employees, they draw from their experiences of previous fraud cases to put the clues together and determine what has happened. Managers and executives, who have relatively little direct experience with fraud, often overlook signs that would immediately trigger the suspicions of a fraud expert. Training management to be aware of fraud risk and providing education about the legal consequences of fraud increases the likelihood fraud will be discovered early and also acts as a deterrent. A number of organizations offer fraud risk training seminars and online classes, and ongoing onsite education programs addressing a company's specific needs can be developed by a fraud professional. Fraud awareness training gives managers and executives the skills and intuitive knowledge that comes from years of dealing with deception. *See Chapter 12 for more information on establishing fraud awareness training programs.*

Internal controls

Generally accepted accounting principles (GAAP) include a number of recommended internal controls, the procedures followed by employees in a company to ensure that accounts are accurate, errors are quickly corrected, and no one has improper access to assets or cash. Among the fraud cases studied for the ACFE's *2008 Report to the Nation*, the median loss for companies with strong internal controls was 30 to 60 percent lower than for companies that did not have strong controls. This is probably because the fraud was either discovered earlier or as soon as the theft became significant enough to trigger an alarm.

Red flags

Each of the following chapters lists some of the "red flags" for asset misappropriation schemes — signs that fraud might be taking place. A red flag should never be ignored. Every company should have a clear procedure for management to follow if illegal activity is suspected. Someone with the proper authority and accounting skills should examine the situation to see if a full-scale investigation is warranted. In most cases, an examination will produce a reasonable explanation for the red flag, or uncover an honest mistake. Occasionally, the red flag will turn out to be the first clue to a complicated fraud scheme. Fraud examiners say the first indication of a fraud is typically just "the tip of the iceberg," and often leads to the discovery of an extensive and complex network of fraudulent activities.

Each list of red flags is followed by techniques and procedures that can be used periodically to check for illegal activity even when it is not suspected. Some of these techniques apply to more than one kind of fraud. Many of these techniques for detecting fraud also serve as deterrents by making it more difficult for employees to commit fraud. Following these procedures creates a sense that employees are being monitored and that those engaging in illicit activities will be discovered and punished.

CHAPTER 5

Asset Misappropriation and Embezzlement

You cannot detect fraud without first being aware of the many types of fraud schemes and the circumstances under which fraud occurs. Each fraud scheme is unique because it arises out of the specific situation in which it occurs: the type of access the fraud perpetrator has to an organization's assets, the inherent weaknesses in the organization's financial processes and controls, and the personalities of the perpetrator and his or her supervisors and associates. This and the following chapters describe common fraud schemes, the warning signs that indicate fraud might be taking place, the methods used to detect various types of fraud, and the internal controls that help to deter fraud. You will learn some of the standard procedures used by accountants and fraud examiners to detect fraud, and how technology is increasingly being used for fraud detection. A checklist for each type of fraud will guide you in determining how fraud might occur in your business or organization.

Though many frauds are first uncovered through tips or by accident, company executives and managers can take positive steps to prevent asset misappropriation and detect it quickly when it does occur. The discovery that "something is missing" is typically the first clue that embezzlement or theft has occurred. Inventory is not found where it was supposed to be, or cash reserves are lower than expected, and there does not seem to be a logical explanation. When a good system for processing accounts, logging inventory, collecting data, and monitoring employees is already in place, that discovery is likely to happen much sooner. By the time a fraud scheme is discovered, it is often too late to recover the misappropriated assets.

Approximately 90 percent of occupational fraud involves asset appropriation, in which employees take cash or property from a business and attempt to cover their tracks so that their theft goes undiscovered. Asset misappropriation includes all theft of cash or property. Among the cases of occupational fraud studied for the ACFE's *2008 Report to the Nation*, 16.3 percent involved the theft of company property, inventory, or confidential information. The median loss for these non-cash frauds was $100,000. Approximately 85 percent of the cases in the same study involved the theft or misuse of cash. The median loss for asset misappropriation schemes as a whole was $150,000, considerably lower than the median loss for corruption or financial statement fraud.

Cash appropriation schemes can be as simple as taking few dollars from the petty cash drawer, or as complex as altering checks, forgery, and tampering with company accounts. Cash appropriation schemes are typically carried out by employees who handle cash or by employees in accounting or management positions who have authority over accounts or access to cash. Hundreds of techniques are used in asset appropriation fraud, but they can be classified into three basic categories: skimming, cash larceny, and the most common type of asset appropriation scheme, fraudulent disbursements.

Double-entry bookkeeping

A basic understanding of double-entry bookkeeping will help you to grasp the nature of embezzlement schemes and financial statement fraud. Double-entry bookkeeping is the foundation of modern accounting. If you had a very simple business, such as selling candy bars for cash from a booth at a festival, you could use a single-entry system to keep track of the cash coming in from your sales and the cash you spent to buy more boxes of candy bars wholesale and to pay the rent for your booth. Most businesses are far more complex, involving sales on credit, advertising costs, mortgages and property leases, purchase or lease of equipment, payment of wages, insurance, taxes, loans, and uncollectible debts. Without double-entry bookkeeping, it would be impossible for a business to know whether it is making a profit or operating at a loss, and how much it is worth.

Double-entry bookkeeping, which originated in the 13th century, records every financial transaction in two places — as a debit in one account and an equal and opposite credit in another. A double-entry system has many accounts, each with a debit and a credit column. When a company's accounts were kept manually by a bookkeeper, every transaction was first recorded in a journal with a debit and a credit column. Next to each amount was written the date and the name of the account which was supposed to be debited or credited. The bookkeeper then wrote (posted) each debit and credit in one of the company's general or subsidiary accounts ledgers. Periodically, the books were "balanced" by adding up all the debits and credits to see if the amounts were equal. When they were not equal, the bookkeeper would review all the transactions one by one until the error was found.

Here is an example of three sales and a payment recorded in a journal:

| Journal | | | | |
Date	Account	Debit	Credit	Note
3-Oct-09	Cash	$459.00		Sale
	Revenue		$459.00	Sale
4-Oct-09	Accounts Receivable	$650.00		Credit Sale- Inv. No. 1012
	Revenue		$650.00	Credit Sale- Inv. No. 1012
5-Oct-09	Cash	$203.00		Sale

	Revenue		$203.00	Sale
6-Oct-09	Accounts Receivable		$650.00	Payment - Inv. No. 1012
	Cash	$650.00		Payment - Inv. No. 1012
	Total	**$1,962.00**	**$1,962.00**	

And then posted to general accounts ledgers:

Cash		
Date	**Debit**	**Credit**
3-Oct-09	$459.00	
5-Oct-09	$203.00	
6-Oct-09	$650.00	
	$1,312.00	**$0.00**

Accounts Receivable		
Date	**Debit**	**Credit**
4-Oct-09	$650.00	
6-Oct-09		$650.00
	$650.00	**$650.00**

Revenue		
Date	**Debit**	**Credit**
3-Oct-09	$650.00	$459.00
4-Oct-09		$650.00
5-Oct-09		**$203.00**
	$0.00	**$1,312.00**

In addition, the credit sale and payment are recorded in the customer's subsidiary account.

In double-entry bookkeeping:

- Expenses are always debits
- Revenues are always credits
- The Cash account is debited when cash is received
- The Cash account is credited when cash is paid out

An organization uses a set of accounts designed to fit its particular accounting needs. The list of all the accounts used by an organization to record and sort its business transactions is called its chart of accounts. New accounts can be added when needed, for example, when a company launches a new product. In a chart of accounts, account categories are typically listed in the following standardized order:

- Assets
- Liabilities
- Expenses
- Losses
- Stockholders' (or Owner's) Equity
- Revenues
- Gains

The accounting software widely in use today may not appear to be making entries into two accounts, because when you enter an amount as a credit in one account, the software automatically debits another account, and simultaneously updates the associated general ledger accounts. Accounting software reduces the potential for human error.

In any embezzlement scheme, if cash is paid out, a corresponding debit must be entered in another account, or the account books will not balance and the theft will be discovered. A fraud perpetrator may hide the theft by debiting one of the expense accounts or by adding the amount to an uncollectible customer account in Accounts Receivable that is about to be written off. The theft may also remain undiscovered if the books are not regularly examined, or if the fraud perpetrator is responsible for all bookkeeping functions and falsifies financial reports altogether.

Skimming

Skimming, which is the theft of cash before it enters a company's accounts, can take place at any point where cash enters a business: the cash register, the mailroom, a sales rep authorized to collect payments, or the desk of a clerk in Accounts Receivable. Employees who deal directly with customers or who handle customer payments are most likely to be involved in skimming. Since the stolen money is never entered in the company's books, it never appears in the company's financial statements, and the total amount of the theft may be difficult to document. Internal audits and bank statement reconciliations often fail to detect skimming. Suspicion may not be aroused until revenue falls far short of expectations, or large amounts of inventory disappear without any apparent reason. The most common types of skimming schemes are unrecorded sales, underreported sales, theft of checks sent through the mail, and short-term skimming. Each of these are detailed further in the following sections.

Note:

The term "skimming" is also used to refer to the use of a device to steal someone's credit card number and information recorded on the magnetic strip of a credit card. The "skimmed" data is then used to make counterfeit credit cards, or is sold to criminals. In April 2007, 13 waiters were arrested after they used hand-held devices to record information from diners' credit cards at more than 40 restaurants in New York, Florida, New Hampshire, Connecticut, and New Jersey. Waiters and waitresses would "skim" the cards while they carried them to the cash register to process payments, then sell the information to the ringleaders for $35 to $50 per card. The ringleaders manufactured counterfeit credit cards and paid others to use them to buy thousands of expensive electronics which were then resold to stores in Queens, New York. Skimming devices can be purchased over the Internet and are sometimes placed on gas pumps or ATM machines. Some have cameras that photograph you as you type in your PIN number or zip code. Watch for suspicious devices, camera lenses directed at your card or the keypad instead of at your face, and signs with unusual instructions at these locations, and keep an eye on your credit card when it is *in someone else's hands. Some restaurants now process your credit card payment at the table through portable card readers.*

Unrecorded sales

The most basic form of skimming occurs when an employee sells goods or services to a customer, makes no record of the sale, and pockets the payment instead of turning it over to the employer. Some form of concealment is typically required, such as ringing up a no-sale or a void on the cash register so that it appears that a sale is being recorded, or destroying or altering the cash register tape afterwards. The perpetrator knows how to manipulate the company's sales process and may create false invoices and receipts, so that the customer thinks he or she is dealing with the company.

When a company sells services, such as dry cleaning, the employee can simply omit transactions from the records and keep the money. If sales of goods are not being recorded, the employee must find a way to conceal or explain the fact that the inventory is being depleted. Retailers are concerned with "shrinkage," when the number of items in inventory does not tally with the number of items sold. A certain amount of shrinkage might be attributed to shoplifting or damage, but an excessive amount will alert the business owner to the theft. An employee who both inventories merchandise and handles cash sales is in a position to conceal unrecorded sales. In an industry where inventory is difficult to measure and control, such as the fast food industry, it is easy for employees to skim at the cash register. Many fast-food restaurants now have signs promising customers a reward for reporting when no receipt is given, or asking them to check their receipts against the cash register total.

CASE STUDY: POCKETING CASH AT THE REGISTER

Cashier
Park City, Utah

Last year, I worked a seasonal job as a cashier in a small restaurant located on a mountain among the ski slopes at a popular ski resort near Salt Lake City. Customers arrived on skis or snowboards and came in for a quick lunch, beer, or a cup of coffee. A young woman named Bethany had worked there the previous year, and the other employees knew all about her. The most popular menu items were burgers and wraps made to order by fast food chefs in the kitchen, but there were a few items, like salads, that were pre-packaged in plastic containers. One item, a chicken salad, cost exactly $10. When a customer who was paying cash ordered one of these salads, Bethany would enter the order into the cash register, ring up the chicken salad last, then delete it from the order but take the full amount of payment from the customer. While the cash drawer was open and she was making change, she would slip a $10 bill under the cash register and put it into her pocket later when no one was looking. The restaurant was busy, customers in damp ski jackets weren't interested in receipts, and the restaurant did not take inventory of its salads every day, so the manager never noticed. The employees who knew Bethany said that she sometimes pocketed several hundred dollars a week. She liked to brag about the items she bought with the money she took. She stole money for her friends, too. When her boyfriend asked her for money to repair his car, she stole $500 in a single day. Late in the season Bethany was fired when she was discovered bringing cocaine to work and sharing it with coworkers. Her theft, however, was never discovered by the management.

The most damaging cases of skimming do not occur at the cash register, but in situations where employees have a high level of autonomy, such as employees who work in remote locations without close supervision or as independent salespeople. Skimming can also be done by salespeople on-site who do not use a cash register, such as in a plant nursery or a warehouse. A manager of an apartment building might remove tenants who regularly pay in cash from his records and continue to receive rent payments from them while reporting their apartments as vacant.

Skimming also occurs when an employee continues to operate a business during non-business hours, or uses company equipment and supplies to do work on the side. A plumber who works for a large company might use a company truck to operate his own plumbing business on weekends, or offer discounts to customers who do not ask for receipts.

STRAIGHT FROM THE HEADLINES

Store Clerk Charged with Grand Theft

In August 2009, investigators were called to a Bealls Outlet store in Daytona Beach after store surveillance cameras caught a 23-year-old employee putting items into shopping bags without scanning them. Confronted with the evidence, she admitted to allowing friends and relatives to go through her checkout line without paying for merchandise and estimated that she gave away about $5,000 in merchandise — mostly men's clothing — over two months. She was jailed on $5,000 bail, fired from her job, and told she would be arrested for trespassing if she returned to the store.

Understated sales

Understated sales are transactions entered into business accounts as a lower amount than the customer actually paid for them. This can occur at the cash register when the employee collects the full payment for an item, but rings up a less expensive item in the register or records the sale of one item while actually selling two to the customer. The employee pockets the difference between the amount paid and the amount recorded in the register. An employee might also use a promotional discount code or an employee discount to ring up a false discount on a sale, while charging the customer full price and pocketing the amount of the discount.

Sales can be understated in accounts receivable by altering copies of invoices so that the invoice to the customer shows a higher amount than the office copy of the same invoice. When the customer pays the invoice, the accounts receivable clerk posts the lower amount and keeps the difference.

Theft of checks sent through mail

The rapid implementation of electronic banking and bill payment has reduced the opportunity for this kind of fraud, but in any business where check payments are received through the mail, a dishonest employee can misappropriate incoming checks and cash them or deposit them in a private account using false identification. Situations where a single person prepares and sends out statements and receives and records payments are particularly conducive to this kind of theft. In some cases, fraudsters have changed the address to which payments are sent so that the checks are routed to a private mailbox.

This type of theft requires additional effort on the part of the fraudster because checks made out to the business require an endorsement and must be cashed or converted to the employee's name. The employee may have an accomplice at a check-cashing facility or bank who agrees to overlook suspicious endorsements on the backs of the checks. The employee may use false signatures and IDs to avoid associating his or her name with the stolen check. Some fraudsters register a new business with a name very similar to the company name and obtain the documentation to open a business bank account where the checks can be deposited and the money withdrawn without attracting too much notice. Employees with authority to cash checks, or to open bank accounts on behalf of a company, may do just that — cash checks for themselves or set up dummy accounts with themselves as signatories and deposit checks there.

If cashing stolen checks proves too difficult, some fraud perpetrators take cash out of deposits and substitute the checks from unrecorded payments in its place. Because the total amount of the deposit is correct, the substitution will not be noticed unless someone takes the time to review each deposit and match recorded payments with the cash and checks used to pay them.

This form of skimming is more difficult to conceal because the canceled checks serve as evidence, and a customer who receives a collections notice after he or she has paid an invoice will raise an alarm. In situations where payments are infrequent or irregular, or are not always expected, this type of fraud can continue for a long time without being detected.

STRAIGHT FROM THE HEADLINES

Tribal Secretary-Treasurer/Tax Commissioner Diverts Taxes to Own Bank Account

In December 2008, John C. Richter, U.S. Attorney for the Western District of Oklahoma, announced a federal jury had found a 53-year-old tribal secretary-treasurer guilty of 33 counts of embezzlement from the Apache Tribe of Oklahoma. According to the evidence presented at her trial, Emily Anne Saupitty was elected secretary-treasurer of the Apache Tribe in 1998. In 1999, she was authorized by the Tribe to transact business on behalf of the Tribe's Tax Commission as a Tax Commissioner. Her duties were to receive tax checks from oil companies and deposit them in an Apache Tribe bank account in Andarko, Oklahoma. In January 2003, Saupitty used her home address to open a bank account named "Apache Tax Commission" in the town of Lawton without the knowledge of the Tribe and made herself the sole signatory. In 2003 and 2004, Saupitty deposited eight checks totaling $107,627.65 for oil and gas taxes, payable to the "Apache Tax Commission." She then paid the geologist and attorney who had assisted her in collecting the taxes and used the rest of the money to buy a home computer, travel with her friends, and spread her political influence in Tribal elections.

"The violation of trust placed in this defendant by the Apache Tribe is appalling," said U.S. Attorney Richter. "She not only used her positions in a public corruption scheme to satisfy her own greedy needs, but also for her own political gain."

Short-term skimming

In short-term skimming, an employee "borrows" incoming payments and places the money in a personal interest-bearing account, or a short-term investment for a few days or weeks, before retrieving it and posting the payments to customer accounts. The skimmer profits from the interest earned while the money is in his account. People engaged in this type of fraud often do not regard it as a criminal activity because the "borrowed" money is being repaid. From the company's point of view, they are stealing interest which the company should have earned and depriving the company the use of its money.

Concealment of skimming schemes

Unrecorded and underreported sales can be concealed with relative ease because the transactions are never entered into company accounting records. Cash register tapes, receipts, invoices, and inventory counts may be altered, "lost," or destroyed to remove any evidence that the transaction occurred. Unrecorded sales of services may never be detected, but when sales of goods are unrecorded, employees must find a way to conceal the fact that merchandise is disappearing from the inventory.

Fraud involving theft of receivables or stolen checks is more difficult to conceal because the company is expecting payments from its customers. When a payment is not recorded, the customer's account becomes overdue and questions are likely to arise. To conceal a theft of receivables, the fraudster must somehow account for the missing payment. Fraud perpetrators resort to a variety of methods to prevent employers from recognizing that incoming payments are being stolen. The following sections describe these methods:

Lapping

One method of accounting for missing payments, called lapping, is to use money from a later payment to make up the amount missing from an earlier payment. Now, the later payment is short, and money must be taken from still another payment to make up the difference. This process can be repeated over and over, with money continually being taken from the most recent payments to make up delinquencies in earlier payments. The same method can be applied to cash stolen from bank deposits. By depositing receivables two or three days after they are collected, a fraudster can take money from today's payments to make up a shortfall in yesterday's deposit. Incoming checks and cash do not always match the missing amounts, and a lapping scheme can become very complex as the fraudster continues to steal while moving credits around from account to account. Often, the fraudster keeps a written record of the stolen payments, or even a separate set of books.

Lapping can continue indefinitely until the stolen money is finally returned, the fraud perpetrator is caught, or a journal entry is made to adjust the accounts receivable balance. Sometimes, the fraudster does this by transferring delinquent amounts to old accounts that are about to be written off as uncollectible debts, eliminating the shortfall from the company's books forever. Some companies use "error" accounts to account for bookkeeping or other mistakes, and delinquent amounts can gradually be posted to these accounts.

Forgery

Stolen checks must be endorsed when they are cashed or deposited. Fraud can go undetected when canceled checks are not closely examined by the companies or individuals who issued them. Many banks no longer return the physical canceled checks to the account holder; they scan them and store images online instead. It may be difficult to verify that a signature has been forged when viewing an image instead of the original check.

Misdirected, stolen, or altered statements

Customers who received statements or late notices indicating missing payments are likely to expose the fraud by making inquiries. An employee who prepares and sends out customer account statements, or who has access to customer records, can steal or misdirect these statements by intercepting them before they are mailed, or by altering customer addresses so that the statements are returned as undeliverable. The returned statements can be retrieved from incoming mail and destroyed. Another strategy is to direct statements to a private mailbox belonging to the fraud perpetrator.

If statements are sent by e-mail or maintained online, the perpetrator of a lapping scheme who has access to electronic customer records may be able to prevent late notices from being sent out by temporarily altering the electronic data in the company system until the missing money has been replaced in an account. Because statements are typically sent out at regular monthly intervals, the data can be altered for a period between the due dates of the previous payment and the next payment, then changed back without being noticed. A typographical error can be inserted into a customer's e-mail address to prevent e-mailed statements or e-mail alerts from reaching their intended recipient.

Some fraudsters create and send out fake statements to replace stolen ones. This is relatively easy to do using a personal computer and company letterhead or accounting templates.

Making false entries into accounts

Stealing or altering statements may prevent customers from raising the alarm, but theft of incoming payments, known as receivables, must also be concealed in company accounts. One way to do this is by creating false accounting entries in the company's books so that overall debits and credits balance. When a payment is made, the bookkeeper ordinarily posts a credit to the customer's account and a debit to cash. Instead of debiting cash, a fraudster might conceal the missing money by debiting an expense account used for purchases of supplies, shipping, or travel expenses. The customer's account will not become delinquent, and the company's books will reconcile. The fraud will not be discovered until someone questions excessive or unsupported debits to the expense account.

Discrepancies in the accounts are also concealed by adding the missing amounts to accounts that are already delinquent and will soon be written off, or by moving those amounts to an account for a fictitious customer. The fictitious account will eventually age and be written off as a bad debt. In an industry such as health care or auto repair, where individual customers often pay for one-time services rather than maintain ongoing accounts, an employee with authority over billing may simply steal a customer's incoming payment and then write off that account as a discounted payment or an uncollectible debt.

Skimming red flags

Skimming is very common because it takes place among the large number of employees who deal directly with the public and handle incoming cash or payments. Direct evidence of skimming will not be found in a company's accounting system because the theft takes place before cash receipts are recorded. It is necessary to look for other signs, such as suspicious activity by certain employees, tampering with sales receipts, or disappearance of inventory.

- **Cash receipts do not match expected revenues**
  Based on previous sales figures, inventory counts, and customer traffic, a business is usually expected to bring in a certain amount of revenue. If the amount of cash receipts is lower than anticipated and there is no reasonable explanation, it is possible that employees are skimming or stealing incoming payments.

- **Unexplained change in normal business patterns**

  Changes in normal business patterns, when compared with past activity, are also cause for concern. There may be a good reason for a drop in business revenue: a recession, a new competitor operating nearby, negative publicity, or road construction obstructing access to the business. If there is no obvious cause, the business should be carefully evaluated.

- **Increase in inventory shrinkage**

  A certain amount of inventory shrinkage is expected due to damage, obsolescence, and shoplifting. If the percentage of shrinkage increases from one financial period to the next without an obvious explanation, it may be due to unrecorded sales.

- **Employee regularly comes in early or stays late**

  An employee who regularly finds a reason to remain alone and unsupervised before or after business hours should be monitored.

- **Customers always ask for a particular sales clerk**

  Multiple customers coming back repeatedly to the same sales clerk or an unusual familiarity between the sales clerk and customers could mean they are collaborating in a skimming scheme.

- **Employees are responsible for counting their own cash drawers**

  An employee who counts his or her own cash drawer and tallies sales has an opportunity to falsify totals or alter counts to cover up missing cash.

- **Excessive numbers of canceled sales, refunds or discounted sales**

  An employee may be taking from customers and making adjustments to the register by ringing up refunds or canceling the sale in the register and pocketing the cash.

- **Inappropriate telephone calls from clients**

  Client phone calls that seem to be outside the normal requirements of doing business could indicate the employee is selling company goods or services on the side.

- **There are damaged, altered, or missing receipts and cash register tapes**

  Some skimming schemes are concealed by manually altering cash register tapes or receipts, or by destroying incriminating documents.

- **Undocumented returns**

  If customers are regularly returning merchandise without sales receipts, or if returns are not accompanied by a customer name, address, and telephone number, an employee might be taking cash from a sale without issuing a receipt or working with accomplices to "return" stolen merchandise for cash.

- **A check-cashing institution questions a check endorsement**

  When an employee tries to cash a stolen check made out to the company by altering the payee name or forging an endorsement, the check-cashing institution may call to verify the check.

Techniques for detecting skimming

- **Surprise inventory counts and cash register audits**

  Unannounced cash register audits and inventory counts, conducted by employees other than those who ordinarily handle cash and inventory, may uncover discrepancies and missing inventory. Taken by surprise, the fraud perpetrator may not have time to conceal the theft in the usual way.

- **Analysis of sales records and trends**

  A comparison of sales records with those from previous years or with the sales records at other business locations may reveal an unexplained drop in sales revenue due to skimming.

- **Ratio analysis**

  Key ratios, such as the ratio of revenue to cost or revenue to returns, can be compared or different business periods. Unexplained differences could indicate skimming. *See "Ratio Analysis" in Chapter 9 for more information.*

- **Monitoring employees**

  Many retailers now use video cameras to monitor their cash registers and warehouses. Not only is evidence of thefts caught on tape, but employees who know they are being monitored are less likely to engage in skimming schemes. Employees can also be physically observed by an alert manager or by anonymous security personnel.

- **Careful review of cash and inventory accounts**

  A careful review of cash and inventory accounts may turn up evidence of skimming, such as false credits to inventory, unsupported entries to cash accounts, excessive write-offs of obsolete merchandise, or of outstanding accounts.

- **Sophisticated inventory control procedures**

  In addition to a simple inventory count, procedures such as logging inventory in and out, reviewing purchase orders, shipping documents and receiving documents, analyzing trends, and the statistical sampling of documents for analysis are likely to detect inventory shrinkage due to unrecorded sales.

- **Dummy bank accounts**

  In several of the real-life fraud cases described in the first chapters of this book, the fraud perpetrator opened a dummy bank account, sometimes under a name similar to the company name, and used it to deposit checks made out to the company. A social security number or tax ID is needed to open a new bank account. If you suspect an employee might be using a dummy bank account for a fraud scheme, you may be able to find it by running a credit check on the employee. A lawyer may be able to assist with a search for bank accounts with names similar to the company name.

Cash Larceny

Cash larceny is the theft of money that has already entered a company's accounting system. The most common type of cash larceny is the taking of money from a cash register, but employees also steal from petty cash accounts, bank deposits, and customer accounts. Cash larceny is commonly believed to be a crime committed by lower-level employees in a company, but among the cases studied by the ACFE for its *2008 Report to the Nation*, more than 65 percent of the cash larceny schemes were carried out by business owners, management, and the accounting department. Smaller businesses with fewer than 100 employees were victims of cash larceny more often than larger businesses, most likely because they have fewer controls and because a single employee may be responsible for multiple accounting functions.

Cash larceny is more likely to be detected by internal controls than other types of fraud because it creates immediate discrepancies in the accounts. Common cash larceny schemes include cash register theft, theft of sales and receivables, theft from bank deposits, and credit card fraud, which are explained further in the following sections.

Cash register theft

Taking money out of a cash register creates an imbalance between the register tape and the amount in the cash drawer at the end of a shift. At the end of the shift, the cash register prints out a report of all the transactions, and the cash in the drawer is counted and recorded as a cash count. Many companies will tolerate small discrepancies between the cash count and the total on the register tape because cashiers often make honest mistakes counting out change. An employee may disguise cash register theft by stealing from other employees' registers or signing on to a register as another employee to throw suspicion on someone else. Sometimes the thief maintains the correct cash balance in the drawer with some form of I.O.U. — such as a personal check from the employee for the missing amount or a note that a certain amount in small bills was loaned to another register as change.

An employee may attempt to mask cash register theft by destroying or recreating register tapes that reveal details about transactions. Another method is to alter the amounts recorded for cash counts at the end of a shift to match the totals on the register tapes, or to manually alter register tapes to match the cash counts. If the employee has the authority to process voids or returns, he or she may simply reverse transactions to make the register tape match the cash in the drawer.

Theft of sales and receivables

Earlier in this chapter was a description of "skimming" of receivables and sales before they are recorded in the company's books. A person handling incoming payments may also steal the money after it has been credited to customers' accounts and conceal the theft. A person who has full control over a company's accounts will be able to cover the theft by making unsupported entries to expense accounts, or by reversing sales and entering them as refunds, returns, or discounts. In some cases, the perpetrator may conceal a theft by simply "losing" or destroying all the pertinent records.

Theft from bank deposits

Most companies have procedures in place to ensure that money is not stolen from a deposit on the way to the bank, but often, these procedures are not strictly followed. If a single employee is responsible for preparing bank deposits, taking them to the bank, and entering them into the company's accounting records, it is easy for that person to take cash out of the deposit and cover his or her tracks. If bank copies of deposit slips are not regularly compared with the deposit slips that were written in the office when the deposit was prepared, a theft may be overlooked. A thief may also alter the office copies to reconcile with the bank deposit slips. Cash can also be stolen from bank deposit bags that are left unattended, even for a brief period of time, or taken by someone who secretly obtains access to them.

Theft from bank deposits can be concealed by lapping — delaying bank deposits by one day and using money from the next day's sales to make up a deficit in the previous day's bank deposit. This scheme can continue indefinitely as long as the same person continues to prepare bank deposits, until the amount stolen begins to exceed the amount of cash available to make up the difference. Another way to cover the theft is to record the missing cash in company accounts as a "deposit in transit" (DIT) — a deposit that has not cleared the bank and will appear in the next day's bank statement.

STRAIGHT FROM THE HEADLINES

Utilities Billing Clerk Steals $1.7 Million in Public Funds

In August 2009, a 38-year-old billing clerk was arrested for allegedly embezzling more than $1.7 million in public funds from the city of Los Baños, California. According to a city press release, between March 2005 and April 2009, she took cash from daily deposits at city hall and made up the missing amounts with checks from other deposits, including building department fees. A criminal investigation was launched when city staff discovered discrepancies in bank deposits in April 2009. The clerk resigned her position with the city shortly after the investigation began. Her personal banking records showed that the money was used to purchase real estate, vehicles, home furnishings, and electronics, and to pay for home remodeling projects, personal living expenses, entertainment, vacations, and travel. The city attorney and the police department were able to recover $7,000 in cash and $13,349 in restitution payments. The clerk deeded to the city two residential properties worth approximately $70,000 each; the cash was recovered during a warrant search of her home. An audit by a forensic auditing firm determined the scope of the theft was more than $1.7 million, and no one else was involved.

The city attorney said, "The city is and will continue to attempt to acquire as many of these assets as we can locate and identify." City officials announced the implementation of new measures to help prevent future theft, including the monitoring of daily deposits by an accounts supervisor, the bonding of all cash-handling employees, a video surveillance system covering the desk where cash is balanced and processed, and a policy that all building department fees should be paid directly to the accounting department.

Other types of larceny

Theft can occur any time an employee has access to cash. Many companies maintain a petty cash account or petty cash box to cover miscellaneous day-to-day expenses. It is easy to steal from petty cash and then create a false entry or receipt to account for it. Incoming checks and cash payments are vulnerable if they are not immediately locked away, or if controls are weak. Many larceny schemes takes place in banks, where employees are in contact with large amounts of money and are entrusted with varying degrees of authority.

An employee may even take cash and report it as a robbery. Most cash larceny schemes are carried out by individual perpetrators, but there are cases in which multiple employees conspire to rob their employer or enlist outside accomplices.

STRAIGHT FROM THE HEADLINES

Bank Employee Steals $110,000 From Client's Account

In July 2009, the New York Police Department's Organized and Identity Theft Task Force arrested Robin Katz, a 25-year-old investment advisor at the Midtown headquarters of Chase Bank, for stealing $110,000 from the bank account of a wealthy client. Approximately a month after Katz had left the bank to go to California for a family emergency, the client discovered money was missing from his account.

Auditors found Katz had ordered a duplicate ATM card made for the client's account and used it to withdraw cash dozens of times over the period of a year. The theft went undiscovered for a year because the account balance was so large that its owner did not notice the missing amounts right away. The ATM card and four receipts were still in Katz's wallet when she was arrested. Katz told authorities that she stole the money because she had trouble paying her bills.

Detecting cash larceny

Skimming schemes may not leave any trace in the company's books except an unexplained disappearance of inventory. Cash larceny schemes typically involve manipulation of documents or company accounts to hide the theft and can often be detected through extensive monitoring and review of the accounting system.

Monitoring can be done in several ways. It happens automatically when a procedure of checks and balances requires a second person to review a transaction and approve it or to compare cash receipts and sales documents before processing them. Another form of automatic monitoring is the security system on a computer network that controls which employees have access to certain accounting processes. Accounting software may also reject entries that do not reconcile with other data. Manual monitoring involves verification of documents such as invoices, packing slips, contractor bids, and purchase orders; manual bank reconciliations and review of canceled checks; careful examination of complex transactions; and the physical supervision of employees. Accounting and fraud detection software can be set up to scan millions of records for possible red flags and can monitor transactions as they are taking place. Later in this chapter we will discuss data mining — using computerized searches to find possible indications of fraud.

Red flags for cash larceny

- **A large number of voids, discounts, and returns**

  Stolen cash receipts must be accounted for in some way so the books still balance. Often, the missing cash is concealed by recording those amounts as voided sales, discounts, or returned merchandise. *See "Double-Entry Bookkeeping" in Chapter 5 for more information.*

- **Discrepancies between bank deposits and posting**

  The amount deposited in the bank should always equal the total cash receipts for that period. Discrepancies between the amount deposited and the cash receipts posted in the company's accounts suggest that money is being removed from the deposits.

- **Opening of unauthorized bank accounts**

  An employee who opens an unauthorized bank account in the name of the company may be using it to deposit stolen checks.

- **Sudden activity in a dormant banking account**

  When a bank account that has not been active suddenly begins receiving deposits or wire transfers, these transactions should be carefully verified.

- **Notices arriving for nonpayment of taxes**

  A common cash larceny scheme involves an accountant stealing money that is set aside for payroll taxes, then not filing an annual company tax return. The arrival of delinquent tax notices, or complaints from employees that they have received such notices, is definitely a red flag.

- **Presence of personal checks in the petty cash or cash register drawer**

  Personal checks from the employee responsible for petty cash found in the petty cash box indicate that the employee has "borrowed" money.

- **Excessive or unexplained cash transactions**

  A large number of cash transactions, or transactions not supported by documents, may indicate an employee is using lapping or moving cash around to cover up a theft.

- **Large number of accounts being written off**

  Outstanding accounts that remain unpaid for a long period are typically written off as uncollectible after a certain amount of time has passed. A large number of accounts being written off in this manner could mean someone is stealing incoming payments and then writing off those accounts, or moving outstanding amounts to old accounts and writing them off to make the books balance.

- **Bank accounts that are not reconciled on a timely basis**

  An embezzler who is responsible for reconciling bank statements with company accounts may conceal missing amounts or by reconciling bank statements at irregular intervals. Any company that does not regularly reconcile its bank accounts is creating an opportunity for fraud to go undetected.

- **Employees regularly volunteering to work overtime or on weekends**

  Employees who regularly insist on working overtime or coming into the office after hours and on weekends when there is little supervision may be using those opportunities to make alterations to accounts or carry out other activities related to fraud schemes.

- **Employee red flags**

  In the ACFE study for its *2008 Report to the Nation*, the most commonly reported employee behaviors associated with fraud were living beyond one's means and having personal financial difficulties. Other common behaviors were excessive gambling, a belligerent attitude, and inability to produce bank reconciliations and reports when asked. If behaviors like these are attracting the attention of coworkers, it is worth taking a closer look at that employee's activities in the workplace.

Techniques for detecting cash larceny

- **Regular internal audits**

  Regular audits of company accounts may not uncover fraud schemes because adjustments have already been made to the books to conceal the theft. They do provide a picture of a company's regular business activity and detect unexpected changes that might signal a fraud. The audit process typically includes a review of control processes and sampling of supporting documents, increasing the likelihood that irregularities will be discovered. Most perpetrators continue to steal larger and larger amounts; when the fraud creates too many discrepancies in accounts, it may be picked up during an audit. *Learn more in the discussion in Chapter 6.*

- **Surprise audits**

  Unannounced audits and inventory accounts may detect a fraud because the fraud perpetrator does not have time to make adjustments to accounts or conceal incriminating evidence. A surprise audit should be carried out by someone who does not work directly with the accounting system on a daily basis.

- **Mandatory job rotation**

  Moving employees from one position to another at regular intervals increases the likelihood that fraud will be discovered when the accounting system is seen with "a new pair of eyes." Job rotation also changes the relationships among employees in the workplace and prevents a fraud perpetrator from becoming entrenched in a situation where he or she has dominance or the cooperation of accomplices.

- **Mandatory vacations**

  A mandatory two-week vacation removes an employee from the office long enough for evidence of a fraud to surface: returned checks, bank statements or notices for nonpayment of tax in the mail, unusual phone calls and visitors, or changes in business patterns. The person taking over the absent employee's responsibilities may notice something outside of ordinary business activity.

- **Careful monitoring of customer credits or write-offs, adjustment accounts, and delinquent accounts**

  Close attention should be paid to accounts used to make adjustments for uncollectible debts, warranties, and returned merchandise. Details of customer credits and write-offs should be examined for supporting documentation. If there are any questions about a credit, contact the customer and make inquiries. If the numbers and amounts of these write-offs seem unusually large, it could be that an employee is using them to account for stolen money.

- **Analysis of the cash receipt and cash recording process**

  A careful walk-through of the cash receipt process — from the moment the sale is entered into the cash register or the customer's payment enters the company premises, through the recording of sales and preparation of bank deposits, to the arrival of the deposit in the company bank account — may identify weaknesses in the system and uncover where theft is taking place.

CHECKLIST FOR CASH RECEIPTS ANALYSIS

This checklist can be used to guide an examination of the processes used to receive and record incoming payments.

At what points do cash payments enter the company?

Cash Register

✓	Are the cash registers in a secure location?
	How is security maintained?
	Do employees have individual log-ins?
	Are cash registers ever left unattended? When?
	Who counts the cash in the register at the beginning and end of each shift?
	Does cash counting take place in a secure environment?
	Is the person doing the cash count different from the person operating the register?
	What is the policy for handling discrepancies and errors?
	What is the procedure for authorizing voids and returns?
	Do register tapes reconcile with the cash counts in register drawers?
	Do register tapes show signs of being altered or damaged?
	Are employees visually monitored at the cash registers?
	Are there security cameras filming the registers?
	What happens to merchandise when it is returned or rejected?
	What are the procedures for opening and closing the store and registers?
	Has anyone reported suspicious activity related to cash registers?

Mail

✓	Is the mail secure after it enters the building?
	Who sorts the mail, and how is it distributed?
	Who opens the mail?
	What is done when a payment by check is received?
	Is there a log for incoming checks?
	Are checks kept in a secure place?
	What is the procedure for recording and processing an incoming payment?

Electronic

✓	What is the process for recording an electronic payment in the accounts?

	If the payment is made online, is the connection secure?
	Are there any software glitches that could cause or allow a duplicate payment?
	How is information such as addresses, e-mail, and credit card numbers verified?
	If the payment is made over the telephone, who enters the information and how?
	Is there a confidentiality policy for employees to follow?
	Who has access to the data for electronic payments?
	Does anyone have the ability to alter or update the data?
	How are cancellations and returns for online payments handled?
	Do security logs show that employees' activity in the computer network coincides with their work schedules?
	Is the database password-protected?
	Who has access to these passwords?
	Has anyone every hacked into this system? What were the circumstances?

Preparation of Deposits	
✓	Is cash handled in a secure environment?
	Is there legitimate documentation for each cash receipt (such as a cash register entry or invoice)?
	Is an independent list of cash receipts prepared before they are submitted to the bookkeeper?
	Are deposits complete and equal to each day's total cash receipts?
	Is the total cash receipts verified against the deposit slip by an independent person?
	Are the bank deposits prepared and taken to the bank by separate people?
	Who prepares the deposits?
	Who takes deposits to the bank?
	How soon are deposits made after cash has been received?
	Are authenticated deposit slips kept and reconciled to the amounts in the cash receipts records?
	Does an independent person check the authenticated bank receipts and deposits listed in the bank statement against the amounts in the cash receipts journal?
	Are there any times when someone else might have access to the deposit before it reaches the bank?

- **Complaints from customers and financial institutions**

  No complaint from a customer, vendor, or financial institution should be ignored. Even a minor complaint about a missing statement or a question about a check endorsement could be the first clue to a major fraud scheme. Telephone receptionists and company employees should be trained to screen incoming calls carefully and obtain as many details as possible, then direct the complaint to someone with the authority to investigate it.

- **Monitoring the cash registers**

  The same monitoring procedures described in the section on skimming in this chapter apply to underreported sales and theft from cash registers after sales have been made: assigning a different employee to count cash in the register at the end of a shift and reconcile it with the cash register tape; following security procedures; video cameras and physical observation of employees.

- **Review of cash accounts**

  The explanation on double-entry bookkeeping in this chapter describes how every transaction involves a credit entry in one journal and a debit in another, so that the books are always in balance. Computerized accounting systems automatically credit cash accounts when debits are recorded for other accounts, such as bad debts or accounts receivable. A review of cash accounts may reveal unusual or unsupported entries that may be a cover for embezzlement.

- **Analytical review**

  A comparison of current sales and inventory figures, costs, and cash reserves with those of earlier periods, or with those from another location of the same business, may reveal an aberration that does not have a logical explanation, such as an increase in the price of raw materials, higher shipping costs, or a new discount incentive program. For example, a sudden increase in the cost of raw materials could indicate that someone is ordering surplus supplies and stealing them.

Business cycles should follow similar patterns to earlier years, unless something obvious has happened to change them. *See the section on ratio analysis in Chapter 9 for how you can use certain ratios to compare various types of business activity during different periods.* An unexplained change in a ratio from one period to the next could indicate fraud.

- **Sophisticated inventory control**
  The same inventory controls described in the section on skimming in this chapter can expose theft: review of shipping documents and packing slips, receipt confirmations, and purchase orders; logging of inventory; and statistical sampling and analysis. Many large retailers use computerized inventory systems that assign individual barcodes to each item, record when it passes into and out of inventory, and place new orders automatically.

- **Review of computer security reports**
  Many companies have security systems on their computer network that determine who can have access to which account databases and maintain a log showing when specific employees log in and out of the system. These logs should be reviewed regularly to see when and how often data is being accessed. Abnormal activity may indicate fraud. For example, if the logs show an accounting manager is logged in while that person was known to be out at lunch, someone could be using a stolen password to access the system and manipulate data.

- **External audits**
  Periodic external audits, conducted by an independent accounting firm, are required if a company is publicly traded and recommended for government entities funded by taxes, as well as for nonprofits that rely on donations or public money. External audits are also advisable for a private company when it is suspected that a fraud is being perpetrated by someone in a high position of authority such

as a CEO, CFO, chief accountant, or comptroller. Such a person would be able to manipulate an internal audit to conceal the fraud. Auditors who have experience with fraud may have a different perspective on the company's business activities.

Credit card fraud

According to Cybersource Corporation, retail losses due to online credit card fraud reached a record $4 billion in the United States and Canada in 2008. This amount is expected to rise through 2010. Although credit card fraud is typically perpetrated by someone outside a company who uses a stolen credit card to purchase goods or services, it must be mentioned because it is so widespread, and because companies can take measures to prevent it. A recent study by Mercator Advisory Group (**www.mercatoradvisorygroup.com**) quantified the "street value" of stolen credit cards, ranging from $1 for a simple credit card number to $1,000 for a plastic card together with identification.

Companies are victimized by credit card fraud in several ways. Unless a merchant has purchased chargeback insurance against cardholder fraud, it loses the cost of goods or services bought with stolen credit cards, plus any associated fees. When customers' credit card information is stolen from a company database, the company can become a target of legal action. Many states have laws requiring companies to inform their customers when their private financial information has been compromised. Even if this is done tactfully and with discretion, many of these customers may no longer trust the company and may take their business elsewhere. If there is evidence that stolen credit card numbers are being used for fraud, banks and credit card issuers typically change account numbers and issue new credit cards to customers with compromised accounts, a process that costs about $10 per card.

Many effective deterrents to credit card fraud are already in use. Most retailers require their cashiers to ask for a photo ID when a customer presents a credit card for payment. Companies that process credit card sales for merchants frequently update data on stolen credit card numbers and notify cashiers when a stolen card is being used. Similar controls are applied when credit card numbers are submitted for online payments. Onsite computer software can also be used to scan transactions for indicators of fraud. Online retailers are increasingly using software verifying the IP address of the computer from which a purchase is being made, or requiring customers to register and create a profile with the Web site. Online customers are asked to enter the security code printed on the back of each credit card to confirm they have the credit card in their possession and not just the number.

CASE STUDY: SCANNING FOR SUSPICIOUS CREDIT CARD TRANSACTIONS

Internet Marketing Developer
Florida

While working at a local visitor's bureau, I helped to create a sales reporting and processing system for online sales of attraction tickets. Because the project was initially an experiment on a small scale, management preferred to create the reporting system in-house rather than purchase an expensive online sales application. Each day's sales were double-checked, and reports were carefully reconciled with inventory and sales figures. If there were any doubts about an order, staff members took the time to call the customer and verify each item before mailing out the attraction tickets. One day, the credit card company called to say that a recent purchase had been made with a stolen credit card. An investigation revealed that over a period of five months, 15 sales had been made using different stolen credit card numbers, but all with the same shipping address — an apartment in New York. Thousands of dollars' worth of theme park tickets had been sent to that address. The visitor's bureau had not wanted to pay the extra merchant fees for chargeback insurance against fraudulent purchases and had to shoulder the entire loss. In spite of all the precautions taken by the staff, a year's worth of profits from the ticket sales was lost. The theft could have been detected at the second transaction if customer records had been regularly scanned, manually or automatically, for duplicate shipping addresses.

CHAPTER 6

Fraudulent Disbursements

Fraudulent disbursements, in which an employee deceives a company into paying out money through apparently legitimate channels, are the most common type of asset appropriation scheme. The ACFE classifies fraudulent disbursements into four major categories: billing schemes, payroll schemes, check tampering, and abuse of expense accounts. Often a fraud involves more than one of these categories.

Of the cases studied by the ACFE for its *2008 Report to the Nation*, almost 24 percent involved billing schemes, in which the perpetrator induces a company to issue payments for false invoices. Check tampering, the theft of company checks or alteration of checks issued for legitimate expenses, was involved in 14.7 percent of the cases. Expense account abuse occurred in 13.2 percent of the cases studied; and payroll schemes, in which employees caused a company to pay compensation for labor or services that were never rendered, occurred in 9.3 percent of the cases. The greatest median loss ($138,000) occurred in schemes involving check tampering.

Billing Schemes

In a typical billing scheme, the perpetrator abuses a company's purchasing and payment procedures to pocket payments for goods and services that are either fictitious or overpriced. Most companies require several documents, such as purchase order, invoice, receipt, or delivery confirmation, which must be authorized and acknowledged by various managers. A file containing all of these documents, called a voucher, is then sent to the accounting department where the payment is disbursed. Billing schemes often involve the fabrication or alteration of one or more documents, or the forgery of authorizing signatures. Situations where most or all of the purchasing functions are handled by one person, or where an accounting executive has uncontrolled access to documents or overriding authority to approve payments, are ripe for abuse. Several of the case studies in this section illustrate how highly placed accounting managers were able to act with impunity in disbursing hundreds of thousands of dollars in company funds to themselves.

Shell companies

Many billing schemes involve a "shell company," a fictitious entity created specifically to receive stolen funds. A shell company may be nothing more than a fabricated name and a post office box. The embezzler may find it necessary to open a bank account in the shell company's name to receive checks made out to the shell company and electronic payments. This usually requires registering the business with state and local authorities to obtain the necessary documents — a fairly simple process. A clever fraudster will use the name and address of a friend or relative to disguise his or her ownership of the shell company. For a small annual fee, the shell company can operate under a fictitious name, adding another level of disguise. The name and address of the shell company can then be used to fabricate invoices and submit them to an employer for payment. Professional-looking invoices can be produced on a personal computer or in the print department of an office supply store.

In some cases, a fraud perpetrator is in a position to approve payment of his or her own fraudulently submitted invoices. Company policies may make it necessary for a fraudster to forge another employee's signature or to fabricate realistic-looking corroborating documents such as purchase orders. Some billing schemes involve collusion among several employees who are responsible for different aspects of the purchasing and payment process.

Most billing schemes involve payment for some sort of service rather than goods or supplies, because suspicion would be aroused if goods that had been paid for were never delivered. Fraudulent invoices are often for services such as "consulting," "repairs," or "research" that cannot be easily documented and verified.

Pass-through schemes involve shell companies, usually set up by an employee in charge of purchasing, to sell goods and services required by the employer. Rather than buying directly from a legitimate vendor, the employee authorizes purchases from the shell company, which charges a higher price for the goods and services. The employee pockets the difference.

STRAIGHT FROM THE HEADLINES

More Than $1.6 Million Stolen Through Fictitious Company

In September 2009, Vivian K. Williams, 49, admitted to stealing more than $1.6 million from her employer, Women's Apparel Inc., a distributor of women's clothing in Easton, Pennsylvania. Between 1997 to June 2008, Williams held many positions in the company, including administrative assistant to the president and director of human resources. Her responsibilities included sales, marketing, and merchandising, and she had authority to sign purchase checks for up to $75,000. According to the plea memo, in 1999 Williams created a fictitious company called "The Copy Connection," which had a New York City mailing address with a P.O. box number. She then submitted invoices from The Copy Connection to her employer, which paid all of them. No services were every performed by The Copy Connection. The money went into a basic business checking account in the name of Williams, trading as The Copy

Connection, and was later transferred into one of Williams' personal checking accounts. According to the IRS, Williams under-reported her real taxable income from 2004 to 2007 by more than $1.06 million and owes back taxes of $327,774, not including interest and penalties. At her sentencing in December 2009, Williams faced a maximum possible sentence of 92 years in prison, a $2 million fine, five years of supervised release, and an $800 special victims/witness assessment.

Mishandling of legitimate invoices

Invoices from legitimate vendors can also be used to perpetrate billing schemes. An employee responsible for preparing invoices for payment may "accidentally" pay an invoice twice, then request that the vendor return the excess payment. When the check for the repayment arrives in the mail, the employee takes it. Another strategy is to mail out legitimate payments to the wrong vendors, steal the payment checks when they are returned, and process the vouchers for payment a second time to the correct vendors. Legitimate invoices could also be duplicated or altered and resubmitted so that the employer issues extra payments to a legitimate vendor. The fraudster steals the checks for these extra payments, forges an endorsement, and deposits them in a personal account.

STRAIGHT FROM THE HEADLINES

Accounting Supervisor Indicted for Embezzling Millions from Employer

On September 2, 2009, U.S. Attorney Tim Johnson announced Diana Simon, 49, a former accounting supervisor at Kaneka Texas, had been charged with embezzling more than $3.6 million from her employer, Kaneka Texas. Kaneka Texas is a wholly owned subsidiary of Kaneka Japan, a Japanese chemicals company with headquarters in Pasadena, Texas.

According to a press release from the U.S. Department of Justice, "The indictment alleges that as an accounts supervisor with Kaneka, Simon was responsible for processing invoices submitted by Kaneka's vendors for payment and allegedly used that process to create and implement a false and fraudulent scheme to cause $3,621,220 from Kaneka's bank ac count to be wired to her own bank account at a Houston area bank from June 2006 through February 2008." An investigation was conducted by the FBI after Kaneka discovered the embezzlement in 2008.

Working with investors to fabricate investors

In a billing scheme, an employee submits fabricated or altered invoices for payment and diverts the payment to his- or herself. Some billing schemes involve collaboration with vendors who bill a company for services that are never performed and give a percentage of the proceeds to the employee who authorized the payment.

STRAIGHT FROM THE HEADLINES

Accounting Manager Embezzles Almost $750,000 from Navy Exchange

A press release from the U.S. Department of Justice in September 2009 announced that Glenda Roberts, 49, a former accounting manager for the Navy Exchange at the Naval Amphibious Base in Little Creek, Virginia, had pleaded guilty in Norfolk federal court to one count of theft of public property. According to the press release, Roberts "used her position to concoct a scheme" for embezzling almost $750,000 from the Navy Exchange. The press release stated, "Roberts would create bogus invoices on her home computer and submit them to the Navy Exchange for payment. Once the checks were approved, Roberts would request the checks be sent directly to her, and she used these checks to pay her own personal bills. To conceal the fraud from auditors, Roberts created invoices for phony companies." Roberts was able to operate this scheme for 7 years, from 2001 to 2008, before it was detected by Navy auditors. Roberts apparently used the money to pay her bills and renovate her house.

Red flags for billing schemes

- **Vendor address is a P.O. box**

  Every vendor should have a physical business address, a contact telephone number, and an e-mail address. If the vendor has requested that payments be sent to a post office box, there should still be a physical address for that vendor and a phone number to call and verify that the postal address is legitimate. Lack of a physical address indicates the vendor is not a registered business, or an employee has fabricated invoices from a nonexistent vendor.

- **Vendor address is the same as an employee address**

  A vendor that has the same physical address or mailing address as an employee is a conflict of interest, even if the vendor is legitimate. It is more likely the employee has created a shell company, or the vendor is nonexistent.

- **Vendor name is not a registered business**

  The vendor should be registered as a business under a personal name or business name (a DBA — "doing business as") and should have a license to do business in the state or country where the business is registered.

- **Invoices are incomplete, altered, or otherwise unclear**

  Invoices that do not clearly state the unit cost or breakdown of the items or services being purchased should be questioned.

- **Invoices cannot be matched with accompanying documentation**

  Every invoice should be accompanied by documents showing that the goods were delivered or services were performed to the satisfaction of the company.

- **The person who selects vendors is also responsible for authorizing purchases**
  A situation in which the person who selects vendors also receives goods and authorizes payments can be easily abused.

- **Business costs have increased from previous years**
  If the costs associated with operating a business are higher than in previous years, and there is no obvious explanation, such as inflation or higher prices of raw materials, then money may have been siphoned off in false payments.

Techniques for detecting billing fraud

- **Compare invoices and purchase orders with inventory levels**
  The same sophisticated system of inventory control that can detect and prevent larceny and skimming is also an effective way of detecting billing schemes. Such a system would show goods listed on the invoices have not been received or the value of the inventory does not equal the amount spent to acquire it. Many billing schemes occur in small companies where a single employee is responsible for ordering goods such as office supplies and services, authorizing payments, and verifying the goods have arrived or the services have been performed. These duties should be divided between at least two individuals or overseen by a supervisor.

- **Regularly review vendor lists and accounts payable**
  Vendor information should be reviewed and verified at periodic intervals, and any unusual listings should be investigated. A shell company may come to light when the goods or services offered by each vendor are closely examined.

- **Regularly analyze purchases**
  Purchasing levels should be analyzed on a monthly and yearly basis, and abnormal levels should be scrutinized.

- **Check for duplicate invoice numbers and purchase order numbers**

  Most companies use a unique number for each invoice and purchase order. Two documents with the same number indicate that one might be a forgery, or that the same invoice is being submitted twice for payment.

- **Review invoices and compare with receiving and shipping reports**

  Invoices and accompanying documentation should be regularly examined. The information on invoices should be complete and should match the information on receiving and shipping reports. Check the addresses to which goods were delivered and the signatures of the employees who received them.

- **Reconcile bank statements and review credit card statements**

  Any unusual amounts or irregular payments should be investigated and matched with invoices and documentation.

- **Review journal entries to inventory accounts**

  A careful review of journal entries to inventory accounts may reveal irregularities or unusual entries, such as broad terms like "consulting fees," that require further examination.

- **Search employee and vendor databases**

  Employee and vendor databases can be searched for vendors and employees who have the same physical address, mailing address, telephone number, or e-mail and for vendor names that match an employee's initials or the name of an employee's family member.

- **Interview coworkers**

  If an employee is suspected of billing fraud, information may be discovered by interviewing coworkers regarding the purchasing and receiving process. Employees may give differing explanations for the same procedures or drop hints that they have observed something unusual.

- **Conduct a step-by-step review of the purchasing and payment process**
  A careful examination of the purchasing process from order to payment may reveal weaknesses in the system that could be exploited or demonstrate that procedures are not being followed.

The following checklist can be used to review purchasing procedures.

CHECKLIST FOR EXAMINATION OF PURCHASING PROCESS
This checklist can help expose weaknesses in the purchasing system and identify individuals who might have the opportunity to commit billing fraud. Multiple functions performed by a single individual is a red flag.

Organization of the Purchasing Department	
✓	Does the company have a purchasing department? If not, who does the purchasing?
	Is the purchasing department independent of the accounting and receiving departments?
	Are purchasing and receiving duties done by different employees than those who handle invoices, general ledgers, and accounts payable?
	How are purchases initiated? Are purchases made only after purchase requisitions have been authorized?
	Who authorizes purchases?
	Does the company use a budget system? Are purchases checked against the budgeted amounts?

Receiving	
✓	Who receives incoming purchases?
	Is a log kept of received goods?
	Are incoming purchases checked against the invoice and purchase order, and are goods examined to verify they are in good condition and are the same quantity and quality that was ordered and invoiced? Who does this work?
	Where are incoming goods stored, and how are they secured? What happens to goods after they have been received?
	What procedure is followed when only partial shipments are received?

Purchase Orders

✓	Does the company use purchase orders?
	Are purchase orders sent to vendors for all purchases, or just for those above a certain amount?
	How does an employee obtain a purchase order?
	Are purchase orders logged when they are given to employees?
	Are purchase orders numbered sequentially with printed numbers?
	Is a list kept of outstanding purchase orders and regularly reviewed and updated?
	Does the business maintain any blanket purchase orders (standing orders that maintain inventory at a specified level)?
	Are quantities received under blanket purchase orders monitored, and are excess amounts returned to the vendor?
	Who gets copies of receiving reports, and where are they filed?

Vendors

✓	What process is used to select vendors? Who selects vendors?
	Does the company maintain an approved vendor list? What are the requirements for approved vendors? Are certifications and references checked?
	Is vendor information (physical address and contact information) complete and up-to-date?
	How often is vendor information reviewed, verified, and updated?
	Is vendor information checked against employee addresses, phone numbers, and initials?
	Is there a bidding process? Are items purchased only after bids have been obtained and reviewed?
	How are vendors notified the company is seeking bids for goods or services? How are they notified when a winning bid has been selected?
	What procedures are in place to ensure the company gets the lowest price?
	Is there a procedure to ensure that any available discounts or special offers are taken advantage of?
	Is there an unusually close relationship between a company employee and a vendor?
	Is there a policy regarding the types of thank-you gifts and favors company employees may accept from vendors?
	Is purchasing staff rotated periodically?

Accounting

✓	Are vendor invoices matched with purchase orders and receiving reports before they are recorded as accounts payable?

Does someone check invoices carefully for prices, discounts, shipping costs, and totals? Who?
Are vendor invoices, purchase orders, and receiving reports checked before payment is made?
Who approves invoices for payment?
How are payments made? Who signs checks or submits electronic payments?
If payments are made by checks through the mail, how is mail returned as "undeliverable" handled?
Who authorizes adjustments to accounts payable?
Are statements from vendors regularly reviewed and matched against accounts payable?
Is the accounts payable ledger regularly reconciled with the general ledger control accounts?
Who assigns categories to purchases in ledger accounts?
Are unmatched documents regularly investigated?
When goods are returned to vendors, how are the transactions processed in the accounting system?
What procedure is followed to avoid paying duplicate invoices?

Making Purchases with Company Accounts

Another type of fraudulent disbursement scheme involves getting an employer to pay for purchases and personal expenses directly out of company accounts. The perpetrator must have some kind of legitimate access to expense accounts or the authority to sign off on purchases. These schemes take several forms, including abuse of expense accounts and company credit cards, and the purchase of items or inventory for personal use through the company's purchasing system. These schemes are described in further detail in the following sections.

Credit cards

Instead of stealing cash, some fraud perpetrators devise ways to get their employer to pay for their personal expenses. A common scheme is the abuse of a company credit card that has been issued to a manager or company representative to cover the costs associated with doing business for the company. Most companies require the holders of such credit cards to submit expense reports and receipts to show how the money was spent. In an environment where controls are less stringent, the card holder may be able to get away with charging personal expenses to a company credit card. He or she may avoid submitting receipts by claiming that they have been lost or misplaced. Accounting staff may be too busy or uninterested to look carefully at expense reports. In some cases, senior executives in a position to authorize their own expenditures have charged thousands of dollars' worth of luxury travel, clothing, home renovations, and other personal indulgences on company credit cards.

A company credit card can also be "borrowed" or stolen from the legitimate holder and abused by another employee. For example, an executive assistant might use his or her superior's card to make purchases and then destroy the credit card statements to hide the fraudulent purchases. Because online purchases can be made by simply typing in the credit card number, billing address, and security code, an employee needs only to write this information down to be able to shop online and have purchases shipped to another address. Some companies issue gas cards to employees who drive company vehicles so they can buy gasoline on a company account. A dishonest employee could use a gas card to buy fuel for a personal vehicle or for a friend in return for cash or a favor.

Requisitions and purchase orders

Most accounting control systems include a purchase order or requisition that must be authorized by senior management before an invoice can be paid. Typical purchase orders are printed with serial numbers, and each one is logged in a journal when it is issued to an employee who needs to place an order with a vendor. The employee completes the purchase order and then takes it to a manager who signs it before it is sent to the vendor. Fraudulent purchases can be made by stealing, altering, or tampering with purchase orders. A fraudster may forge an authorizing signature, add purchases to an existing order that has already been authorized, or generate counterfeit purchase orders. Authorization for a purchase is sometimes obtained by misrepresenting the nature of the item or service being purchased and altering the description on the accompanying invoice to support the deception.

When a company is already purchasing items such as electronic equipment or building supplies for its business, an employee may be able to place an order using a company account and then divert the supplies for his or her personal use. Sometimes this is done by adding items to a legitimate purchase order and intercepting the items when they are delivered, or by directing their delivery to a different shipping address.

Many companies require executive approval for purchases over a certain amount, but allow individual managers to authorize expenditures below that amount. A fraudster may split a large purchase into several smaller purchase orders that he or she can freely authorize.

It is the job of the accounting department to scrutinize purchase orders and ascertain they have been properly authorized before paying the accompanying invoices. Fraud can be committed by anyone who is familiar with any weaknesses in this procedure or who has an opportunity to tamper with the documents at some point during the process.

Expense accounts

Many companies reimburse employees for business-related expenses such as travel, vehicle mileage, the cost of entertaining clients and, in some cases, even clothing. Expense account fraud occurs when an employee submits fraudulent expenses for reimbursement or re-characterizes personal expenses so that the company pays the bills.

Among the fraudulent disbursement cases studied for the ACFE's *2008 Report to the Nation*, 13.2 percent involved reimbursement for fraudulent expenses. The median loss for these cases was lower than for other types of fraudulent disbursement schemes. Expense reimbursement schemes perpetrated by business owners resulted in losses five times greater than those perpetrated by lower-level employees, probably because a business owner is able to authorize his or her own expenses. In some cases, business owners used the company account as a personal checking account.

The most common ruse is simply mischaracterizing a personal expense such as travel or dining out as a business expense and submitting a request for reimbursement. If the request is not carefully reviewed, the mischaracterization will go undetected and the reimbursement will be processed. Mischaracterization schemes are frequently carried out by upper-level management and may involve large payments.

Another expense reimbursement fraud strategy involves overstating expenses. Receipts for legitimate expenses may be altered to overstate the amount due to the employee. Expenses can be overstated, especially for travel, by purchasing a high-priced airline ticket and submitting the receipt for reimbursement, then returning the ticket for a refund and traveling for a much lower fare. The employee pockets the difference between the high-priced ticket and the economy fare.

Some employees obtain blank receipts or letterheads and fabricate supporting documents for fictitious expenses. Another scheme is to submit multiple reimbursement requests for the same expense, using different supporting documents.

Not all expense reimbursement schemes are initiated by the employee submitting the reimbursement request. There are cases in which a supervisor asks subordinates to submit fictitious expenses and approves the requests, then shares or pockets the proceeds.

Red flags for expense account fraud

- **Missing receipts and documentation**

  Whether an employee is using a company credit card or turning in an expense report for reimbursement, there should be a receipt or other document to support each item.

- **Attitudes of employees with company credit cards and expense accounts**

  In the section on employee red flags in Chapter 5, certain types of behavior were described that might indicate an employee is committing fraud. An employee who shows little respect for rules and regulations, or one with a "wheeler-dealer" attitude, may abuse privileges such as a company expense account.

- **Senior executives dominate or intimidate the accounting department**

  An accountant may not want to question undocumented expenses or refuse payment for a personal expense for fear of losing his or her job.

- **An unusual number of items or supplies charged to an expense account, or an unusually large reimbursement to an employee for business expenses**

  Expenditures typically follow a pattern associated with company business cycles or a specific employee's job responsibilities. Deviations from these patterns, such as unusually large reimbursements or an abnormal amount of activity, are a sign that the employee may be charging personal expenses on the account.

- **Lax enforcement of company policies**

  Employees are more likely to abuse expense accounts if they are under the impression that no one will notice or that such behavior is a matter of course.

Techniques for detecting expense account fraud

- **Compare expense accounts to budgeted amounts**

  Amounts charged to expense accounts should be reviewed and compared to the amounts allocated for these expenses in the annual budget. If the expenses significantly exceed the budgeted amounts, closer examination is needed. Either the budget is unrealistic, the employee's legitimate business expenses exceed allowed amounts, or the expense account is being padded with unauthorized expenses in disguise.

- **Compare expenses to previous years**

  A historical comparison of current expenses with expense account totals from previous years may reveal significant discrepancies. These might be due to changes in marketing activities, company policies, or prices, but they could also indicate an employee is using the account to pay for personal expenses.

- **Careful examination of the receipts and documents accompanying expense reports or credit card statements**

  It should be routine for a supervisor or a person in the accounting department to go over expense account charges and reimbursement requests and verify the receipts, ticket stubs, credit card slips, and hotel bills are for legitimate business expenses and match the totals on the expense reports. This can be done by comparing the hours on an employee's time sheet or work schedule to the dates on the receipts and by confirming the employee used the purchases for business purposes. Some companies designate specific hotels and restaurants to be used for business by employees and limit the dollar amounts that will be reimbursed. Even when company policies are strictly enforced, employees may be able to get away with being reimbursed for personal expenses — for example, by charging a family dinner to a company credit card during a business trip and recording it as entertainment for a client. Supplies and materials purchased on account for a company project should be compared to inventory totals, and the receiving and shipping documents should be examined to see when and where materials were delivered.

CASE STUDY: EMPLOYEE ABUSE OF EXPENSE ACCOUNTS

New York banker

My first job was with a major U.S. banking firm. I was just a trainee when I accompanied my boss on our first business trip. I was sitting next to him on the plane when he suddenly turned to me and said, "Let's play poker!"

I said, "I'm sorry, I can't. I don't have any money."

He answered, "We can play for our expense accounts."

"What?" I asked, puzzled.

"Our expense accounts. You know we're allowed to spend up to $900 cash from our expense accounts without having to account for it. I'll play you for the cash from your expense account."

So we played poker with our expense accounts. In my position, I really couldn't do anything else. The first thing I learned from my boss was how to cheat on my expense account.

Payroll Schemes

Payroll schemes are perpetrated by falsifying time sheets, time cards, and sales reports to cause a company to pay out compensation for nonexistent employees or work that was never done. Among the cases studied for the ACFE's *2008 Report to the Nation*, more than half of the payroll schemes occurred in small companies with fewer than 100 employees. Nevertheless, the median loss for payroll schemes in large companies was double the median loss in small companies.

Many employees commit small-scale payroll fraud when they leave work early, take long lunch breaks, or come in late without reporting it on a time sheet. Payroll fraud schemes typically involve more serious transgressions, such as collecting a second paycheck or claiming overtime pay for hours that were never worked.

Ghost employees

A ghost employee is a fictitious person or a non-employee who is added to the company payroll. People who have the authority to add new employees to the payroll are the most likely suspects in ghost employee schemes. Fictitious ghost employees are sometimes given names similar to the names of existing employees, so that they do not attract the notice of a payroll clerk. Sometimes employees who have already left the company are kept on the payroll, and someone else collects and cashes the payroll checks.

STRAIGHT FROM THE HEADLINES

CFO Pays $655,710 to Ghost Employee

In September 2009, Elias Castellanos, 43, a former chief financial officer for the Housing Authority of New Orleans (HANO), created by the state to provide safe and affordable housing for low-income families, pleaded guilty to embezzling more than $900,000 from the agency. According to U.S. Attorney Jim Letten, the theft was uncovered during an unrelated investigation involving HANO, which is now insolvent and in federal receivership under the Department of Housing and Urban Development.

Between September 2006 and June 2009, Castellanos submitted fraudulent time sheets under his wife's maiden name and billed HANO for $655,710 for work his wife didn't perform. Castellanos was also accused of fraudulently billing the agency for an additional $245,217 in work. His wife, who lived in Miami, was not accused of wrongdoing. Authorities were able to recover $675,037 of the stolen money.

Letten commented that Castellanos "violated the public trust in the worst way" because his job was to protect public money set aside to help "the most vulnerable among us. You had the fox guarding the chicken coop."

Proper documentation such as personnel forms must be supplied for each ghost employee, and regular time sheets prepared and submitted as if the person had really worked for the company. Typically these time sheets are approved by a supervisor before being sent to the accounts department for processing. Often the perpetrator is a supervisor who has the authority to add new employees and approve time sheets, such as a department supervisor or human resources officer. A person responsible for managing subcontractors sometimes fabricates records of additional hours worked by legitimate contract laborers, submits them for payment, and intercepts the extra paychecks.

STRAIGHT FROM THE HEADLINES

Employee Creates Fictitious Insurance Agent

In September 2009, employees of Aviva USA, an insurance company headquartered in Des Moines, Iowa, discovered that a coworker had embezzled an estimated $5.9 million over a period of five years. The woman, who had worked for Aviva and its predecessor for 35 years, allegedly devised a computer program to divert commissions from sales by a fictional agent into a bank account belonging to her and her partner. She was arrested by the FBI on fraud charges, and Aviva has also filed a civil lawsuit against her for defrauding the company.

Paychecks may be mailed out to employees, deposited directly into their bank accounts, or handed out in the office. It is easy for supervisors responsible for handing out paychecks in the workplace to remove a ghost employee's check from the stack of envelopes. When the ghost employee is a fictitious person, the fraudster cashing the paycheck will have to forge an endorsement on the check, obtain fake identification with the ghost employee's name on it, or find an accomplice in a bank or check cashing facility. If the ghost employees are real people, they may cash the paychecks themselves and give a share to the fraudster.

STRAIGHT FROM THE HEADLINES

Director of Charity Pleads Guilty to 148 Counts of Embezzlement

In September 2009, Anna M. Naukam, former executive director of the Oklahoma CASA Association, pleaded guilty to 148 counts of embezzlement and one count of conspiracy and was sentenced to 15 years in prison, 20 years on probation, and payment of $549,024 in restitution. For almost ten years, Naukam was executive director of the Oklahoma branch of Court Appointed Special Advocates (CASA), a taxpayer-supported private association that provides volunteer advocates to represent neglected and abused children in court.

During the investigation, 51-year-old Naukam told state auditors, "I was very good at cooking the books." In 2001, soon after she and her husband had filed for bankruptcy, Naukam obtained a CASA credit card. A year later, she had a CASA credit card issued for her husband, who was not an employee.

In 2006, Naukam added her husband to the CASA payroll with a salary of $40,000, but told the organization he was just a volunteer. She fabricated invoices, altered checks, forged meeting minutes, and signed other peoples' names to organization checks. An audit revealed that the couple had misused more than $650,000. At her sentencing, Naukam showed no remorse for taking money intended to help abused children, telling the judge instead that the experience had been "hard on her." Naukam's embezzlement was discovered when the CASA Board of Directors began investigating questionable practices at the organization.

Overcompensation

Overpayment of wages is the most common type of payroll fraud. Most employees are either paid an hourly rate or a yearly salary. Wages paid at an hourly rate can be overstated by either increasing the number of hours worked or the amount paid per hour. Salaried employees receive the same wages regardless of the number of hours worked, so they can only increase compensation by somehow inflating their salaries. Only a person who has access to personnel and payroll data can alter the amount that an employee is due to be paid.

Hourly workers typically report their hours in one of three ways: punching in and out on a time clock, logging in and out of a computer workstation, or manually writing in their hours on a time sheet. If they can escape detection, employees may devise a way of adding a few extra hours to a workweek by having another employee punch in or log in for them, or they may leave the premises unnoticed after logging in. In most companies using manually prepared timesheets, the timesheet must be approved by a supervisor before a paycheck is issued. A worker might create a falsified timesheet, forge a supervisor's signature, and submit it to the payroll department in place of the real timesheet. Another strategy is to alter the timesheet after the supervisor has signed it. A supervisor may be in collusion with employees and approve falsified timesheets in return for a kickback or personal favors.

Many companies pay a higher hourly rate for overtime — hours worked beyond the regular workweek, usually to meet a deadline or complete an urgent project. Employees may be able to get away with recording unworked overtime hours on their timesheets because the hours worked are outside of regular work periods or on weekends when fellow workers are not present.

Another way to steal from the payroll is to take vacation or personal leave without reporting it. Poorly supervised employees may be able to get away with reporting they were in the office on days when they were absent or with spending part of the day out of the office. The absence of managers or executives may go unquestioned because of their seniority. Cell phones permit an employee to be in contact with the office from almost anywhere. An increasing number of employees work at home and telecommute. Many companies do not have clear policies defining what is required of employees outside the office, and the policies that do exist are difficult to enforce.

Rubber-stamp supervisors

In many payroll fraud cases, "rubber-stamp supervisors" approve time sheets without ever examining them. A supervisor may be too inattentive or lazy to look closely at timesheets before approving them. In other cases, supervisors trust their employees so completely that they never question the hours recorded on a timesheet. Employees who are aware of the supervisor's lack of attention may take advantage of it to regularly inflate the amount of time worked.

Supervisors who work closely or develop strong personal relationships with their employees may become sympathetic and willing to overlook the extra hours recorded on a timesheet. The supervisor may be afraid of offending or losing a valued employee, or may depend on that employee to carry out administrative responsibilities.

Working another job on company time

The widespread use of computers and the Internet has greatly increased the incidence of another type of payroll theft: employees who use company resources and time to operate side businesses or do other work while in the office. For example, an employee may spend several hours of his or her workday on a cell phone arranging appointments to show real estate properties after work hours. Many web designers and graphic designers freelance by doing work for private customers at night and on weekends. It is easy to access the internet from the office and work on a personal project or process orders for an online business on company time. An employee may even use expensive software programs licensed to the company to do work for private customers.

A recent survey by Vault.com, reported on **www.emarketer.com**, revealed that 25 percent of workers spent at least 10 minutes a day on the Internet at work for personal activities such as shopping online, checking e-mail, or looking up movie schedules. Thirteen percent reported they spend two hours per day. Workers are increasingly surfing the Internet or playing computer games on company time. Human resource theory typically considers that an employee will use one hour of the work day, in addition to breaks, for personal needs rather than productive work and factors that into employee salaries. Excessive amounts of time spent pursuing personal activities on the Internet represent an economic loss to the employer. According to the 2007 annual Electronic Monitoring and Surveillance Survey, conducted since 2001 by the American Management Association (AMA) and The ePolicy Institute, more than 67 percent of companies surveyed now monitor their employees' use of the Internet to some extent.

Sales commissions

Workers who are paid commissions on the sales they make may fraudulently inflate sales figures in order to increase their compensation. The strategy used depends on the industry and the manner in which sales are recorded and reported. On a retail sales floor, an employee might ring up fictitious sales or take credit for sales made by another employee. A sales representative may inflate his or her monthly sales total by recording fictitious sales near the end of one month and then processing them as returns or cancellations at the beginning of the next month.

A sales representative may also increase commissions by inflating the value of sales. For example, the customer might pay a discounted price for merchandise or services, but the sales representative will alter the invoices to reflect the full price in order to receive higher commissions.

Just as with hourly compensation rates or salary rates, a person with access to the payment system might be able to alter the percentage of sales due to a sales representative as a commission.

Workers' compensation and insurance fraud

Workers' compensation is a state-administered insurance program guaranteeing medical care and reasonable compensation for workers injured on the job. In addition, many companies offer optional short-term medical insurance that compensates a worker who is unable to work for a short period due to an illness or injury. An employee fakes or exaggerates an injury and collects the insurance payments while not working. In some cases, the fraudster collaborates with a doctor to file claims for bogus medical treatments.

The immediate victim of insurance fraud is the insurer who must pay the claims. Over the long term, however, the employer and other employees become victims when insurance premiums are raised because too many claims have been paid out.

Red flags for payroll fraud

Payroll fraud involves two basic types of schemes: drawing a paycheck for a nonexistent employee, and inflating the salary, commission, or number of hours worked in order to receive a larger paycheck. The best place to look for red flags for payroll fraud is in personnel records, timesheets, and employee schedules. The following are signs payroll fraud could be occurring:

- **More than one employee with the same name, address, or phone number**
  A quick alphabetical search of an employee database may reveal that several paychecks are being issued to employees with the same address, name, or telephone number. There could be a legitimate reason, such as two or more family members employed by the company and sharing the same address, but it is also possible that two paychecks are being issued to the same person.

- **Duplicate social security numbers**
  Social security numbers are an important form of identification and are linked to bank accounts, tax records, and retirement sav-

ings accounts. Each employee has a unique social security number. Duplicate social security numbers indicate either undocumented workers sharing a social security number, or a worker receiving more than one paycheck.

- **Duplicate bank account information**
  If the same bank account information appears on the records of two employees, they either share a joint bank account or are the same person.

- **Missing tax forms and social security numbers**
  A personnel record that is missing documentation, such as a tax-withholding form or photocopy of a social security number could indicate a ghost employee.

- **Excessive claims for overtime pay**
  Claims for overtime pay that exceed budgeted amounts or company policy, or that do not coincide with periods of business activity, may be fraudulent or overstated.

- **A time clock that can be easily accessed by other employees**
  If a time clock is not password-protected, or some method exists for an employee to clock in for someone else or to alter the time record retroactively, there is an opportunity for employees to cheat on their hours.

- **A single individual responsible for authorizing time sheets and handing out paychecks**
  The same person who approves workers' timesheets should not be responsible for distributing paychecks; that person would have an opportunity to submit timesheets for a fabricated employee or to collect kickbacks from employees who have been overpaid.

- **Discrepancies between time sheets and employee schedules**
  If an employee's time sheet shows he or she was working on a day when that employee was not scheduled to work or had requested

vacation time or medical leave, he or she may be trying to claim wages for time spent out of the workplace.

- **An employee receiving a significantly higher paycheck than another employee in the same job position**
  Employees should receive similar amounts of compensation based on the company pay scale and seniority. When one employee receives a much larger paycheck than someone else in a similar job position, it may be because salary information has been altered on his or her record.

- **Employee personnel records accessed inappropriately**
  A computer security log showing that an employee's personnel records were accessed after hours or during a lunch hour should trigger an investigation to see if any salary data was altered.

- **A large number of canceled sales or returns after the end of a pay period**
  An employee paid on commission may inflate sales figures by reporting false sales in one pay period and then reversing them as cancellations or returns during the next.

Techniques for detecting payroll fraud

- **Search personnel files**
  Personnel files should be regularly monitored for duplicate addresses, similar names and, when payment is made by direct deposit, duplicate bank account information.

- **Review and update personnel files**
  A review of personnel files should be conducted at least once a year to make sure that every employee's documents are on file and that any employee who has left the company is no longer on the payroll or receiving benefits. Each employee's most recent paycheck should be compared to his or her authorized wages or salary.

- **Compare payroll amounts to budgeted amounts**
  Discrepancies or excessive payroll costs should be investigated to see why they do not match the budgeted amount.

- **Rotate the job of distributing paychecks**
  Responsibility for distributing paychecks should be rotated from time to time, without prior notice, to another employee. This will thwart or expose attempts to pocket paychecks for nonexistent employees or collect kickbacks from overpaid employees.

- **Have every employee sign for his or her paycheck**
  If ghost employees are suspected, conduct a one-time exercise in which every employee must personally claim his or her paycheck or pay stub and sign a register. This should be administered by a person from outside each department and in such a way that no employee will be able to appear twice and claim two paychecks.

- **Conduct a thorough step-by-step analysis of payroll procedures**
  Walk through the entire payroll process, from the creation of personnel records for new employees to the distribution of paychecks and reconciliation of the bank statements and ledgers. Look for possible weaknesses and identify the employees that handle each responsibility.

CHECKLIST FOR PAYROLL PROCEDURES ANALYSIS

This checklist incorporates many of the recommended procedures and controls for maintaining the integrity of the payroll process. Separation of duties is the most important safeguard against payroll fraud. If this checklist reveals that the same person is handling multiple responsibilities related to the payroll, the situation should be closely examined.

Human Resources	
✓	Are reference and background checks done for all new employees? Who does this and how is the information recorded?
	Is there a social security number and tax-withholding form for every employee?
	Are forms for tax-withholding and payroll deductions completed, signed, and on file for each employee?

	Who authorizes wage and salary rates for employees? Is there a signed wage authorization on file for each employee?
	What is the procedure for making changes to an employee's wage rate or salary?
	Are bonuses, overtime, and commissions in line with company policies?
	Who approves bonuses, overtime, and commissions? Are they approved in advance?
	Are sick leave, personal leave, and vacation time approved, verified, and checked to see if they comply with company policies?
	How are work hours verified? Is there a time clock?
	Is the time clock secure, and does someone supervise the punching of time cards?
	Are time cards or time sheets reviewed and signed by a supervisor at the end of each pay period?
	Are employee time sheets and production reports compared to production schedules and employee schedules?

Accounting

✓	Are personnel records maintained by the same person who verifies timesheets and prepares the payroll?
	Is payroll accounting done by the same person who makes entries to the general ledger?
	Are payroll registers reviewed for employee names, hours worked, deductions, salary and wage rates, and agreement with paychecks, and are they approved before paychecks are disbursed? Who does this?
	Who distributes payroll checks?
	Is the payroll paid out of a separate bank account?
	Who has access to blank paychecks, signature plates, and computer programs that issue checks?
	Are bank statements for the payroll bank account reconciled regularly? Are canceled checks compared to the payroll register and are the endorsements examined?
	Who does this bank reconciliation?
	Are payroll registers reconciled with the general ledger?
	What procedures are followed for the filing of tax returns and the payment of payroll taxes?
	Are records kept of vacation and sick pay owed to employees, and are these amounts reconciled to the general ledger control accounts?
	Are payroll amounts periodically compared to budgets and estimated costs, and are variations investigated?

Check Tampering

In check tampering schemes, the employee takes company checks and physically alters them to make them payable to him or herself. The majority of check tampering frauds are perpetrated by employees in upper management or accounting departments because the employee must have access to company checks and, most likely, bank statements. Many check tampering frauds involve forgery. In several of these asset appropriation schemes, the employee steals checks that have been issued to someone else and then tampers with them in order to cash them.

Among the cases studied for the ACFE's *2008 Report to the Nation*, the median loss for check tampering fraud ($138,000) was higher than any other type of fraud except fraudulent statements, and the largest losses were incurred by employees in high positions. On the average, schemes involving check tampering lasted several months longer before being detected than other types of fraud, except for financial statement fraud. Check tampering occurred more frequently in smaller businesses, presumably because accounting controls are less stringent and because responsibility for several accounting functions may rest in the hands of a single employee. Check tampering frauds were more likely to be discovered by accident than other types of fraud.

There are five basic kinds of check tampering schemes: forged maker schemes; intercepted checks and forged endorsements; altered payee and altered check schemes; concealed checks and blank checks; and authorized maker schemes. The following sections describe these five types of check tampering schemes.

Forged maker schemes

The person who signs a check is the "maker" of the check. A forged maker scheme is one in which the perpetrator forges an authorized signature on a stolen company check. The fraudster must either have legitimate access to company checks or be aware of an opportunity to steal checks undetected. For example, a secretary might know where the boss keeps the key to a locked area where checkbooks are kept, or a careless manager might leave a few blank checks in a desk drawer or folder. Several pages of checks might be stolen from deep within a checkbook so that their absence is not immediately obvious. If company checks are computer-generated, then anyone who has the password to access the accounting system may be able to generate and print unsigned checks. An employee may have access to old, unused checks that have not been destroyed.

The stolen checks must be signed with a reasonable approximation of a legitimate signature. The perpetrator may get away with freehand forgeries by depositing the checks at places that do not verify signatures carefully. A legitimate signature can also be scanned and then printed onto the checks. Some companies use rubber stamps, automated check signers, or a computer program that prints signed checks. An employee may be able to gain access to the rubber stamp or the security passwords for printing signed checks. Canceled checks with automatic signatures can easily pass the scrutiny of the accounting department.

Once a fraudster has obtained blank checks, he or she must find a way to convert them to cash. If a check is made out to a fictitious person or to a third party, a falsified identification may be needed to cash it. Many fraudsters simply make out forged checks to themselves, even though this increases the chances of discovery. If the fraudster has a business bank account or a shell company, checks are usually made out to the business name so the cancelled checks appear more legitimate. Checks may be made out to friends or family, or a fraudster may have an accomplice at a bank or check-cashing facility who processes the checks without asking questions. A check may also be used to purchase goods or services for personal use directly from a vendor.

STRAIGHT FROM THE HEADLINES

Trusted Accountant Steals Cash and Forges Payroll Checks

In September 2009, Ruth Ellen Sons, 62, of Tucson, Arizona, was sentenced to five years in prison for embezzling $973,000 from the Tucson Museum of Art, where she had been employed as an accountant for 18 years. Between 2003 and 2008, Sons stole cash out of the deposits from the museum gift shop and hid the thefts by manipulating the museum's general accounting ledger. She also forged officials' signatures on payroll checks and then cashed them. According to a search warrant affidavit filed by police, investigators had records showing Sons forged and cashed 209 Tucson Museum of Art checks in amounts ranging from less than $600 to just shy of $1,900 at two check-cashing businesses, amounting to a total of $323,256 between May 13, 2006, and November 11, 2008.

Tucson Museum of Art Executive Director Robert Knight said the museum discovered that between $200,000 and $300,000 was not accounted for during a full, independent audit of its books late in 2008 and contacted police. Sons, who was well-liked and trusted by her coworkers, resigned around the same time.

Sons' daughter told the media her mother has a gambling addiction, and said, "She was always waiting for that big win to pay it all back; it's heartbreaking." The search warrant affidavit also stated police had investigated a Desert Diamond Casino players card in Sons' name and that Sons had logged "approximately $2.4 million" in casino play.

Intercepted checks and forged endorsements

Another form of check tampering involves intercepting company checks that have already been prepared and signed. Some of these tactics have already been described: sending out payments to false addresses and intercepting them when they are returned in the mail, misdirecting checks to a postal address belonging to the employee, and collecting paychecks made out to nonexistent ghost employees. Sometimes signed checks are stolen before they reach their intended payees because of weak controls or because too much trust is placed in an employee handling the checks.

A check that is not made out to the person who is cashing it is called a third-party check. A third-party check cannot be cashed unless it is endorsed on the back by the payee. In forged endorsement schemes, intercepted checks are endorsed with the payee's forged signature and cashed or deposited in the fraudster's bank account. If identification is required to cash the check, the fraudster may forge the payee's signature as though the payee had signed the check over to them, then endorse it with his or her own name. This is called a double-endorsement, and should always be regarded with suspicion when bank statements are being reconciled.

Altered payee and altered check schemes

After intercepting a check, the fraud perpetrator may alter the check by inserting a new payee instead of forging an endorsement. This might be done using white-out or simply by scratching out the payee name, writing a new name, and initialing the change. Sometimes, the payee name can be altered by adding a few strokes to change some of the letters or by adding a person's name above the payee's company name.

An employee who prepares checks might write the payee name so it can easily be altered after the check has been signed by an authorized person, for example, by writing it with erasable ink.

Blank checks and concealed checks

When the person authorized to sign checks for a company is very busy or inattentive, an employee who prepares and brings checks to be signed may be able to get away with leaving the payee section blank. After the checks have been signed, the employee fills in his or her own name on the blank check.

In concealed check schemes, the employee slips fraudulent company checks in among legitimate ones and submits them to be signed, knowing that the person signing the checks will not notice. The employee submitting checks for signing may be so trusted that the check signer never suspects them. Concealed check schemes often occur when the person who regularly signs checks is away from the office and someone else is temporarily in charge, or when normal procedures are disrupted for some reason.

Authorized makers

Cases where employees authorized to sign company checks write checks to themselves are the most difficult to detect. Someone with authority to sign checks typically occupies a high position in the company and can override procedures designed to prevent fraud by intimidating subordinates. Employees may not question their boss's actions because they do not want to lose their jobs. Sometimes, a business owner or partner uses company checks to pay personal expenses or writes checks to friends or family members. A high-level manager whose superior is absent or at another location can use his or her authority to override controls.

Authorized maker fraud occurs most often in companies where accounting controls are less stringent. The person authorized to sign checks takes advantage of weaknesses in the accounting system to write checks and record them as payment for legitimate expenses or to move money from one account to another. In some companies, a single person prepares checks, signs them, and mails them out. Persons who are given unsupervised authority over a special account, such as an account for a construction or renovation project, can easily abuse their privileges.

STRAIGHT FROM THE HEADLINES

School Administrator Wrote Checks to Himself

Leonard Eugene Robinson, 52, of Fresno, California, pleaded guilty in May 2009 to embezzling some $422,000 from the Orange Center Elementary School where he had been employed as business manager for 21 years. Robinson admitted to writing checks to himself from school district accounts and hiding the thefts by controlling the books and records.

Robinson was also charged with one count of burglary for allegedly taking a school district computer's hard drive in an attempt to remove evidence of his actions. According to prosecutors, Robinson wrote checks to himself over a three-year period between October 2005 and January 2009. Robinson's attorney, Glenn LoStracco, accredited his client's actions to a gambling addiction.

Orange Center School Superintendent and Principal John Stahl said: "It was a shock. I couldn't believe it. The individual had been here 21 years... It's been difficult for all of us. It was like a member of the family stealing from you." The theft was discovered when the school found itself short of money to fund essential programs during a yearly audit in January 2009. Fortunately, the school district's insurance covered approximately $415,000 of the loss. Stahl announced a system of checks and balances had been implemented for the new business manager, but said that for him, the loss of trust was the biggest issue. Orange Center Elementary School is the only school in the district and has only 350 students, making it a tightly knit community.

Concealment of check tampering

Most check tampering schemes are not one-time affairs. The employee is able to conceal his or her activities and continue stealing from the company. Among the cases of fraud studied for the ACFE's *2008 Report to the Nation*, check tampering frauds and financial statement frauds had the longest duration until discovery: a median duration of 30 months, compared to 26 months or less for other types of fraud. The perpetrator of a check tampering scheme must conceal the theft in the company accounts and, in the case of intercepted checks, find a way to prevent the intended payee from raising an alarm.

Many perpetrators of check tampering schemes are involved in reconciling their company's bank statements. This gives them the opportunity to intercept the fraudulent cancelled checks when they are returned by the bank and destroy or alter them. Checks must typically be recorded in a disbursement journal and assigned to an expense category. The fraudster may be able to get away with recording the fraudulent check as a voided check or omitting it from the journal altogether. This will create a discrepancy between the bank account total and the company accounts. The fraudster may be able to get away with "forcing" a reconciliation by falsely reporting that the two totals match. In some cases, according to the ACFE's report, companies that rarely reviewed their accounts overlooked such discrepancies for months. The stolen checks can also be recorded in the disbursement journal under false names or assigned to rarely used vendor accounts. Missing amounts can be accounted for by overstating other payments in the disbursement journal.

In forged maker and authorized maker schemes, the perpetrator may hide the theft by altering the bank statement. For example, if the fraudulent checks are not in numerical sequence with legitimate checks, it may be possible to simply delete them from the statement. A fraud perpetrator who is not involved in reconciling bank statements may still be able to intercept and alter the statements to remove the stolen amounts.

Altered payee and intercepted check schemes require additional concealment because the intended payee is still waiting for payment. In some cases, an employee stole checks that were going out to payees who did not expect them or who did not receive payments on a regular basis. The employee may cover up the fraud by resubmitting invoices with a new purchase order and having another payment issued to the payee. If the employee altered a payee's name, he or she may escape detection by using the same method to change it back to the original payee.

Perpetrators of authorized maker schemes may fabricate a voucher, including invoices, purchase orders, and receipts, to document an expense in the amount of the stolen check.

STRAIGHT FROM THE HEADLINES

CFO Issued Checks, Altered Accounts to Conceal Theft

James W. Foremsky, 62, and Susan A. Foremsky, 57, of Topeka, Kansas, pleaded guilty in March 2009 to stealing $2.6 million from Vektek, where James Foremsky was chief financial officer from June 1995 to November 8, 2007. According to the Kansas Chamber of Commerce, Vektek is a privately owned manufacturing company with 120 employees and annual sales estimated at $7.2 million. As CFO, Foremsky had control over all of Vektek's finances, including the company's bank accounts. The indictment announced by the office of Eric Melgren, U.S. Attorney for Kansas, described that Foremsky issued checks on Vektek accounts, cashed them, and recorded them as "void" on internal company spreadsheets; ordered wire transfers from the Vektek account to pay personal credit card bills for himself and his family; and moved funds between company accounts to cover up the thefts. On one occasion, Susan Foremsky obtained a cashier's check for $18,130 from Vektek to pay off the mortgage on the family's home. The indictment also stated the money paid for a lavish lifestyle for Foremsky and his family, including expensive vacations, bar tabs, meals at restaurants, new vehicles, mortgage payments, and a hobby maintaining and showing jumping horses.

CASE STUDY: THEFT FROM A CHURCH

Ronald E. Keener
Church Executive
4742 N 24th Street, Suite 340
Phoenix, AZ 85016
http://churchexecutive.com/index.asp

Excerpt from "Fast growth and few controls invite employee embezzlement: Pastor shocked by people who said they would not prosecute wrongdoers for theft of monies from their congregations," an article by Ronald E. Keener. Keener is editor of Church Executive *magazine, a monthly publication for senior pastors, executive pastors, and business administrators of America's large Christian churches.*

Keener interviewed senior pastor Linn Winters of Cornerstone Christian Fellowship in Chandler, Arizona, for the article. Winters agreed to the interview in hopes other churches might recognize the dangers of employee theft and know what to look for.

A church accountant and member of the church's executive management team had stolen close to $521,000 from Cornerstone Christian Fellowship.

Winters said that suspicions were first aroused when "we started not getting the types of reports we felt we ought to get, and we weren't getting them in a timely manner. We'd ask questions, and the answers were a little fuzzy." Church executives believed that the accounts had grown beyond the treasurer's capabilities. "She'd been here since the beginning. I think her family attended the second Sunday of our church opening and had worked tirelessly on behalf of the church in the past. It came out as this spirit of trust and camaraderie and hard work, but at some moment her heart turned, and she began to abuse that trust."

One red flag was a $50,000 check with the name of the church's mortgage company on the memo line, but the church's bank as the payee. The accountant had convinced church executives that she was taking the check to the bank and making a wire transfer to the mortgage account. Instead, she got cashier's checks made out to her personal bank rather than to an individual payee. She would then go to the bank and divert the funds to her own account.

"We had gone through such rapid growth...one of the things that happens with rapid growth is you tend to assess departments that look like they're struggling, and for the first 10 years of the church it [finance department] didn't appear to be struggling. We felt we were fine. [In truth, the finance department] was too 'ma and pa;' it was too far behind who we were as a church."

"The majority of the money taken was from our building fund. That was the place that was most able for money to leave and for us not to notice... A building fund is incredibly susceptible because you had people walking up to her and handing her a check. They'd say, 'Here's my $40,000 contribution to the building fund.' Well, it would never get there. And the rest of us didn't know someone had walked up and handed her a check in the lobby for the building fund."

"There should have been what I call separate hands — the hands that were taking the money in should have never touched the books because when those two things are separated, then the bookkeeper is going to catch the person taking the money in, or the person taking the money in is going to be able to say, 'Hey, wait a minute, we shouldn't be that short.'"

"But when those two hands belong to the same person — that was our mistake. We lost our accountant and, in the meantime, those two hands came back together, and she never rehired. That was the vulnerability. She took over the books during that year and a half. I said, 'You've got to get that accountant back in here; that's too much work for you to be doing.' 'No, I'm fine, we can do this for a while,' she said. We allowed the hands to come back together."

"We were shocked at how many letters we got from churches in the immediate area who said, 'We are praying for you. This happened to us.' The reality is that church theft is much more prevalent than people know," said Winters. "It's just that we are larger, and the amount that was stolen was larger." Unfortunately, Winters' church was insured for only $50,000. As the church and its budget had grown over its 12 years, the coverage had not been changed.

Note: The accountant was arrested in 2007, and in April 2009 was sentenced to five years in prison for embezzling $495,000 from Cornerstone Christian Fellowship. Police in Chandler, Arizona, said they found $250,000 in cash, traveler's checks, money orders, and prepaid gift cards in her home, including $100,000 in cash stuffed in a backpack. They also recovered $150,000 in property, including cars, jewelry, and high-end electronics.

Red flags for check tampering

Check tampering is often part of a larger embezzlement scheme, so the red flags for check tampering should be considered along with indications of other types of fraud such as cash larceny or billing fraud. The checks being examined for fraud may be checks issued by the company, or they may be checks received from customers as payment.

- **Voided checks listed in the check register**

  An employee with access to company checks may have cashed a company check or deposited it into a personal account, charged the stolen amount to an expense account, and listed the check as "void." All voided checks should be kept on file and should be visually compared with the check register. Bank statements should be searched for the voided check number.

- **Checks made out directly to employees**

  Except for paychecks, any check made out to an employee is suspect and should be accompanied by a good explanation.

- **Missing checks or checks out of sequence**

  Missing checks may have been stolen, and a stop payment order should be issued for each one. Check numbers out of sequence on a bank statement might indicate someone has taken checks out of a new, unused checkbook, forged, and cashed them.

- **Returned checks with dual endorsements, altered endorsements, or altered payees**

  Canceled checks returned with the bank statement should be visually examined. Manual alterations, dual endorsements, and apparent forgeries should all be confirmed with the original payee and the person who is supposed to have signed the check.

- **Duplicate or counterfeit checks**

  The bank will be able to trace where the checks were deposited or cashed.

- **Deposit dates that do not match customer accounts**

  Checks not deposited on or near the date the payment was recorded on a customer account require further examination — they suggest a lapping scheme or lax procedures in receiving and depositing payments.

- **Customers complaining their accounts are still marked unpaid after their bank records show they have made a payment**
An employee could be intercepting checks as they arrive in the mail and stealing them. Cooperate with the customer and the customer's bank to find out who cashed the check or where it was deposited.

- **An unfamiliar payee or abnormal payee address on a check**
Compare the check with invoices and supporting documentation. Is the payee on a list of registered vendors? Does the address match an employee's address?

- **Cash advances**
Any cash advance should be looked at closely to make sure it is fully documented.

Techniques for detecting check tampering

- **Order and reconcile cut-off bank statements**
Ask the bank for a statement ending two weeks after the end of the company's monthly accounting period, and compare it to income and expenses recorded in company accounts. This may reveal a fraud carried out between accounting periods and hidden by making adjustments to the accounts just before the end of the period. Online banking makes it possible to view and export a statement for any time period. Randomly examine online bank statements for unusual payments and discrepancies.

- **Check the online bank statement against the bank reconciliation**
Check the bank reconciliation prepared by the accounting department against an online bank statement to see whether fraud is being concealed in the bank reconciliation.

- **Examine canceled checks**

  Arrange for your bank to send you canceled checks for each month. Most banks will do this for a small monthly fee. Compare these checks to the amounts on the invoices or statements associated with them. Closely examine each check for signs of forgery, altered payees, double endorsements, and other signs of fraud.

- **Do your own bank reconciliation**

  Get copies of statements and bank reconciliations for all bank accounts including checking accounts, savings accounts, money market accounts, CDs, and investment accounts. Do your own bank reconciliation and double-check all the balances. Fraudulent disbursement schemes often target a dormant bank account or a savings account that is not actively in use.

- **Conduct a careful review of the procedures for preparing, signing and processing checks**

  Review each step of the process for preparing, signing, sending out checks, and reconciling the bank statements to see if there are weaknesses in the process or individuals who have the opportunity to commit check fraud.

	CHECKLIST FOR BANK RECONCILIATION
	Use this checklist to test bank reconciliations for signs of fraud.
✓	Who does the bank reconciliations?
	How are bank statements received (by mail or electronically) and who receives (or downloads) them?
	Are reconciliations done in a regular, timely manner?
	Are there any signs the bank statements have been altered?
	Are the bank reconciliations mathematically accurate?
	Trace the balance on the bank statements back to the cut-off date or compare with online bank statements.
	Compare the balance with the company's ledger.

	Trace pending transactions and deposits in transit (DITs) on the statement to see whether they were recorded in the account books for the proper accounting period.
	Look at canceled checks closely. Compare them with a list of outstanding company checks.
	Look at invoices and documentation associated with outstanding checks for large amounts.
	Examine invoices and receipts associated with checks written for large amounts.
	Look at current activity for investment accounts, CDs, savings accounts, and money market accounts. Verify balances, interest rates, maturity dates, and the institution where each account is held.
	Is interest accrued for investment accounts, CDs, savings accounts, and money market accounts recorded in the company books?

CHECKLIST FOR CHECK TAMPERING

This checklist will help to identify weaknesses in financial controls that could create an opportunity for check tampering.

✓	
	What is the procedure for requesting checks?
	What is the procedure for preparing checks?
	Who prepares checks?
	Who signs checks? How are they signed?
	Does the person signing checks review them before signing?
	Is the same person preparing checks and signing them?
	What happens to a check immediately after it is signed?
	Are bank statements and checks regularly reviewed? Who reviews them?
	Are bank reconciliations done immediately after the bank statement cut-off date?
	Who does bank reconciliations?
	Are bank reconciliations done by the same person who prepares or signs checks?
	Who reviews bank reconciliations?
	Who registers checks and assigns them to expense categories?
	Are canceled checks stored and filed in a secure place?
	Are blank checks stored in a secure place?
	Who has the keys or access to the place where blank checks are stored?
	If checks are printed or signed electronically, who knows the password to access the check printing function?
	Does someone review and approve the printed checks before they are sent out?

Are paper checks used for large payments to vendors?
Are old checks and checkbooks destroyed?
Are inactive bank accounts regularly reviewed?
Are computer network security procedures carefully observed, passwords guarded, and activity logs scrutinized or tagged for unusual activity?
Are the persons responsible for handling checks routinely rotated?
What happens to a check that is returned in the mail?
Is a list maintained of outstanding checks?

CHAPTER 7

Corruption

A lmost 200 years ago, the seminal economist Adam Smith remarked, "People of the same trade seldom meet together, even for merriment and diversion, but the conversation ends in a conspiracy against the public, or in some contrivance to raise prices." Human nature has not changed a great deal over the past two centuries.

Corruption in the business world occurs when a company employee deliberately disobeys company policies and business regulations to influence business transactions for personal gain at the expense of the company, its customers, or its vendors. Corruption undermines market forces by unfairly raising prices through price rigging and bribery, and circumvents regulations and standards intended to protect the consumer. An employer can also land in serious legal trouble when it is held responsible for the criminal activities of its employee.

STRAIGHT FROM THE HEADLINES

"The Informant!" Price-Rigging in Archers Daniel Midland

The 2009 movie "The Informant!," directed by Steven Soderbergh, is based on a book with the same title written by journalist Kurt Eichenwald and published in 2000. The book documents in detail the story of Mark Whitacre, a corporate vice-president of the agricultural conglomerate Archer Daniels Midland (ADM), who became an FBI informant and revealed that company executives routinely collaborated with competitors in Europe and Asia to fix the price of lysine, a food additive widely used in diet foods and drinks. After almost three years of investigation, ADM and its co-conspirators paid an antitrust fine of over $100 million and three executives served jail sentences. According to ADM's 2005 annual report, ADM also paid $400 million to settle a class action antitrust suit. Food companies who used lysine in their products had to raise their prices to consumers to compensate for ADM's artificially orchestrated increases in the price of lysine.

As a result of the investigation, anti-trust prosecutors concluded price-rigging was more widespread than previously thought. Investigations of other companies led to convictions and fines for price-rigging of vitamins, fax paper, and graphite electrodes.

Ironically, Whitacre embezzled $9 million from ADM while he was cooperating with the FBI during the investigation. He violated his immunity arrangement with the government, and because of the additional charges, he ended up serving a longer prison sentence than the ADM executives he had exposed.

Most corruption cannot be detected by reviewing company accounts and documents for irregularities because it involves some form of collaboration with personnel outside the company. The absence of a paper trail makes it difficult to find conclusive evidence of wrongdoing. Corruption is often discovered by chance or by accident, and substantiating it may require professional investigation, including price comparisons and market data analysis, personal interviews, and police intervention.

The ACFE's *2008 Report to the Nation* reported that nearly one-third of the fraud cases studied involved corruption, sometimes in combination with asset appropriation schemes or financial statement fraud.

The U.S. Federal Bureau of Investigation (FBI) emphasizes the serious economic impact of corruption in its *Federal Bureau of Investigation Strategic Plan 2004 – 2009*. The white-collar crime section within the report states, "The ability of the U.S. government and industry to function effectively is likewise threatened by complex frauds. The amount of taxpayer funds involved in the government procurement process is staggering, as billions of dollars are spent each year on everything from highways to rockets. The U.S. Government Accountability Office (GAO) estimates that as much as 10 percent of appropriated funds for domestic programs may be lost to fraud in the government procurement and contracting process, and this type of crime is critically linked to public corruption imperatives." The procedures for securing contracts to supply goods and services for government agencies and projects are sometimes abused, and as much as 10 percent of the budget for certain programs is lost to fraud, including overcharging for goods and services and billing for services that are never performed. Fraud not only causes financial losses, but subverts legislation intended to guard resources, protect consumers, or advance disadvantaged groups. Some suppliers abuse affirmative action programs by fraudulently representing themselves as companies owned by women, minorities, or disabled veterans. The GAO maintains the fraud hotline FraudNET "to facilitate reporting of allegations of fraud, waste, abuse, or mismanagement of federal funds."

How to contact GAO FraudNET:
Online report: www.gao.gov/cgi-bin/fraudnet.cgi
Telephone: 1-800-424-5454 (an automated answering system)
Fax: 202-512-3086
E-mail: fraudnet@gao.gov
Mail: GAO FraudNET
441 G Street NW, Washington, DC 20548

The next sections briefly describe various types of corruption schemes and provide some real-life illustrations, along with red flags and techniques for detecting each type of fraud scheme. Corruption schemes can be classified into four basic categories: conflicts of interest, bribery, kickbacks and illegal gratuities, and corporate espionage. It is difficult to quantify the exact amount of damage caused by a particular corruption scheme because the extent of it may never be known. Entrepreneurs and start-up companies can be forced out of business because they do not have fair access to a market for their products; individual consumers can be forced to pay higher prices for goods and services; substandard materials are often used in construction and manufacturing; and businesses might be paying more than they should for supplies and equipment. Most corruption schemes involve two or more parties, with losses on all sides.

Conflicts of Interest

A conflict of interest occurs when an employee has a personal or economic interest in a business transaction. For example, a family member of a company executive might be among the bidders for a contract, or an employee might be a partner in a business that supplies goods to his or her department. In such circumstances the executive would stand to benefit, directly or indirectly, if the contract is awarded to a family member, and the employee might be willing to authorize a higher price for the supplier's goods because he or she will receive some of the profit.

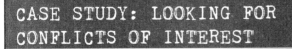

CASE STUDY: LOOKING FOR CONFLICTS OF INTEREST

During the early 1970s, a small group of student activists at Northwestern University spent weeks gathering the names and addresses of the directors of Chicago corporations, politicians, government officials, media companies, hospitals, and charities, and the membership lists of Chicago social clubs and professional associations. Each name and its association was keypunched on computer cards and run through the only computer on campus, which occupied a whole building. The process took several hours. The hundreds of pages of printouts revealed a network of tightly correlated business and social relationships among the directors of corporations and the owners of companies that supplied those corporations with goods and services. For example, the same people who served on the boards of hospitals and clinics were directors or owners of companies that supplied these institutions with laboratory services and medical supplies, or of the funeral homes and nursing homes where patients were sent when they left the hospital. While this was not solid proof of conflicts of interest, it demonstrated that corruption could certainly exist. Today's personal computers are able to conduct a similar comparison in minutes, and much of the research can be done on the Internet.

A common example of a conflict of interest is when a purchasing department employee creates a "shell company" to procure goods and sell them to the employer, often at inflated prices. Even though other suppliers may outbid it, the employee authorizes purchases only from the shell company and pockets the profits.

STRAIGHT FROM THE HEADLINES

Employee Conspires with Vendors to Submit Fraudulent Invoices

In April 2009, a former fleet department manager of Ferrellgas Inc. a propane gas company based in Overland Park, Kansas, pleaded guilty to embezzling more than $3.5 million from the company. According to court documents, an internal audit at the company revealed a significant theft had occurred over a period of several years. The suit alleged the fleet manager, who worked at the company for ten years, conspired with employees of at least three vendors to submit false or fraudulent in voices to Ferrellgas. Two of the companies submitted invoices for work that was never done. A third company serviced vehicles for Ferrellgas, but charged excessive amounts on its invoices. The fleet manager met with employees from each of the companies to coordinate how and when the invoices should be sent. When the invoices were paid, the companies kept 5 percent and were instructed where to forward the remainder. The money was deposited either in the fleet manager's personal bank account or in the bank account of "a non-profit business entity of which he was the founder, chief executive officer, and a member of the board of directors." One of the conspirators was also listed as a director of the non-profit. Of the $3.5 million that was embezzled, the fleet manager retained $3 million. He was also accused of attempting to conceal stolen money by transferring assets to his wife's name as part of a divorce settlement.

STRAIGHT FROM THE HEADLINES

McDonald's "Monopoly™" Game Promotion Undermined by Fraud

During the 1990s, McDonald's Corporation began using contests and games to promote its business. One of its most popular games was a "Monopoly™" game in which customers who purchased certain menu items received game piece stickers that could be collected and attached to a game board. Players who acquired certain game pieces won grand prizes of $1 million, and others won assorted valuable prizes. McDonald's also partnered with Hasbro, Toys "R" Us, and Best Buy to offer coupons and smaller prizes. In 2001, McDonald's was suddenly embroiled in a public relations nightmare when the FBI arrested eight people for fixing the outcome of the contests.

The ringleader, Jerome P. Jacobson, 58, was a security official with Simon Marketing, the company hired by McDonald's to run the games. He had been responsible for placing the high-winning game pieces into circulation since 1995. Although court documents stated that Simon Marketing's policy included constant supervision of the game pieces from printing to distribution by at least two, and sometimes three, people, Jacobson was able to steal the high-level game pieces and distribute them to family members and friends who acted as recruiters. According to then-Attorney General John Ashcroft, "these recruiters then solicited others who falsely and fraudulently represented that they were the legitimate winners of the McDonald's games." Prosecutors alleged that Jacobson charged $50,000 cash for $1 million game pieces, usually be fore handing them over. The recruiters also got a commission. Winning pieces for lesser prizes such as luxury cars and electronics were sold by recruiters.

The fraud was uncovered after one of the participants in the scheme "blew the whistle" on the ringleaders. Acting FBI Director ThomasPickard said that the FBI received court authority to investigate the collaborators after it was found that "many of the winners were of the same family or were closely related. All appeared to be connected in some fashion, even though a variety of tricks were used to conceal their relationships and their locations." Eventually, 21 individuals were charged in connection with the fraud. Jacobson testified that he stole 80 percent of the prize-winning game tickets between 1995 and 2001.

Jacobson and his crew defrauded McDonald's Corporation of approximately $13 million in prizes, but the damage went much further. McDonald's immediately announced a new $10 million instant cash giveaway to make up for the fraudulent games and made a commitment to allow its customers a second opportunity to win every cash dollar that had been stolen. Simon Marketing, which had handled almost all of McDonald's major promotions, including its "Happy Meal™" menus, abruptly lost one of its biggest clients. The scandal undermined the goodwill generated by the promotion and the creativity, effort, and expense that had gone into the promotion, including millions spent on advertising.

Bribery

Bribery involves giving or receiving cash or something of value to influence the future outcome of a business transaction. The bribe could be in cash or in the form of a special privilege or benefit, such as football tickets, use of a luxury vacation accommodation, or even a promise of future employment. A person bidding on a contract might give an employee cash or a gift in return for the assurance that he or she will be chosen above other bidders, even though their prices are lower. Bribes are also offered to entice an employee to look the other way during an illegal transaction or to ignore company regulations. An employee may also spend a company's money on bribes to secure a sale or contract without the knowledge of senior management, and mask the missing cash by attributing it to other expenses.

In some countries, bribery is regarded as part of the cost of doing business. The Foreign Corrupt Practices Act of 1977 (FCPA) prohibited U.S. companies from making "corrupt payments to foreign officials for the purpose of obtaining or keeping business." Concerned that the FCPA might put U.S. companies at a disadvantage when competing with their foreign trade partners, the U.S. government initiated negotiations in the Organization of Economic Cooperation and Development (OECD), and in 1997, the United States and 33 other countries signed the OECD Convention on Combating Bribery of Foreign Public Officials in International Business Transactions. In 1998, the U.S. Congress ratified this Convention and enacted implementing legislation. Since then, several firms have been the subject of civil and criminal enforcement actions by the Justice Department because they bribed foreign officials. The penalty for bribery of a foreign company or government entity can be severe: large fines, prohibition from working on government contracts, and jail sentences for employees and company officers. In 2000, computer giant IBM agreed to pay $300,000 to settle allegations that its subsidiary in Argentine had bribed government officials to win a contract to upgrade computer systems in a government-owned bank. In 2007, global telecommunications provider Alcatel-Lucent agreed to pay $2.5 million to settle charges that Lucent Technologies, which it bought in 2006, had paid for hundreds of trips for Chinese officials in order to win contracts. In May 2009, the *San Francisco Chronicle* reported an admission by computer and technology services vendor Sun Microsystems Inc. that it may have violated anti-bribery laws at a location outside the United States. If a violation is found, Sun could lose its contracts with the U.S. government, its major source of revenue. To avoid similar consequences, many companies have implemented strict anti-bribery compliance policies and accounting controls.

Kickbacks and Illegal Gratuities

Kickback schemes are typically perpetrated by employees who have authority to authorize purchases. Kickbacks are arrangements in which vendors or contractors give an employee a percentage of the proceeds of a sale as a reward for purchasing from them. A vendor may be charging higher prices than competitors, selling substandard goods, or simply seeking an advantage over its competitors when the playing field is otherwise equal. In some cases, the employee arranges for a vendor to be paid for goods that were never delivered. Kickbacks are harmful because they interfere with purchasing policies and procedures intended to save the company money and encourage competitive bidding among vendors. The employee is essentially transferring his or her loyalty from the employer to the vendor. Instead of saving the company money by discounting its prices, the vendor is putting money into a dishonest employee's pocket.

Illegal gratuities are payments or gifts given after a transaction is carried out to the satisfaction of the giver. For example, after a bid has been accepted and a contract signed, a vendor might reward a purchase agent with expensive tickets to a football game or a free vacation, or may simply hand over a cash payment. Like bribes and kickbacks, the payment of illegal gratuities undermines the selection process used by a company to obtain services, goods, and raw materials at the best possible prices. The company may pay more for goods and services because its purchase agent approves a bid from a particular vendor even when other vendors have made lower offers. Typically, companies specify the types of gifts their employees can accept from vendors or customers. Many companies allow their employees to accept small thank-you gifts such as Christmas baskets, bottles of wine, or lunch invitations, but place a dollar limit on their value. Illegal gratuities paid to secure a contract or a sale are hidden expenses, and are often concealed in expense accounts or disguised as other payments — providing a false estimate of the real cost of operating a business.

STRAIGHT FROM THE HEADLINES

Illegal Gratuities Helped Win the 2002 Winter Olympics for Salt Lake City

In January 1999, Frank Joklik, President of the Salt Lake Organizing Committee (SLOC), resigned after acknowledging cash payments and other benefits were provided to members of the International Olympic Committee to influence their selection of Salt Lake City for the 2002 Winter Olympics. The scandal came to light in November 1998, when a Salt Lake City television station received a copy of a letter from the Senior Vice President of the SLOC to the daughter of an IOC member from Cameroon, telling her that a $10,000 tuition payment would be her last.

Marc Hodler, a senior International Olympic Committee (IOC) official from Switzerland, revealed that as many as 25 of the 114 members of the international committee had sold their votes in recent elections to choose Olympic sites. Hodler charged that there had been extensive bribery to influence IOC selection votes since at least 1990, when Atlanta was chosen as the host city for the 1996 Summer Games, and that similar scandals allegedly underlay the selection of Nagano, Japan, for the 1998 Winter Games and Sydney, Australia, for the 2000 Summer Games. Hodler also spoke about several middlemen who had profited by acting as brokers to sell the votes of IOC members from Africa and the Middle East, who knew they could never win selection for sites in their own regions but whose votes could tip the balance in the competition among North American, European, and Asian cities. According to the Canadian press, the SLOC paid $58,000 to one of these middlemen, a former Egyptian Olympic athlete who had become a successful Toronto businessman after immigrating to Canada. He had recently been hired as a "marketing consultant" for a series of successful Olympic bids.

The SLOC, which had previously acknowledged paying for housing, travel and education expenses for relatives of members of the IOC, was found to have made direct cash payments to "a number" of I.O.C. members and their families. Jean-Claude Ganga, the IOC member from Democratic Republic of Congo, admitted he had received $70,000 in direct payments, as well as free medical care and a favorable position in a Utah real estate deal, which netted him $60,000. Ganga described such arrangements as "normal." There were allegations SLOC officials made campaign contributions to an IOC member who was running for mayor of Santiago, Chile and provided college tuition for the children of IOC members from Ecuador and Libya. A cash contribution went to another

IOC member from the Netherlands. According to an ethics panel of the Salt Lake City organizing committee, eight members of the international committee received gifts during the selection process.

As a result of the scandal, the president and senior vice president of the SLOC quickly retired. The Mayor of Salt Lake City announced she would not run for a third term, renouncing her dream of presiding over the Olympics. Some members of the IOC were pressured to resign because they had abused their positions.

STRAIGHT FROM THE HEADLINES

Defense Contractor Employees Get Kickbacks for Referring Business to Another Company

In September 2009, two former employees of a high-tech defense contractor in Red Bank, New Jersey, pleaded guilty in federal court to conspiracy to accept kickbacks in the awarding of subcontracts. Their employer was a scientific, engineering, and technology applications company with contracts with the federal government, including the Department of Defense. During a two-year period when their employer was not able to directly fill orders for communications systems equipment, the two men accepted kickbacks for referring buyers to another company based in California. According to a press release from the U.S. Attorney's office, their kickback fee was based on a percentage of their employer's business that was referred to the other company. The defendants admitted they received approximately $150,873 in kickback payments. Their employer was unaware of the kickbacks. Each man faces a maximum prison sentence of 5 years and a fine of $250,000.

Detecting Bribery and Corruption

Bribery and corruption are difficult to detect because transactions are often in gifts or cash paid to an employee by someone outside the company. Corruption schemes are most often uncovered through tips from employees and disgruntled vendors or by accident. They cannot be easily detected by examining a company's books or by electronic monitoring of transactions, because they are deeply concealed in regular business practices and do not typically involve alterations of accounts or check tampering. The most significant internal evidence of corruption can be found by analyzing how well a company is adhering to its own policies regarding selection of vendors, acceptance of gifts and favors, solicitation of bids, quality control, granting of discounts to customers, and compliance with U.S. laws regarding payment of bribes to foreign officials.

Prevention and detection of corruption depend largely on the enforcement of clear policy guidelines by company management and on the maintenance of communication channels through which tips can be received confidentially. Employees should receive periodic education about what behavior is allowed under company policies and what is unacceptable, and should be encouraged and rewarded for reporting suspicious activity. Easy access to legal counsel should be made available to employees in situations where they might unwittingly become part of a corruption scheme.

Bribery is a federal crime only when it affects federal government offices or federally regulated industries such as securities, banking, and health care. Commercial bribery — bribery in the context of a corporation or a private organization — can often be prosecuted at the federal level as mail fraud or in connection with other offenses committed by companies that sell goods or services to the federal government. The Anti-Kickback Act of 1986 prohibits government contractors and subcontractors from issuing or accepting kickbacks, or from forcing an employee to kickback part of his or her compensation. Title 18, Section 874, of the U.S. Code (the general and permanent laws of the United States) makes it a federal crime to solicit kickbacks from any person employed in the repair of any public building or anyone employed in any work financed in whole or in part by loans or grants from the U.S. government. Title 12, Section 2607 of the U.S. Code explicitly prohibits kickbacks and unearned fees connected with the settlement of a federally related mortgage loan.

The Bank Bribery Amendments Act of 1985 prohibits any bank representative from receiving anything except a legitimate salary, wages, and fees in connection with bank business. The IRS allows an annual tax exemption for one business gift worth $25; any amount over that is taxable as personal income. Commercial bribery is a criminal offense in approximately 25 states, punishable by jail time, fines, and restitution. Crimes of bribery are often prosecuted in civil suits as well as criminal courts.

Exposure of illegal activities like bribery and kickbacks seriously damages a company's reputation. While the public might easily believe a company is an innocent victim of embezzlement, terms like "bribery" and "kickback" connote a culture of greed and somehow imply the company has failed to protect public interests. The public disclosure that one or more employees are being prosecuted for bribery and corruption can be a painful experience requiring extensive public relations efforts to restore confidence in the company.

STRAIGHT FROM THE HEADLINES

A Payroll Kickback Scheme

In August 2009, residents of Okaloosa County, Florida, were shaken when the Okaloosa County sheriff and five of his employees were arrested on both state and federal charges for their involvement in a payroll kickback scheme. According to the arrest affidavit from the Florida Department of Law Enforcement, from 2006 to 2009 the sheriff paid bonuses to his employees and had them return part of the money to him in cash. Funds were transferred into the employees' checking accounts, and the employees were then notified of the bonuses and asked to return part of it to the sheriff or his chief administrator. Employees were told that the money was to be used for charitable purposes, but the five staff members knew otherwise. In three years, the sheriff collected more than $100,000 in kickbacks from employees. Each year, the scheme widened to include more employees. The sheriff's chief deputy received $98,000 in "bonuses" and helped to suppress employees' questions by assuring them that what they were doing was legal and acceptable.

The Okaloosa County Sheriff's Office's (OCSO) director of administration directed staff members to deposit bonuses in employee accounts, collected the kickbacks, and monitored the funds. She testified the sheriff approached her in 2006 and said that, as he could not be paid anything more than his salary, he wanted to pay bonuses to her and have her return part of the money to him. She received $96,000 in bonuses, and "concealed and falsified personnel records relating to the kickback scheme." The OCSO finance administrator calculated the bonus payments, and oversaw the transfer of funds into employee bank accounts. She received $89,000 and also falsified her own timesheet by logging 140 overtime hours in a single two-week period. Another employee received $149,000 in "bonuses" — his bonus for 2008 exceeded his annual salary.

Early in 2008, employees observed that the sheriff seemed to have an inappropriately close relationship with a newly hired female chief of staff. The bonus scheme escalated as he bought her gifts and paid her bills, and the sheriff kept her on the payroll even when she was living in another city and working at another job. The sheriff issued her OCSO vehicles, a fuel card, and a firearm. In addition to the bonus kickback scheme, the sheriff was charged with using free inmate labor and official vehicles to run his wife's estate sale business and for remodeling done on his home.

The OCSO employees were charged with racketeering and the sheriff's former chief of staff was charged with grand theft.

Red flags for corruption

As previously mentioned, an employee's behavior might be the most obvious clue that corruption is occurring. Some bribe recipients, however, remain discreet and conceal the fact that they have received large payments. Corruption always involves at least two people, so look for behavioral red flags among several employees, vendors, customers, and employees.

Behavioral red flags

- **An employee appears to be living beyond his or her means**
  This is the most common behavioral red flag for all types of fraud. An employee takes expensive vacations, buys a new home, or drives a luxury car that someone with his or her income could not ordinarily afford.

- **Unusually close relationship between employee and vendor or between employees**

  Among the corruption cases studied for the ACFE's *2008 Report to the Nation*, the second most common behavioral red flag for corruption was an abnormally close relationship between the employee and the vendor who was paying bribes. An employee and vendor who do not appear to have much in common socially may meet frequently outside the office. Employees whose relationship with each other seems inappropriate may be sharing more than friendship.

- **"Wheeler-dealer" attitude**

  The third most common behavioral red flag for corruption in the 2008 ACFE study was a wheeler-dealer attitude — an employee who is always looking for ways to make money and trying to strike a deal with someone. A person with this approach to life is likely to seek out opportunities to profit and to place his or her own interests above the interests of the organization.

- **Controlling attitude; unwillingness to share responsibilities**

  When an employee does not want to relinquish control or share responsibilities with other employees, it may be because he or she is afraid of being found out or will lose the opportunity to solicit bribes or kickbacks unobserved.

- **An employee who ignores company policies and breaks rules**

  An employee who improperly asserts authority or forces subordinates to bend rules and ignore standard procedures is likely to have his or her own agenda in mind.

- **Frequent employee turnover in a department**

  If there is frequent employee turnover in a department, without apparent reason, employees may be quitting because they are not comfortable with the activities of their coworkers or superiors and do not want to be implicated in a corruption scheme.

- **Employee who actively seeks out and accepts "freebies" and corporate gifts**

  An employee who seems eager to get "something for nothing" and readily accepts corporate gifts even when they are inappropriate is likely to be susceptible to bribery.

- **Financial pressures and personal problems**

  As with all types of fraud, a person who is struggling with debt, divorce, personal instability, marital infidelity, exceptional medical expenses, addiction to drugs, or gambling is more likely to become involved in a corruption scheme as a perceived solution to his or her problems.

- **A vendor or customer who routinely offers generous gifts**

  A business does not ordinarily distribute gifts unless it has something to gain by doing so. A vendor or customer who routinely offers lavish entertainment or inappropriate gifts may offer other inducements to employees who can grant favors.

- **A vendor or customer with a reputation for being involved in pay-offs or other schemes**

  If a company or its representative is known in the industry for participating in kickback or bribery schemes, dealings with that company should be carefully watched.

- **A vendor or customer who is a one-man business**

  An independent sales representative or middleman is not subject to the same controls and accounting restrictions as a representative of a larger, more highly organized company. Such as person may rely on bribes and kickbacks to gain an advantage over competitors or may be used by a larger company as a conduit for bribes.

Accounting and inventory red flags

- **Unexplained increase in the cost of goods or services**

  Goods and services may cost more than in the past because of inflation or an increase in demand, but if there is no reasonable explanation for higher prices, someone in the company could be allowing vendors to overcharge. Look to see if there has been a change in vendors since the price went up.

- **Decrease in the quality of goods being delivered**

  Deliveries of goods should be routinely examined to see if they are the same quality that was ordered. A vendor could be delivering goods of lower quality and paying the difference as a kickback to the employee authorizing the purchase.

- **One supplier being used consistently**

  When the same vendor consistently wins bids, the bidding process should be closely examined to see whether this vendor's prices and services are competitive with those of other vendors. A vendor who continually resubmits bids at the last minute could be receiving confidential information about competitors' prices.

- **Excess inventory or inventory ordered before it is required**

  Inventory ordered in overly large quantities, or before it is needed, may be a sign the employee responsible for purchasing is receiving kickbacks.

- **Complaints from vendors**

  Any complaint from a vendor regarding unfair treatment during the bidding process should be investigated.

Techniques for detecting corruption and bribery schemes

- **Educate employees about fraud and encourage reporting**

  Review company policies regarding acceptance of business gifts, relationships with vendors, and purchasing procedures, and make any necessary changes. Then, hold reeducation sessions for all employees to explain these policies and procedures, and emphasize noncompliance is unacceptable and policies will be enforced. Educate employees about what constitutes fraud and about the warning signs of fraud. Provide an anonymous employee hotline to receive tips and easy access to legal counsel for employees who may have become embroiled in a corruption scheme. If appropriate, conduct individual interviews with employees in key positions. When employees clearly understand company policies and know that certain activities are criminal, they will be inclined to report suspected fraud.

- **Analytical review of inventory costs**

  Compare the current cost of goods and services purchased by the company with costs in previous months and years. Check inventory costs against the annual budget. Look for unexplained changes, aberrations, or patterns in inventory purchases related to particular employees, vendors, or customers.

- **Mandatory job rotation**

  Periodically rotate the jobs of sales representatives, buyers, and employees who authorize purchases, so no individual becomes too entrenched or has the opportunity to develop a long-term relationship with a vendor or customer. Personal relationships may be important in sales, but potential losses due to corruption far outweigh the temporary disadvantages of changing sales representatives. Emphasize the vendors' and customers' relationships with the business as a whole rather than with individual employees.

- **Exit interviews with employees**

  During an exit interview with an employee who is leaving the company, ask about his or her future plans for employment. Employees who have been offered employment by a vendor or customer, directly or indirectly, are suspect. Even if it cannot be proved that particular employee accepted a bribe, the vendor's or customer's future relationship with the company should be closely watched. After an employee has left the company, compare the addresses of his or her subsequent employers with vendor addresses to find out whether a vendor has hired the former employee.

- **Compare employee addresses with vendor addresses**

  If a member of an employee's family is the owner of a vendor company, the vendor address may be the same as the employee's home address. Vendors who use post office boxes as their addresses should be closely examined to discover why they are not using their physical addresses.

- **Review vendor profiles**

  When a vendor is selected for a contract, the vendor's ownership information, address, and qualifications should be reviewed. Watch for:

  - A vendor address that is a P.O. box or that matches an employee address.
  - Employee or member of an employee's family who is an owner of the vendor.
  - A vendor who does not have the appropriate licenses or certifications, or who is not bonded.

- **Electronic submission of bids**

  Use a standardized online system to advertise contracts, send out bid packages, and receive bids from vendors. Vendors are asked to register and create passwords, and can be required to update their own information at regular intervals. An electronic bid system reduces the opportunity for vendors to exert personal influence on buyers and tracks dates and times when bids were submitted and bid packages were sent out to vendors. It also allows automated searches of vendor records, bid comparisons, and analytical reviews. Security procedures should protect the bidding submission system so the dates and times when an employee accesses the bids are logged. If an employee is suspected of leaking information on competitors' bids, it will be possible to verify when those bids were looked at, and by whom. Last-minute alterations to bids can also be easily detected.

- **Consistent posting of requisition requests on the internet**
  By posting outstanding requisition requests and solicitations in an area for vendors on the company Web site, the company can be sure all vendors have timely access to them and are not excluded from the bidding process. To be successful, the solicitations need to be continually updated and maintained, and instructions and deadlines for submitting bids must be clearly stated.

- **Examine pricing policies and customer invoices**
  Examine company pricing policies and confirm that customers who receive discounts or favorable treatment are receiving them legitimately.

- **Examine purchasing and bidding policies and processes**
  Examine the purchasing and bidding process for irregularities and signs that policies are not being followed. The following checklist contains some of the signs of improper treatment of vendors.

CHECKLIST FOR RED FLAGS FOR BRIBERY IN THE BIDDING PROCESS

This checklist will help to identify problems in the bidding and contract process that may indicate a vendor is bribing an employee. Obtain a detailed description of company policies regarding the process of soliciting, evaluating, and selecting bids from contractors and suppliers. This includes copies of bid packages — the information package that is given to vendors who want to submit a bid for a particular project or commodity.

Vendors

✓	Are vendors required to register with the company before submitting bids?
	How is this registration done? How long does it take?
	Does the company assign a portion of its purchases to vendors owned by minorities, women, and disabled veterans? If so, how do vendors qualify? Are their qualifications verified? How often? By whom?
	How often is the vendor list updated and reviewed?

Bid Solicitation

✓	For what types and amounts of purchases are bids solicited? Is there another purchasing process for smaller amounts?
	How are bid solicitations advertised? Are they posted on the company Web site? When are they posted? Who updates this area of the Web site?
	How are bid packets sent to vendors? Who does this?

Bid Submission

✓	How are bids submitted?
	What happens to a bid after it has been submitted?
	What is the policy regarding deadlines and late submissions?
	What is the process for altering a bid after it has been submitted?

Vendor Selection

✓	How is the winning bid selected? Who makes the decision? What are the criteria?
	Are company policies strictly adhered to? Why or why not?
	How is the vendor notified?
	If the first choice falls through, how is a replacement made?
	What is the procedure for verifying that a vendor charges prices as promised in the contract?

Electronic Bid Submission

✓	Does the electronic bid submission system work smoothly, or does it exclude some types of contractors?
	Are vendor registrations approved in a timely manner?
	Are electronically submitted bids acknowledged and reviewed in a timely manner?
	What procedure is followed to review electronically submitted bids?
	Is there both an electronic submission and a manual submission process? Are manual submissions treated differently?
	Who has access to electronically submitted bids? What kind of access?
	Is there any way an employee might have the ability to make alterations to an electronically submitted bid, intercept it, or prevent it from being included in the bidding process?

Red Flags

✓	Requirements that eliminate competition are included in the initial documents preparing the bid solicitation, such as: • Specifications that exactly fit the product or work of a specific contractor. • Specifications that were not included on previous similar solicitations. • Requiring prequalification or preregistration that automatically eliminates competitors. • Using specifications prepared by a contractor who is participating in the bidding. • Unnecessary or falsified documents justifying non-competitive bidding.
	Irregular sharing of information with some potential bidders and not others: • Permitting consultants who helped prepare the specifications or design to become subcontractors or consultants under the winning contract. • Splitting up requirements among several contracts, so that contractors can "share" the job. • Sharing information from design or engineering firms that prepared the plans with certain contractors.
	A major contract is split up into several smaller jobs to avoid review, when contracts over a certain amount must be reviewed and authorized by management.
	Deadlines for submitting bids are so short that only vendors with advance knowledge have time to prepare and submit a bid.
	Bid solicitations are posted in obscure publications, during holiday periods, or in such a way that they are difficult to find on the company Web site, so only a few vendors see them.

	The instructions and deadlines for submitting a bid are vaguely worded so they are difficult to understand.
	Bid solicitations are not updated when the company makes changes that affect the bid.
	Bid packages are not sent out according to a regular procedure.
	"Bid conferences" are held in such a way that competitors have the opportunity to communicate with each other and potentially engage in bid rigging.
	Purchasing agents have improper contact with contractors or their representatives at trade shows, professional meetings, or social events.
	Purchasing agents have a financial interest in a vendor company.
	Purchasing agents assist contractors in preparing bids or refer them to specific suppliers or subcontractors.
	Purchasing agent has received a job offer from a vendor.
	Documents have been falsified to allow the submission of a late bid.
	A low bidder withdraws and becomes a subcontractor for another bidder.
	Contractor's qualifications to do the job are misrepresented, or certifications are false.
	A late bid is accepted against company policy.
	Changes are made to a bid after other bidders' prices are known.
	One bidder's price is revealed to another.

Corporate Espionage

Proprietary information, such as specialized manufacturing techniques, data, industry secrets, product designs, a list of clients, or information on pricing and bidding, is often at the heart of a company's business. Many companies require employees who have access to such information to sign confidentiality agreements — legal contracts stating they will not share the information with anyone outside the company. Corporate espionage occurs when an employee sells proprietary information to a competitor or someone who will use that information illegally. There have been several recent cases in which employees of retailers or car dealerships sold lists of credit card numbers or the personal information of customers to identity theft rings. When cases of fraud like these are discovered, a company must go to considerable expense to inform all of its customers, and banks must assign new credit card numbers to all the accounts that have been compromised. Competitors may attempt to purchase confidential information on a company's bidding process so they can offer lower prices.

STRAIGHT FROM THE HEADLINES

Renault Files Complaint Against Employee(s) for Industrial Espionage

Great secrecy surrounds the release of the newest automobile models, and car magazines are willing to pay for photos and information before it is made available to the public. In July 2007, the French carmaker Renault filed an industrial espionage complaint after *Auto Plus* magazine published photos of an as-yet unreleased model. *Auto Plus* published numerous photos and detailed information on the next-generation lower-medium Megane, slated for release at the Paris auto show in October 2008. The complaint was filed against unnamed employees for leaking photos and internal information about future products under development. A company spokesman told *Automotive News Europe* all Renault employees sign standard confidentiality agreements prohibiting them from releasing information on new models or discussing new models with the press, and that "when a car is revealed to the press before its launch, it has a real and immediate impact on sales of existing vehicles." After French police searched the office of a journalist at *Auto Plus* magazine, editor-in-chief Laurent Chiapello remarked the automotive press has been publishing photos of future vehicles "for 60 years," and he believed the object of the investigation was to end the leaks at Renault.

STRAIGHT FROM THE HEADLINES

IT Executive Accused of Stealing 3.2 Million Customers Data Worth $10 Million

In December 2008, the *Vancouver Sun* reported a former IT executive for a Canadian marketing firm had been accused of taking a computer backup tape containing the names and information of approximately 3.2 million customers, and credit card and bank account information for more than 800,000 customers. An affidavit filed in British Columbia's Supreme Court said the tape could "potentially be marketed as a discrete asset with a value in the tens of millions of dollars." According to the affidavit, the IT executive ordered another employee to bring three backup tapes to his office, where he made copies. Later, only two tapes were found on his desk; the tape containing the customer data was missing. When confronted by the CEO, he repeatedly denied knowing anything about it and soon left his job. The CEO then changed the locks on the computer room and terminated off-site access to the company's computer system. The affidavit described the IT executive as a "problem employee" whose office attendance was irregular, who charged lunches with his friends to the company, and who had informed employees he would be leaving soon.

STRAIGHT FROM THE HEADLINES

Hilton Accused of Corporate Espionage

Early in 2008, Hilton Hotels Corporation began seeking to employ Ross Klein, former president of the hotel chain Starwood Luxury Brands Group, and Amar Lalvani, former senior vice president of the Starwood Luxury Brands Group, who were closely involved with W Hotels, Starwood's lifestyle brand. In June 2008, following its acquisition by Blackstone Group, Hilton hired Klein as global head of Hilton Luxury & Lifestyle Brands and Lalvani as global head of Hilton Luxury & Lifestyle Brand Development. On April 16, 2009, Starwood Hotels & Resorts Worldwide Inc. filed a lawsuit accusing Hilton of "aiding and abetting" the two executives in illegally obtaining information about Starwood's luxury brand. The suit alleges that during their last months at Starwood, the two executives and other Starwood employees they brought with them to Hilton stole more than 100,000 "confidential electronic and paper documents" containing, according to a Starwood press release, "Starwood's most competitively sensitive information." The lawsuit alleges that the confidential information was used to help Hilton reduce the time, the expense, and the risk involved in launching its new Denizen luxury hotel brand.

In a public statement, Kenneth Siegel, Starwood's chief administrative officer and general counsel, said, "The wholesale looting of proprietary Starwood information, including a step-by-step playbook for creating a lifestyle luxury hotel brand, unfairly enabled Hilton to launch a new brand in only nine months instead of the usual three to five years." He added that Starwood considers it "a blatant case of theft of trade secrets, computer fraud, and unfair competition."

Corporate espionage can be very difficult to detect until its consequences become evident. Perpetrators receive payment outside the company and in secret, and may go undiscovered unless they flaunt their new-found wealth. The widespread use of computers makes it easier for dishonest employees to access, copy, and transmit electronic data. Sometimes the information thief is not an employee at all, but a hacker who successfully breaks into the company computer network, as shown in the story below:

STRAIGHT FROM THE HEADLINES

Over 100 Million Credit and Debit Cards Compromised by Hackers

In August 2008, a key Secret Service informant and ten other men in five countries were served with federal indictments in Boston and San Diego in connection with nearly every major breach of U.S. retail networks from 2004 to 2008, including a 2005-2007 intrusion into clothier TJ Maxx, in which millions of credit and debit card numbers were stolen. In addition to TJ Maxx, the defendants were allegedly responsible for intrusions into BJ's Wholesale Club, Boston Market, Barnes & Noble, Sports Authority, Forever 21, DSW, and OfficeMax. Among those named in the indictments was Maksym Yastremski, a Ukrainian in Turkish custody, alleged to be "Maksik," who earned over $11 million selling stolen credit and debit card numbers and magstripe swipes from 2004 - 2006 alone. He worked with Albert "Segvec" Gonzalez of Miami who, along with two other Miami men, allegedly hacked into vulnerable wireless networks at TJ Maxx and other companies and planted packet sniffers — software programs that intercept and log transactions passing over digital networks — to scoop up a total of 40 million credit and debit cards. Gonzalez and Yastremski had also been charged in New York in May 2008 with an intrusion into the Dave & Buster's restaurant chain.

Gonzalez was the key informant in the Secret Service's "Operation Firewall" — the government's 2004 crackdown on the cybercrime supermarket Shadowcrew.com. Gonzalez convinced members of Shadowcrew to use a private VPN service monitored by federal agents. Twenty-eight members were arrested in October 2004, but Gonzalez tipped off his co-conspirators to the operation so they avoided the crackdown. Federal agents were surprised to discover Gonzalez was behind the wave of retail intrusions following Operation Firewall and immediately arrested him. According to the government, the number of credit cards stolen by Gonzalez makes him eligible for life imprisonment.

TJX, parent company of TJ Maxx set aside $250 million dollars to deal with the consequences of the breach, which affected as many as 100 million credit card numbers. The sum included a settlement of up to $24 million with MasterCard Inc. and up to $40.9 million with Visa to reimburse banks and other institutions for computer costs, fraud claims, and expenses related to re-issuing credit cards.

Detecting corporate espionage

A trade secret is defined as a practice, process, design, instrument, pattern, formula, or collection of information that is not generally known to the public or cannot be reasonably arrived at by simple deduction and research, and which gives a business an economic advantage over competitors or customers. Most trade secrets concern technology or the production of goods, but a trade secret might also be a special mailing list of customers or suppliers, a method of bookkeeping, a distribution system, consumer profiles, or a special advertising and marketing strategy. The Economic Espionage Act of 1996 makes the intentional stealing, copying, and receiving of trade secrets both a state and federal white-collar crime. Convicted individuals can be sentenced to fines of up to $500,000 and 15 years in jail, and corporations can be fined up to $10 million. All property and proceeds from the stolen secret can be seized and sold by the government. Most states have adopted the Uniform Trade Secrets Act (UTSA), a model law drafted by the National Conference of Commissioners on Uniform State Laws to better define the rights and remedies of common law trade secrets.

Economic espionage is difficult to prove in court without concrete evidence and may involve a lengthy investigation and costly legal fees. The best method for preventing corporate espionage is also the best method for detecting and documenting it: strong security controls. Sensitive information should be protected with strictly enforced security procedures, and employee access to it should be restricted. In addition, employees with access to sensitive information should be required to sign a confidentiality contract and be informed of the legal and financial consequences of breaching such a contract. Logos, slogans, and brand names should be trademarked, and Web site URLs with similar names and spellings should be purchased and held by the company. Proprietary material such as membership directories or employee manuals should carry a written notice warning there are legal consequences for copying or sharing the information with anyone outside the company. Manuals and other printed copies of sensitive material should be numbered, and employees should be required to sign for them.

Red flags for corporate espionage

- **Lax security**
  Employees carrying laptops containing sensitive information home with them, poorly guarded passwords and employees sharing passwords, employees with unsupervised access to confidential documents and material, a high turnover of temporary contract employees, general disregard for security policies, unsecured storage of company manuals and other proprietary material, and a disorganized hierarchy in the workplace are all situations that could lead to corporate espionage.

- **Close or inappropriate social relationships between an employee and a competitor**
  Employees who have close or inappropriate social relationships with competitors should be watched. Attachment to a significant other who works for a competitor may be stronger than loyalty to an employer. An employee may be meeting with a competitor outside the office to transfer information.

- **Disgruntled employees**
  The same employee red flags for bribery apply to other types of corruption with one addition — an employee who seems socially

isolated, to be a loner, disgruntled, or hypercritical may be likely to become involved in corporate espionage.

- **An employee leaving the company for a job with a competitor**
It is natural for an employee to seek a higher-paying or more desirable job in the same industry, and a competitor will be eager to hire someone with experience, business contacts, and knowledge of the field. When employees are leaving to accept employment with a competitor, it is important to emphasize any confidentiality contracts the employee may have signed and to protect documents, materials, and files from being copied or taken. Computer passwords should be changed immediately, and employment should be terminated as soon as possible after the employee announces his or her intent to prevent further access to proprietary material.

- **Tips, suggestions, or hints from coworkers**
Coworkers may notice changes in an employee's behavior or suspect something is going on, but be reluctant to accuse the employee outright. Supervisors and managers should be sensitive to comments and hints from coworkers regarding the possibility that an employee is acting against the company's interests. If the employee is innocent, a brief and discreet investigation will quickly clear him or her of suspicion. If not, a coworker's hint might lead to the discovery of a scheme that is causing serious losses to the company.

Techniques for detecting corporate espionage

- **Monitor security logs**
Access to computer files should be protected by passwords, and a log should be kept of every time the files are opened. Many computer security programs automatically record who accesses files and the dates and times they were accessed. Regularly examine logs or access reports for files, looking for employees who access files after hours or from remote locations, or who access files that are not re-

lated to their work. Computer security systems can be programmed to alert a department head immediately when a file is accessed inappropriately. Every company should protect its computer system from outside hackers. This includes protecting sensitive data such as credit card numbers while it is being transmitted over the Internet.

- **Keep an inventory count of sensitive documents**
  Printed copies of blueprints, business plans, instruction manuals, and employee handbooks should be numbered and stored in a secure area. Each document should be assigned to a specific employee or department or signed out on a register each time it is removed from storage. If corporate espionage is suspected, the register will show who had access to these materials. A document issued to an employee who does not need it for his or her work is an indicator of corporate espionage.

- **Run background checks on employees**
  Every employee who has access to sensitive information should be subject to a background check before hiring. Many companies now ask employees to sign a document giving permission for the company to run credit checks and use credit scores as a guide in deciding whether or not to hire a new employee. A credit check may reveal whether an employee in serious financial difficulties needs counseling or assistance. In addition to standard background checks, Internet search engines allow informal background checks. Type in an employee's name and you may find a professional profile, a personal or professional Web site, blogs, news articles about the person's activities, membership in professional or social organizations, and profiles on social networking sites such as Facebook and MySpace. A search can provide valuable information about an employee's loyalties and social contacts, and potential red flags for a conflict of interest or participation in a fraud scheme.

- **Exit interviews**

  Exit interviews with employees who leave the company should include questions about future employment and may reveal possible conflicts of interest. Someone may be employed by a competitor as a reward for previous cooperation or because he or she is bringing valuable information from your company to theirs.

Insider Trading

Insider trading occurs when an individual buys or sells shares of a company's stock based on information not available to the public. For example, a person who knows a company will soon announce a merger that will raise the price of its stock might buy up a large number of shares several days before the announcement is made public. After the announcement, when the price of the company's stock goes up, he or she sells those shares and reaps a large profit. The opposite occurs when a person, knowing some future event will cause the share price of a company's stock to drop, quickly dumps shares on the market. One of the most egregious examples of insider trading is the Enron executives who sold large quantities of Enron shares in 2001, days before the public learned Enron had used fraudulent financial statements to hide millions of dollars in losses. Enron stock prices plummeted from a high of $90 to less than $15 a share.

The Securities Act of 1933 and Sections 10(b) and 16(a) of the Securities Exchange Act of 1934 made insider trading illegal and extended the definition of illegal trading to include buying or selling a company's stock while in possession of secret information about the company; tipping off others to such information; buying and selling of stock by a person who has received such a tip; and securities trading by any person who has stolen secret information. The SEC made the detection and prosecution of insider trading violations a priority because insider trading weakens investor confidence in the integrity and fairness of the U.S. capital markets.

STRAIGHT FROM THE HEADLINES

ImClone Founder Warned Family to Sell Stock Before Price Fell

On December 29, 2001, the share price of ImClone, a biopharmaceutical company, dropped sharply when it announced an experimental drug made by the company had failed to get the expected approval from the Food and Drug Administration (FDA). In June 2002, the SEC filed insider trading charges against the company's founder, Samuel D. Waksal, for telling friends and family to sell their ImClone stock and attempting to sell his own before the announcement was made. The SEC revealed six other ImClone executives and several members of Waksal's family sold their stock before the announcement was made on December 28 and before the price of ImClone stock fell 16 percent. On June 10, 2003, Waksal was sentenced to seven years and three months in prison.

In 2004, Martha Stewart, founder of Martha Stewart Living Omnimedia, was sentenced to five months in jail for giving false information to investigators regarding her sale of ImClone shares. She received a tip from her broker, a former employee at ImClone, that Sam Waksal, the president of ImClone, was selling all of his shares in the company in anticipation of the announcement. She avoided a loss of over $45,000 by selling her shares on December 27, the day before the FDA announcement was made public.

CHAPTER 8

Financial Statement Fraud

Financial statement fraud involves the manipulation of a company's financial statements to misrepresent the company's value, revenues, or liabilities to others. Within a company, certain employees may falsify statements to appear as though they are meeting financial goals and objectives, or to qualify for commissions or bonuses. A company may misrepresent itself publicly to elevate the value of its stock, get higher credit ratings, and attract investors. Companies may engage in complex financial transactions to make it look as though they are bringing in more revenue than they really are.

Financial statement fraud differs from other types of fraud because the economic benefit to the perpetrator(s) is indirect. Rather than stealing cash or assets directly from a company, the perpetrator profits from performance-based bonuses and promotions, higher stock prices, or easier and cheaper access to loans and investment capital. Financial statement fraud can also be perpetrated to cover up wholesale theft, such as the movement of cash to hidden offshore accounts. Perpetrators of Ponzi schemes provide entirely fabricated financial statements to their victims to make it appear as though legitimate stock market transactions are taking place.

Among the 959 cases studied for the ACFE's 2008 *Report to the Nation*, financial statement fraud occurred in little over 10 percent of the cases, but was associated with a median loss of $2 million — five times greater than the loss associated with corruption and 13 times greater than the median loss for asset misappropriation schemes. Asset misappropriation schemes and corruption victimize the organization, its investors, and its customers by stealing profits and threatening the viability of a business. Financial statement fraud can have wide repercussions in the stock market, artificially inflating the price of a company's stock and causing millions of dollars in losses that can never be recovered. Misleading financial statements also deceive banks and lenders into violating the policies they have put in place to ensure loans will be paid back.

Chapters 10 and 11 will discuss how individual investors can protect themselves against financial statement fraud. This chapter explores how and why financial statement fraud is committed.

Financial Statement Fraud Perpetrators

Asset misappropriation schemes are perpetrated by employees who have access to cash, checks, and bank accounts; corruption by those who are in a position to offer or receive illegal favors or benefits. The majority of financial statement frauds are committed by business owners and executives because they are the ones who stand to benefit from the fraud and because they have the authority to manipulate reports and set accounting procedures. Managers are sometimes involved in financial statement frauds relating to their particular department or area of influence. Lower-level employees occasionally commit financial statement fraud to cover up a theft or a mistake, or to overstate sales or revenue to meet performance goals.

Organized criminals commit financial statement fraud to obtain bank loans under false pretenses or to generate positive publicity around a stock and raise its price before dumping it on the market.

STRAIGHT FROM THE HEADLINES

Prominent Financier Fabricates References to Obtain $74 Million Loan

On August 25, 2009, Hassan Nemazee, 59, chairman and chief executive Officer of Nemazee Capital Corporation, was arrested in connection with a scheme to defraud Citibank, N.A. (Citibank). Nemazee Capital Corporation is a New York investment company involved primarily in real estate. A complaint filed in Manhattan federal court alleged Nemazee engaged in a fraudulent scheme to induce Citibank to lend him up to $74 million based on false representations he owned millions of dollars in collateral. Further investigation revealed Nemazee had defrauded three banks — Citibank, HSBC, and Bank of America, N.A. — of more than $290 million in loans. His brother-in-law helped him to fabricate phony documents such as account statements and correspondence bearing forged signatures, designed to convince the banks Nemazee had hundreds of millions of dollars in assets and had placed millions of dollars of U.S. Treasury securities in specified accounts as collateral for the loans. E-mail between the two men shows the brother-in-law was creating account statements designed to look like real account statements, but bearing account numbers for accounts that did not exist, with large fictitious balances. The brother-in-law also created a letter on a forged Pershing LLC letterhead, using a real Pershing employee's name but a New York address and phone number belonging to Nemazee, so that if anyone from Citibank called to verify the letter, they would be telephoning a number belonging to Nemazee. Nemazee allegedly made partial repayment of a Bank of America loan with money fraudulently borrowed from Citibank and partial repayment on the loan from Citibank with the Bank of America loan. He repaid Citibank $74.9 million with money from a loan fraudulently obtained from HSBC and was arrested at the airport as he tried to leave the country.

Records show that over the past 15 years, Nemazee and his wife have contributed more than $750,000 to Democratic federal committees and candidates and have been active as political fundraisers. In 1999, Nemazee was nominated by President Bill Clinton to be ambassador to

Argentina, but his name was withdrawn when Republicans raised questions about the propriety of some of his investment activities. The Democratic National Committee, Vice President Joseph Biden, and several other prominent Democrats have pledged to return at least some of Nemazee's campaign contributions or donate them to charity.

Motivation

Each financial statement fraud scheme is unique to the circumstances existing in a particular company or industry. The way in which a financial statement fraud is structured is determined by the evaluation criteria used by those who have power over company management. If sales figures are used as a measurement, the fraud scheme will inflate sales in some way. If performance is judged by the amount of revenue, a way will be found to record non-cash assets as revenue.

Understanding the motivation for financial statement fraud is the key to detecting when and how it might take place. Financial statement fraud occurs because the perpetrator has a reason for misrepresenting a company's financial and material assets, revenues, earnings, inventory, or sales figures. In companies where senior executives set unreasonable financial goals, or where compensation is strongly tied to financial results, managers and department heads may feel strong pressure to demonstrate success at any cost. The interest a company pays on borrowed money is determined by its credit ranking; a company can borrow more and pay less interest if it has more assets to offer as collateral, little debt, and a high potential to produce earnings. Some loan contracts require a company to maintain a specific current ratio — the ratio of current assets to current liabilities. To meet the conditions of the loan, company officials may overstate its assets. Executives who hold stock options may want to prop up the value of a company's stock by exceeding the expectations of stock market analysts.

Some of the reasons why a company's senior managers might want to overstate a company's performance are:

- To inflate the value and perceived earning potential of a business prior to a public stock offering, takeover bid, or sale of the business.

- To increase the size of asset-based loans, to meet a lender's requirements for extending credit, or to borrow money at a lower interest rate.

- To meet the requirement of an existing loan contract.

- To meet performance goals set by a parent company.

- To meet personal performance goals.

- To receive bonuses or performance-based compensation.

- To increase a company's perceived earning potential and support its stock price by meeting or exceeding the expectations of stock market analysts.

- To maintain the appearance of growth when a business that has been growing rapidly begins to slow down.

There are also situations in which senior managers may be motivated to understate the performance of a company:

- To make the business seem less volatile by presenting a picture of steady, incremental growth.

- To diminish current growth so the company will seem to be growing more rapidly in the future.

- To defer earnings to the next accounting period after sales goals have been met for the current period.

- To lower the value of a business in preparation for the owner's divorce settlement.

- To lower the value of a company whose management is planning a buyout.

- To write off all possible losses immediately so future earnings will be higher.

Financial statements may also be fabricated or falsified to cover up another fraud scheme, such as embezzlement, or to hide an embarrassing loss from investors.

How Financial Statement Fraud is Committed

There are three basic ways in which financial statement fraud is carried out. A company's accounting system can be manipulated to produce the desired results by changing the dates on which sales are recorded; recharacterizing liabilities such as bad debts, depreciation, or obsolete inventory as assets; or deferring expenses to a later year. In some cases, companies artificially increase their "sales" by shipping out goods that have not been ordered by customers, or by offering incentives to customers who stock up on excess inventory. Another type of financial fraud involves entering false, unsupported information into the accounting system to produce the desired results on financial statements. A third type of fraud is the creation of false financial statements outside the accounting system, such as the statements sent out in a Ponzi scheme telling investors they have money in an investment account when they really do not.

No company's business cycles fit neatly into the time periods covered by quarterly, biannual, or annual financial statements. For example, an aerospace company might land a large government contract every few years. A film production company produces a blockbuster after two or three years without a major success. American department stores and electronics stores experience their strongest sales during the period just before Christmas. A tourism business is most active during the vacation season. To satisfy investors and stock market analysts who are looking for a pattern of steady, reliable growth, such companies may engage in "creative accounting," or "income smoothing," recording their revenue and expenses in a way that spreads them out evenly over several financial periods. A company actively seeking to boost its profile in the stock market may use "aggressive accounting" practices to produce a picture of steady and substantial growth.

Creative accounting is not necessarily illegal. It does not become fraud until the company fails to fulfill its own expectations of growth, and the information contained in its financial statements becomes inaccurate and deceptive. A company may continue to employ questionable accounting procedures unchallenged until investors have experienced a substantial loss, investigators are called in, and a lawsuit is filed against the company.

Generally Accepted Accounting Principles (GAAP)

No two businesses are exactly alike. The accountants — who are responsible for recording a business's financial transactions, assets, and liabilities in a way that meets the needs of company management while complying with government regulations and Internal Revenue Service (IRS) tax rules — exercise flexibility in choosing which accounting practices to use. Generally accepted accounting principles (GAAP) is a set of commonly accepted accounting procedures and standards set by officially sanctioned policy boards. The use of GAAP standards for all financial statements is intended to provide the users of those statements, including executives, managers, lenders, and investors, with some level of consistency so financial statements from one business can be compared with those from other businesses.

From 1936 to 1959, accounting standards and procedures in the United States were established by the Committee on Accounting Procedure of the American Institute of Certified Public Accountants (AICPA). In 1959, the AICPA created an Accounting Principles Board to oversee this responsibility. In 1973, the Financial Accounting Standards Board (FASB) (**www.fasb.org/home**) was established as a body independent of all other business or professional associations to develop standards for financial reporting and provide guidance in the implementation of these standards. The FASB is overseen and funded by the non-profit Financial Accounting Foundation (FAF), established for that purpose in 1972. The FAF Board of Trustees currently consists of six officers and 13 trustees who, according to the FASB, serve five-year terms and represent "diverse backgrounds and expertise in areas of business, finance, investment, accounting, government, investor advocacy, education, and other professions involved in the activities of the financial and capital markets." The FASB works with several offshoots and affiliates, including the Governmental Accounting Standards Board (GASB) and the Emerging Issues Task Force (EITF) to address issues specific to certain financial sectors and to identify new deviant accounting practices and censure them before they become widely used.

The latest authoritative version of U.S. GAAP was released in July 2009 as FASB Statement No. 168, *The FASB Accounting Standards Codification* and *The Hierarchy of Generally Accepted Accounting Principles*. This version can be found by visiting **http://asc.fasb.org/**.

The AICPA Code of Professional Conduct prohibits its member accountants and auditors from expressing an opinion or stating affirmatively that financial statements or other financial data "present fairly...in conformity with generally accepted accounting principles," if those financial statements contain any departures from GAAP. GAAP is intended to ensure the information in financial statements reasonably and accurately represents a company's financial status.

The standards of U.S. GAAP are not exactly the same as the accounting principles used in other countries. Increasing globalization has resulted in the need for universal accounting standards that would allow an accurate comparison of financial statements from businesses in different parts of the world. In 2007, Financial Accounting Standards Board chairman Robert Herz called for a timetable for moving U.S. companies from GAAP to the International Financial Reporting Standards (IFRS), a set of global accounting standards developed by the International Accounting Standards Board (IASB). A proposed SEC timeline has all U.S. companies switching to IFRS by 2015.

GAAP incorporates eight major standards for judging when a financial statement contains inaccuracies and needs to be restated to reflect the true financial status of an organization. Departure from any of these standards could constitute fraud:

- **Materiality**: An error or discrepancy between the financial statement and the organization's records is considered "material" if it is significant enough to affect the decisions made by prudent users of that financial statement.

- **Matching**: The revenue and expenses reported for a particular financial period on a financial statement should match the amounts recorded in the organization's books and records for that same period.

- **Conservatism**: The financial figures in an organization's books and records should be at least as much as amounts reported on financial statements. Typically, the value of a business as reported on its financial statement should be a little lower than the value reflected in its books to account for errors or possible unreported losses.

- **Going concern**: Financial statements are based on the assumption the business or organization is a "going concern" — that it will continue in business indefinitely. If a business is in danger of folding or about to close its doors, this information must be disclosed in a footnote on financial statements. The value of an active business is greater than the value that can be realized by sale of its assets.

- **Cost**: Assets should be recorded at either their current market value or the price paid for them when they were bought (their cost of acquisition), whichever is lower. Other methods for determining the value of an asset are not acceptable ways to carry cost on a balance sheet. These include "fair value," the price that a willing buyer would pay to a willing seller on the open market (allowed only for certain types of assets, such as securities); "price-level adjusted historical cost," which represents an asset's value as what it would currently cost, adjusting for inflation; "net realizable value," the value of an asset based on the price it will sell for at some point in the future, minus the costs of owning, operating, and selling it; "future profits," which includes an estimate of the future profits a company could earn by possessing the asset; or "replacement cost," the amount it would cost to replace the asset.

- **Objective evidence**: Assets on a financial statement should be valued based on reasonable objective evidence such as contracts, invoices, cancelled checks, and receipts.

- **Consistency**: The methods used for calculating and representing the amounts on a financial statement should be consistent from year to year. If a company changes its bookkeeping methods in any way that has a material impact on its financial statements, it is required to disclose this in a footnote.

- **Full disclosure**: Any deviation from GAAP in the preparation of financial statements, any event that might impact the future earnings potential or value of the business, and any legal liabilities must be disclosed in footnotes to the financial statement.

In other words, GAAP ensures that the numbers on a financial statement are the same as the amounts in a company's accounting records and that they are supported by concrete evidence such as invoices, contracts, and receipts. If an auditor or accountant does not certify that a financial statement conforms to GAAP, it means that questionable accounting practices were used to arrived at the numbers on the financial statement. Users of such a financial statement should be very careful.

Types of Financial Statement Schemes

Financial statement fraud essentially involves making a business look more profitable than it really is, either by inflating the amount of revenue coming in, or by hiding or reducing expenses or liabilities on the company's balance sheet. This is accomplished in a variety of ways. Company executives may elect to use accounting methods that produce more favorable results. Income from other sources, such as sales of assets, loans, interest, or legal settlements may be represented as revenue. Operating expenses may be disguised or written off, and liabilities may be hidden. Finally, financial information may simply be fabricated.

The following sections describe various types of financial statement schemes. *See Chapter 9 for more information on how to detect these types of financial statement fraud.*

Fictitious revenue

Fictitious revenue schemes involve recording sales of goods or services that never occurred. Often, this is done by fabricating phantom customers, but it can also be carried out by writing fictitious invoices to legitimate customers or altering existing invoices to reflect higher sales. In 2003, the SEC issued *Staff Accounting Bulletin Number 104, Revenue Recognition* (SAB 104) giving guidelines for recognizing revenue. It stated that the following conditions must be met before revenue can be considered realized:

- **Persuasive evidence of an arrangement exists**
  Invoices, statements, signed contracts, and remittance slips are all substantial evidence of a sale.

- **Delivery of goods has occurred, or the service has been rendered**

  Revenue is not considered realized until the goods have been delivered or the service has been completed. If only a part of the service or delivery is complete, only that portion can be counted as revenue.

- **The seller's price to the buyer is fixed and determinable**

  Revenue is calculated based on the price stated in a contract or invoice.

- **Collectibility is reasonably assured**

  Revenue can not be recorded unless there is certainty that the invoice will be paid in a timely manner. For example, the buyer has signed a receipt acknowledging delivery of the goods and committed to a payment schedule.

Fictitious revenue schemes can occur wherever there is pressure to increase sales figures, or to boost value and the perceived earning power of a business. On an individual level, a sales rep might report fictitious sales to receive a higher bonus or commission. Managers might collaborate to make it appear as if their unit or department is exceeding sales targets, either for financial rewards or to protect their jobs. On a corporate scale, companies inflate their sales figures to generate positive reports from stock market analysts. Some large-scale frauds have involved the creation of offshore bank accounts and shell companies that "sold" assets to each other, reporting these transactions as "revenue" when the assets were only being transferred from one branch of the company to another.

STRAIGHT FROM THE HEADLINES

Banks Helped Enron to Generate Fictitious Revenue

The bankruptcy of Enron, one of the world's leading energy and communications companies, in 2001 was one of several wake-up calls that led to the passing of the Sarbanes-Oxley Act by U.S. Congress. Enron's reported 2000 revenues of nearly $101 billion turned out to be based on systematic, institutionalized financial statement fraud. Investors, pension funds, and Enron employees whose retirement savings were all tied up in company stock lost more than $25 billion. In April 2002, the University of California, the lead plaintiff in the Enron shareholders lawsuit, filed a 485-page consolidated complaint in the U.S. District Court for the Southern District Court of Texas in Houston, alleging the Enron fraud succeeded because of the active complicity of several prominent banks and law firms. The complaint laid out the scheme in detail and named J.P. Morgan Chase, Citigroup, Merrill Lynch, Credit Suisse First Boston, Canadian Imperial Bank of Commerce (CIBC), Bank of America, Barclays Bank, Deutsche Bank, and Lehman Brothers as key players in a series of fraudulent transactions. According to the complaint, a number of top executives at these banks profited personally from the schemes.

Several of the financial institutions named in the complaint helped to set up clandestinely controlled Enron partnerships, used offshore companies to disguise loans, and facilitated sham sales of overvalued Enron assets, allowing Enron executives to move billions of dollars of debt off its balance sheet and artificially inflate the value of Enron stock. The complaint describes the elaborate scheme as "a hall of mirrors inside a house of cards." Bank executives helped conceal the true state of Enron's precarious financial condition, while securities analysts at the same banks made false, rosy assessments of Enron to entice investors. As underwriters in the sales of Enron securities, the banks also misled the public by approving incomplete or incorrect company statements.

Bank loans to Enron, which should have been recorded as debt, were made to look like profits from sales. In other instances, Enron and the banks made loans appear to be investments. Bank officers were aware that if the price of its stock fell, Enron would be required to issue additional stock, diminishing the company's investment rating. The complaint revealed that some of the financial institutions had strong incentives to keep Enron afloat because they had written millions of dollars of "credit default puts" on Enron securities, requiring them to make good on

Enron's publicly traded debt if the company defaulted.

When Enron's financial manipulations became public and the stock collapsed in November 2001, executives from J.P. Morgan Chase and Citigroup pressured Moody's, a top credit rating agency, to keep Enron's credit rating in place until the banks could arrange a bailout sale of Enron to avoid insolvency and forestall a full-scale investigation into the company's dealings. The proposed sale fell through, and Enron filed for bankruptcy on December 2, 2001.

Another type of fictitious revenue scheme is making "sales with conditions" and reporting them as revenue. For example, a retailer might agree to purchase inventory on the condition that it will only pay for items sold during the next four months, and unsold items can be returned to the wholesaler. The wholesaler, wanting to boost its sales figures, might record all of the inventory as sold when part of it will probably be returned during the next financial period. In this case, collectibility — a necessary qualification for revenue to be considered realized — is not "reasonably assured" under the SEC guidelines mentioned above, and the sale should not be recorded as revenue until after the unsold goods have been returned and subtracted from the invoice. Another example of a sale with condition is software sold on a trial basis, where the customer has the option of canceling the sale within a 30-day period if the software proves unsatisfactory. The software company should not record this as a sale until after the end of the 30-day period.

A sales contract or invoice may be accompanied by a secret "side letter," offering the customer additional discounts or return options reducing the amount of revenue the company will receive from the sale. The company reports the full amount of the invoice as a sale and hides the discount in an expense account.

Manipulation of timing

Financial statements can be altered by manipulating the time periods when certain transactions are recorded in the company's books. Costs associated with the sale of goods or services should be recorded in the same financial period as the sale of those goods. One way to inflate sales figures is to record these costs in a different financial period. Reporting costs on a later financial report will make a company's sales figures appear higher than they really are. In some cases, costs for future financial periods are reported in an earlier period to give the appearance the company is experiencing higher sales and, therefore, rapid growth in the ensuing periods.

Profits reported on a financial statement can be artificially inflated by moving expenses — such as advertising and marketing, the purchase of equipment and supplies, or the opening of a new store or facility — to financial periods other than the periods when they are incurred.

Premature revenue recognition is a scheme in which revenue is recorded in the accounts before sales are complete. For example, a contract may exist, but the payment arrangements are incomplete; a customer may have placed an order, but the goods have not been shipped; or the goods have been delivered, but the customer has not yet paid for them and has the option to return them.

A company may report revenue from a long-term contract in one of several ways: It may record the revenue and expenses after a contract has been completed (completed contract method), or it may record a portion of the revenue, with associated expenses, based on the percentage of the contract that has been completed during each financial period (percentage of completion method). The latter method is easily abused because project managers have considerable freedom in the methods they use to estimate costs and measure the degree of completion. If a project overruns its budget, the revenue reported on earlier financial statements will be incorrect.

Sales figures are sometimes manipulated by extending the closing date of a financial period to include sales made after the financial period would normally have ended.

Channel stuffing is the practice of inducing customers or distributors to "stock up" on excess goods or unneeded supplies just before the end of a financial period. Sales figures for that financial period are increased, but future sales will be impacted when the excess inventory is disposed of.

STRAIGHT FROM THE HEADLINES

Coca-Cola Disciplined by SEC for False Disclosures Relating to Channel Stuffing

In April 2005, the SEC announced an enforcement action against The Coca-Cola Company "relating to its failure to disclose certain end-of-quarter sales practices used to meet earnings expectations." The SEC began its investigation after an ex-worker claimed the company had overstated revenue and engaged in bogus transactions.

SEC investigators found that "at or near the end of each reporting period between 1997 and 1999, Coca-Cola implemented an undisclosed 'channel stuffing' practice in Japan — known as 'gallon pushing' — for the purpose of pulling sales forward into a current period...Japanese bottlers were offered extended credit terms to induce them to purchase quantities of beverage concentrate the bottlers otherwise would not have purchased until a following period."

Coca-Cola typically sells gallons of concentrate to its bottlers in amounts corresponding to the amount of finished product sold to retailers. As a result of gallon pushing, from 1997 to 1999 Coca-Cola's Japanese bottlers' concentrate inventory levels increased at a rate more than five times greater than the rate of their finished product sales to retailers.

The SEC concluded "gallon pushing pulled forward sales from subsequent periods and made it likely that Coca-Cola's bottlers would purchase less concentrate in subsequent periods. This practice contributed approximately $0.01 to $0.02 to Coca-Cola's quarterly earnings per share and was the difference in eight out of the 12 quarters from 1997 through 1999 between Coca-Cola meeting and missing analysts' consensus or modified consensus earnings estimates. Despite the impact to current earnings and the likely impact to future earnings, Coca-Cola failed to disclose its gallon pushing practice in its periodic reports."

Although the SEC did not find a problem with Coca-Cola's accounting treatment of sales made in connection with gallon pushing, it concluded that Coca-Cola's failure to disclose the impact of gallon pushing on current and future earnings, as well as the false statements and omissions within a Form 8-K, violated the antifraud and periodic reporting requirements of the federal securities laws.

Coca-Cola agreed to settle the proceedings by consenting to a cease-and-desist order and voluntarily took steps to strengthen its internal disclosure review process to prevent future violations.

Understated expenses and concealed liabilities

One way to boost profits on a financial statement is to understate or omit some of the expenses associated with operating the business during that financial period. A legal settlement, fine, or a loss on investment capital might not be recorded in the books at all, even though it impacts the company's overall financial status. Debts and other financial liabilities might be represented as another type of transaction or disguised by moving funds from one bank account to another. Concealing this type of information makes a company look more profitable than it really is.

Capital expenses and revenue-based expenses are treated differently on financial statements. A capital expense is an expenditure on items such as computers, computer software programs, or manufacturing equipment benefiting the business over several accounting periods. Revenue-based expenses are directly associated with generating revenue during a specific accounting period. Capital expenses are amortized over a period of years, while revenue-based expenses are subtracted from the revenue earned during the accounting period when they were incurred. A company may increase its revenue by "capitalizing" revenue-based expenses — misrepresenting them as capital expenses and subtracting them over several accounting periods instead of all at once.

STRAIGHT FROM THE HEADLINES

AOL Penalized for Capitalizing Advertising Costs

You may remember receiving countless unsolicited CDs through the mail from America Online (AOL) during the 1990s and early 2000s, promoting its newest upgrades and pricing plans. In May 2002, America Online Inc. agreed to pay the U.S. government $3.5 million to settle a civil lawsuit brought by the SEC charging AOL with recording the cost of sending out those CDs (and other advertising costs) as an asset rather than a charge in financial statements between 1995 and 1996.

On December 29, 1993, the Accounting Standards Executive Committee of the American Institute of Certified Public Accountants issued Statement of Position 93-7, *Reporting on Advertising Costs* ("SOP 93-7"), setting forth the rules governing accounting for costs of advertising to gain subscribers. SOP 93-7, ¶ 26, requires advertising costs "be expensed either as they are incurred or the first-time advertising takes place." For fiscal years 1995 and 1996, AOL capitalized most of the costs of acquiring new subscribers, including the costs associated with sending CDs to potential customers and the fees paid to computer equipment manufacturers who bundled AOL software onto their equipment, as "deferred membership acquisition costs" (DMAC) and reported those costs as an asset on its balance sheet, instead of expensing those costs as incurred. According to SOP 93-7, the cost of advertising directly to customers who respond by buying a product can be recorded as an asset and expensed over several accounting periods only if the company can reliably predict its revenues and demonstrate it will be able to recover the advertising costs within a certain time period. AOL was not able to do this because it was operating in a new and unstable market, and the rate of response to AOL's advertising had already begun to slow.

The amount of DMAC reported on AOL's balance sheet grew from $77 million in 1995 to $314 million in 1996. Had these costs been properly expensed as incurred, AOL's 1996 reported pretax income of $62 million would have become a pretax loss of $175 million. The effect of capitalizing DMAC was that AOL reported profits for six of eight quarters in fiscal years 1995 and 1996, rather than losses that it would have reported had the costs been expensed as incurred.

AOL did not admit or deny the charges and issued a statement saying, "The agreement with SEC calls for the company to treat those costs as expenses in the period during which they were incurred. As a result,

America Online will restate its historical results from 1995 to 1997 to reflect that changed treatment."

Every business must allow for goods returned by dissatisfied customers or goods returned because they are damaged. The value of these goods and the expense of processing the returns should be deducted from the amount of net sales on a financial statement. A company selling products under warranty must estimate the expenses that will be incurred during the warranty period and record that amount as a liability. Some companies overstate their sales figures on financial reports by underreporting returns and liabilities, or by omitting them altogether.

Overstated assets

Banks and creditors are concerned with a company's current assets, including cash on hand, prepaid expenses, accounts receivable, and inventory and marketable securities that can be converted to cash in less than a year. Current assets serve as collateral because they can be liquidated to pay off a debt and because they ensure a company has the necessary cash to operate its business. Loan covenants often require the borrower to maintain a specific current ratio, the ratio of current assets, such as accounts receivable, to current liabilities. A company in midst of financial difficulties may misclassify long-term assets, such as property or equipment, as current assets in order to appear more solvent.

The value of an asset must often be estimated based on current market price, depreciation, and other factors. This process can be easily abused. The accounting rule of thumb is that the value of an asset should be its cost when it was purchased or its current market value, whichever is lower. A company might report a higher value for an asset than it is really worth. Inventory having lost value since it was purchased may be recorded at cost rather than at its current market value.

There are many ways of overstating inventory. Inventory that has become obsolete and damaged should be written off. Companies sometimes continue to carry obsolete inventory on their books, even though it has no value because it can no longer be sold. Inventory stock that has been sold and paid for may still be recorded as being in the warehouse unsold. Inventory counts can be tampered with and the numbers altered. There are even cases in which stacks of empty boxes in warehouses were disguised as inventory.

Accounts receivable can be inflated through various fictitious sales schemes, as described above. After a certain period of time has elapsed, invoices for which payment cannot be collected should be written off as bad debt. Some companies increase their reported assets by maintaining phony customers or bad debts as legitimate accounts receivable.

Fixed assets, such as real estate, should be valued at the price paid for them, even if their market value has increased. Some schemes value fixed assets at a higher "market price" instead of the amount for which they were acquired. Other schemes falsify ownership documents for fixed assets that do not really belong to the company, list the same fixed assets for more than one branch of the company, or list leased assets as though they are owned by the company. Interest and finance charges incurred by the purchase of an asset should not be included in its cost, but shown on the financial statement as interest expense. Some schemes increase the value of fixed assets by including interest paid on the money borrowed to purchase them as part of their cost.

STRAIGHT FROM THE HEADLINES

Stanford International Bank Overstated Assets in $8 Billion Investment Scam

In February 2009, the SEC charged billionaire Robert Allen Stanford and three of his companies, Antiguan-based Stanford International Bank (SIB), Houston-based broker-dealer and investment adviser Stanford Group

Company (SGC), and investment adviser Stanford Capital Management, with orchestrating a fraudulent, multi-billion dollar investment scheme centering on an $8 billion certificates of deposit program. The SEC also charged SIB chief financial officer James Davis as well as Laura Pendergest-Holt, chief investment officer of Stanford Financial Group (SFG), in the enforcement action.

The SEC alleged that acting through a network of SGC financial advisers, SIB sold approximately $8 billion of so-called "certificates of deposit" to investors by using fabricated historical return data to claim that SIB's unique investment strategy had achieved double-digit returns on its investments for the past 15 years. To keep investors buying its CDs, SIB reported fictional investment income on its financial statements. According to the SEC, Stanford and Davis provided a predetermined return on investment for the bank's portfolio to SIB accountants, who then reverse-engineered the bank's financial statements to reflect investment income that SIB did not actually earn. In its December 2008 monthly report, SIB told investors that the bank had received a "capital infusion" of $541 million on November 28, 2008. In fact, Stanford had contributed Antiguan real estate properties already owned by the bank to its equity. Though the properties had been purchased for $88.5 million only a few months earlier, Stanford valued them at $541 million.

Information given to investors in SIB brochures and "pitch books" was blatantly falsified. Investors were told that SIB invested in a "well-diversified portfolio of highly marketable securities." Instead, significant portions of the bank's portfolio were misappropriated by Stanford and used by him to acquire private equity and real estate. At year-end 2008, the largest segments of the bank's portfolio were undisclosed "loans" to Stanford, private equity, and over-valued real estate. SIB claimed that its investment portfolio was managed by a global network of money managers and "monitored by a team of 20-plus analysts." The SEC's complaint alleges that, in fact, "SIB's investment committee, responsible for the management of the bank's multi-billion dollar portfolio of assets, is comprised of Stanford; Stanford's father who resides in Mexia, Texas; another Mexia resident with business experience in cattle ranching and car sales; Pendergest-Holt, who prior to joining SFG had no financial services or securities industry experience; and Davis, who was Stanford's college roommate." SIB used generous commissions to recruit well-established financial advisors to sell its products, then encouraged them to transfer their client's assets into SIB CDs.

> On February 21, 2009, Antigua's Financial Services Regulatory Commission named a British firm, Vantis Business Recovery Services, as a receiver of Stanford International Bank and Stanford Trust Company. At the end of 2009, Stanford was in a Texas jail awaiting trial.

Improper disclosure

GAAP and SEC regulations require that financial statements disclose any information that might be of interest to investors, auditors, creditors, and any other users of financial statements. The notes and statements from management accompanying a financial statement should contain narrative disclosures and explanations of anything that might impact the present or future financial status of a company. The disclosed information must be accurate and not misleading. Improper disclosure occurs when information is deliberately omitted, misstated, or falsified to conceal or misrepresent a company's true financial circumstances. Additional information that should be disclosed in a financial statement includes:

- **Debt covenants and liabilities**: A company must disclose any liability that has the potential to materially affect the company's earnings or its business operations. For example, as part of a loan agreement, the company may have entered into a covenant to maintain a specific current ratio or accepted restrictions on other financing arrangements that could impede its ability to obtain necessary financing in the future. The company may have agreed to guarantee a loan to a subsidiary or one of its executives, or it may be under contract to cover the costs of completing a construction or software design project. Companies sometimes omit this type of information from their financial statements, hoping it will never come to light.

- **Lawsuits and regulatory decisions**: Events such as lawsuits, court judgments, or regulatory decisions affecting a company's business may occur after the close of a financial period. Failure to disclose such events along with the financial statement constitutes fraud, as these events affect the company's future earnings and materially alter the financial picture presented by the statement.

- **Fraud committed by a company officer**: If it is discovered that someone in a significant position of trust within an organization has committed fraud, this should be disclosed along with the financial statement. The harm done by fraud to an organization is also harm done to investors. The commission of fraud by one individual or department may signal fraud in other parts of the organization.

- **Related-party transactions**: Business transactions between entities controlled by the same management or the same owner are known as "related-party transactions." When related-party transactions are reflected on a financial statement, the connections among the entities and the nature of those transactions should be fully disclosed. Earlier in this chapter, the example "Banks Helped Enron to Generate Fictitious Revenue" gives several examples of related-party transactions that generated millions of dollars in fictitious revenues. The true nature of these transactions was concealed from investors, who later lost billions of dollars.

- **Changes in accounting methods**: Changing the way accounting transactions are recorded from one year to the next may create the appearance of growth or increased value when the opposite is true. A comparison of the figures on two or more financial statements cannot be accurate if the accounting methods used to produce them are different. According to Statement of Financial Accounting Standards No. 154 (SFAS 154), Accounting Changes and Error Corrections, changes to accounting principles, the methods used for making estimates, and the entities included in financial reports must be disclosed along with financial statements.

- **Impaired intangible assets**: Some businesses rely heavily on intangible assets such as patents, intellectual property, brand recognition, and customer goodwill. Anything that has happened during the year to change the status of an intangible asset should be disclosed in the financial statement. Examples include the expiration of a pharmaceutical company's patent on a popular drug, a highly publicized recall, serious flaws in a newly launched software program, or a tainted food scandal.

Misrepresentation of credentials and intellectual property

A company's earning potential may depend on its ability to innovate, develop, and sell new products. Users of financial statements rely on a company's assurances it has the necessary qualifications, licenses, patents, and talent to successfully carry out a new project. During the dot-com bubble of 1998 – 2001, stock prices of Internet start-ups soared as investors who knew very little about the Internet responded to promises of millions of dollars in profits and advertising revenues from online businesses. The investors had no way to evaluate the true earning potential of Internet-business models. Stock prices plummeted, and many companies went bankrupt when the promised revenues did not materialize.

Another example of this type of fraud is a company's lying about the credentials or résumé of a new CEO to boost investor confidence.

Ponzi schemes

Ponzi schemes are named for Charles Ponzi, a famous fraudster of the 1920s. In a Ponzi scheme, a business or "investment company" receives investors' money, typically promising a high rate of return, but never invests it as intended. Instead, money received from new investors is used to make payouts to longtime investors and create the impression their investments are bringing in high returns. Entirely fabricated financial statements are sent to investors showing false account "balances." In some cases, investors receive only verbal assurances their account balances are growing. Perpetrators of

Ponzi schemes avoid regulatory scrutiny by remaining private and unregistered, and they often rely on personality and charisma to recruit new investors and maintain their confidence. A continual influx of new cash is needed to sustain a Ponzi scheme. A number of high-profile Ponzi schemes came to light after trillions were lost in the stock market in 2008 – 2009. Investors who needed their money began withdrawing large sums, and there was not enough money coming into the schemes to make the payouts.

STRAIGHT FROM THE HEADLINES

Bernard Madoff Fabricated Statements for His Clients

On December 11, 2008, many lives were changed forever when Bernard Madoff announced that the highly regarded asset management branch of Bernard L. Madoff Investment Securities LLC was "all one big lie." Investors lost $65 billion, the largest loss incurred to date by a single fraud perpetrator.

Madoff had risen from a humble career as a plumber to serve as the Chairman of the Board of Directors and on the Board of Governors of the National Association of Securities Dealers (NASD). In 1960, he founded Bernard L. Madoff Investment Securities LLC with $5,000; eventually, the company dominated 9 percent of the trades on the New York Stock Exchange. In addition to the legitimate business, Madoff operated a "hedge fund," an investment fund with a special investment strategy that is open to a limited group of investors and is exempt from many regulations, in secrecy from an upstairs office. For the Frontline special "The Madoff Affair," which aired in May 2009, correspondent Martin Smith explored the details of how the scheme was constructed. Madoff enlisted "feeders," like accountants Mike Bienes and Frank Avellino, and fund manager Sandra Manzke, to recruit new clients and channel their investments into his fund. He guaranteed them a 20 percent return, allowing the "feeders" to make easy money by taking a 2 percent commission and offering their clients as much as 18 percent on their investments. In return, the "feeders" agreed not to mention Madoff's name on their prospectuses and to use small, obscure auditing firms for external audits. New clients were recruited through a wide social network extending to wealthy aristocrats overseas, particularly in South America and Russia. Madoff exploited his memberships in various country clubs and professional and religious associations, as well as through sitting on the boards of some of the charities that invested in his "fund." He attracted clients and ensured their cooperation by creating an atmosphere of exclusivity. Sometimes, he would make a generous offer to a new client, saying, "My fund is closed, but because you're a good friend, I'll make an exception for you..."

In 2001, Harry Markopolos, a Madoff whistleblower, was asked by his employer, Rampart Investment Management in Boston, to try to duplicate Madoff's investment strategy. During his research, Markopolos concluded Madoff's fund could not possibly be achieving the returns reported on its statement to investors. In 2005, the New York office of the the SEC failed to grasp the significance of a detailed report submitted by Markopolos and did not pursue an investigation. Editors at *The Wall Street Journal* refused to approve an investigative piece based on the report. Madoff managed to avoid regulatory scrutiny by never registering as an investment advisor, even though anyone advising more than 15 clients is required to do so by the SEC. When the scandal broke in December 2008, many Madoff clients lost their life savings, and others had to give up their homes and severely curtail their affluent lifestyles. Several charities were forced to lay off their staffs and close their doors.

The Connecticut Post reported the Orthopaedic Specialty Group, a surgeons' group with 130 doctors and employees in Fairfield, Connecticut, had invested its entire retirement fund with Madoff. "For some of us, it's an entire career's worth of work," Dr. Robert Dawe told the newspaper. "I'm not an expert on finance; I'm an expert in orthopedic surgery." Some of the group's doctors had been paying into the retirement fund for 40 years. Dr. Dawe told the Post that Madoff had been recommended by a trusted source, and many experts had called him the "best of the best." Twice a year, Madoff met with the group and showed them documents indicating the group's money was being invested in "blue-chip" securities. The town of Fairfield invested $22 million of its pension fund in Madoff's fund over three years in the 1990s and received statements and annual audits saying it had grown to $42 million. First selectman Kenneth Flatto told **www.FOXNews.com**: "The town controller was getting monthly statements and the annual audit reports showing the breakdown and everything. That's why it's just hard to believe."

Some investigators believe the actual loss to Madoff investors could be less than $20 billion, and the initial estimate of $60 billion includes fictitious profits reported in statements to investors over the years. Bernard Madoff was tried in federal court and sentenced in June 2009 to 150 years in prison.

The Sarbanes-Oxley Act of 2002

After losing billions in 2000-2002 following large-scale corporate and accounting fraud at Enron, Tyco International, Adelphia, Peregrine Systems, and WorldCom, investors lost confidence in U.S. capital markets. On July 30, 2002, Congress enacted the Sarbanes-Oxley Act of 2002 (Pub.L. 107-204, 116 Stat. 745) — also known as the Public Company Accounting Reform and Investor Protection Act of 2002, and commonly called Sarbanes-Oxley, Sarbox, or SOX — to help eliminate fraud in publicly traded companies by increasing regulation and raising penalties. The Sarbanes-Oxley Act contains 11 sections setting new standards for the boards and management of all U.S. public companies and public accounting firms. The SEC is responsible for setting rules and requirements to implement the provisions of the Act.

The Sarbanes-Oxley Act sets requirements both for disclosure of important information in the financial statements of public companies and for the implementation and evaluation of internal controls to prevent fraud and financial mismanagement. Executives of public companies are now required to regularly evaluate the effectiveness of internal controls and perform fraud risk assessments.

Public Company Accounting Oversight Board

The Sarbanes-Oxley Act provided for the establishment of the Public Company Accounting Oversight Board (PCAOB) (**www.pcaobus.org**) to protect investor interests by overseeing the audits of public companies, setting audit standards, and investigating acts of noncompliance. The duties of the PCAOB are to register and inspect public accounting firms that audit publicly traded companies; set and adopt standards of quality control, ethics, and independence for audits of these companies; conduct investigations and impose penalties for noncompliance with the Sarbanes-Oxley Act or the PCAOB rules; and to promote high professional standards among public accounting firms.

An accounting firm must be registered with PCAOB in order to legally issue an audit of a publicly traded company. Registration required the accounting firm to list all of its customers from the previous year and the fees they paid. Section 103 of Sarbanes-Oxley, which requires the PCAOB to set standards for audits, includes the following requirements:

- Audit work papers must be preserved for at least seven years.

- An audit must include a concurring review and an approval by a qualified professional other than the one in charge of the audit.

- All audit reports must include a description of how the company's internal control structure was tested, the author's evaluation of those internal controls, and a description of any weakness or non-compliance that was found.

Certification of CEOs and CFOs

The Sarbanes-Oxley Act requires that chief executive officers (CEOs) and chief financial officers (CFOs) take personal responsibility for the accuracy of annual and quarterly SEC filings. There are two types of certifications: criminal certifications and civil certifications. A criminal certification is a signed statement certifying the financial statement complies with SEC standards and fairly and accurately represents the financial status and results of the company's business operations. Criminal penalties are imposed on officers who violate these requirements. A civil certification is a statement that:

- The company officer has personally reviewed the financial report.
- The report does not misrepresent the financial status of the company.
- The officer is responsible for designing and maintaining internal controls, has conducted an evaluation of these controls within the past 90 days, and has included the written conclusions of this

evaluation in the financial report.

- Any material weaknesses in these internal controls and any fraud involving management or significant employees has been disclosed to the auditors.
- Any significant changes made to controls since the previous report have been explained.

Audit committee

Sarbanes-Oxley requires each member of a company's audit committee to serve on its board of directors. Members of the audit committee may not receive compensation for any consulting or advisory work, apart from work done in those two capacities. The audit committee is directly responsible for hiring and overseeing outside auditors and must have the authority to hire legal counsel and other necessary advisors. At least one member of the audit committee should be a "financial expert" — an accountant, comptroller, or CFO who has knowledge of accounting principles and experience with financial reports and audits. If such a person is not present, the SEC must be informed and an explanation given. The audit committee is also responsible for setting up a whistleblower mechanism to receive tips and complaints regarding accounting irregularities.

Auditor independence

One of the problems that emerged during the corporate scandals of 2001 -2002 were apparent conflicts of interest in public accounting firms. The same companies who performed audits were paid millions of dollars in consulting fees to perform other work, impairing their ability to remain objective. Sarbanes-Oxley prohibits public accounting firms from doing other types of work for their audit clients, such as bookkeeping; design or implementation of accounting systems and internal controls; management; human resource functions; investment banking or investment advising; and legal services. A public accounting firm cannot perform an audit for a company that has hired a CEO, comptroller, or CFO who was on its payroll during the past year and participated in the company's previous audit. The lead audit partner or the person responsible for reviewing a company's audit must be rotated every five years.

Auditors must report directly to the audit committee and are required to reveal any discussion they have had with management concerning alternative accounting practices and compliance with GAAP. They must report on the accounting practices and policies used to prepare financial statements and submit any written communications they have had with company management. In addition, auditors must review company management's assessment of the effectiveness of internal controls and present their own evaluations.

It is illegal for any officer of a publicly traded company to attempt to fraudulently influence, coerce, manipulate, or mislead an auditor who is performing an audit of the company's financial statements.

Requirements for financial disclosures

The Sarbanes-Oxley Act requires all annual and quarterly SEC reports to disclose any transactions not reported on the balance sheet that could materially affect the company's financial status, including contingent obligations and relationships with unconsolidated entities that could possibly pose a potential risk to the company's liquidity.

Pro forma financial statements are prepared in advance of a new business venture or a planned transaction, such as a merger, to show the expected impact of the transaction on a company's business results. They may also be used to adjust a company's earnings to account for an unusual one-time financial event such as restructuring costs. Sarbanes-Oxley directs the SEC to issue rules that pro forma statements may not contain untrue statements or omissions that might mislead investors and that they must conform to GAAP.

Section 402 of the Sarbanes-Oxley Act makes it illegal for a publicly traded company to make personal loans to its directors or executives, except in the case of a consumer lender making a loan of the same type and under the same conditions as loans it offers to the public.

The Sarbanes-Oxley Act also requires stock transactions by directors, officers, or owners of more than 10 percent of a public company's stock to be reported to the SEC before the end of the second business day following the transaction. Directors and officers who have received company stock as compensation are prohibited from trading the stock during pension fund blackout periods (periods when participants in a company's retirement plan are restricted from trading in the company's securities).

Public companies must disclose whether they have an established code of ethics for senior officers and give an explanation if they do not. Any changes to or waivers of this code of ethics for a senior company officer must be reported to the public immediately.

The SEC is required to review each company's financial statements and disclosures for accuracy at least once every three years.

Publicly traded companies are required to make disclosures "in plain English" of any material changes in their financial status on a "rapid and current basis." This means investors will be kept informed of significant changes to a company's financial status as soon as they occur, instead of being kept in the dark while a company is foundering.

Whistleblower protection

A "whistleblower" is an employee who reports illegal practices within an organization to a manager or regulator. Section 806 of the Sarbanes-Oxley Act makes it illegal for a publicly traded company to retaliate in any way against an employee who reports suspected misconduct or aids in the investigation of securities fraud, as long as the report is made to a supervisor, a law enforcement agency or federal regulatory agency, or a member of Congress or committee of Congress. This applies not only to retaliation by the company as a whole, but by any individual employee, officer, contractor, subcontractor, or agent of the company. Compensatory damages are awarded to the whistleblower if the company is found to have violated Section 806.

Section 1107 of Sarbanes-Oxley makes it a crime to knowingly retaliate against a person who provides truthful information to a law enforcement officer regarding the possible commission of any federal offense.

Increases in the penalties for financial statement fraud

The Sarbanes-Oxley Act expanded the definition of white-collar crime so people convicted of "attempting" or "conspiring" to commit securities fraud, bank fraud, wire fraud, mail fraud, and health care fraud were subject to the same penalties as people who actually committed those crimes. Section 207 of the Sarbanes-Oxley Act made securities fraud a crime punishable by a maximum of 25 years in prison and a $250,000 fine. Sections 802 and 1102 made it a crime to destroy, alter, or hide documents that could serve as evidence in an investigation or to obstruct or impede any official proceeding.

The Act also implemented rules to prevent some of the worst abuses observed during the corporate scandals of 1998 – 2001. Corporate assets can be frozen during an investigation to prevent them from being moved or distributed. The bankruptcy code was amended by Section 803 so that penalties, settlements, fines, restitution, and disgorgement payments cannot be discharged by declaring bankruptcy. Section 304 states that if a public company has to restate its financial reports because of noncompliance due to "misconduct," the CEO and CFO must reimburse the company for any bonus or incentive-based compensation and any profits they realized from the sale of company securities during the 12-month period after the erroneous financial statement was filed. The Act does not specify the CEO and CFO must be involved in the misconduct leading to the restatement of the financial reports.

Consequences of the Sarbanes-Oxley Act

A great deal of debate and discussion has emerged since the passage of the Sarbanes-Oxley Act, along with an entire compliance industry involving auditors, legal firms, and fraud investigators. Some of the debate concerns the degree to which government should intervene in the affairs of corporations. Another subject of debate is the cost of compliance with the Act, not only for companies who must pay for accountants and auditors, but for taxpayers who fund the expanded regulatory operations of the SEC. Many financial experts agree the implementation of the Sarbanes-Oxley Act has helped to restore investor confidence and resulted in more accurate, more conservative, and more transparent financial statements. In the years immediately following its passage, the number of financial reports being restated after their initial releases increased. These numbers declined after companies settled into compliance. Several other nations, including Japan, Canada, Germany, and Australia, have passed similar legislation regulating public companies.

Critics of the Sarbanes-Oxley Act claim the government's excessive intrusion into corporate affairs has made U.S. public companies less able to compete with foreign companies. Critics also contend the cost of implementing its requirements is prohibitive and discourages smaller companies and foreign businesses from registering with U.S. stock exchanges. The Advisory Committee on Smaller Public Companies, chartered by the SEC, concluded in its 2006 final report that the costs of complying with Sarbanes-Oxley were disproportionately higher for smaller companies and recommended the requirements be scaled down for them. Though Sarbanes-Oxley applies only to publicly traded companies, it also has an effect on private companies. Private companies expecting to go public in the future, or that hope to be bought by a public company, must already plan for Sarbanes-Oxley compliance.

An annual survey by Financial Executives International (**www.financialexecutives.org**), an association of 15,000 CFOs, comptrollers, and treasurers, indicates the cost of complying with Section 404 of Sarbanes-Oxley, which sets requirements for internal controls, is gradually decreasing as companies become more efficient in implementing these controls. The 2007 survey, which polled 185 companies with average annual revenues of $4.7 billion, reported compliance with Section 404 required an average of 11,100 internal people hours in 2007, a decrease of 8.6 percent from the previous year. The average cost of compliance with Section 404 in 2007 was $1.7 million.

Despite the costs of complying with Sarbanes-Oxley, there is evidence that public companies benefit from effective internal controls. A 2006 study by Lord & Benoit, LLC, a Sarbanes-Oxley Research and Compliance firm, concluded that from 2004 – 2006, "companies that either historically operated organizations with no material weaknesses in their internal controls or were able to identify and correct material weaknesses in a timely manner experienced much greater increases in share prices than companies that did not."

CHAPTER 9

Detecting Accounting
Fraud Within an Organization

Financial statement fraud can occur on any level in an organization. It involves altering or falsifying financial records so the statements based on these records give incorrect information about the organization's financial status. As described in Chapter 8, an employee may alter financial records to cover up embezzlement or payroll theft, to receive a higher performance-based bonus or sales commission, or to make it appear as though a target goal is being met. Senior executives of an organization may use questionable accounting practices or falsify financial information to misrepresent their company's financial status to investors and lenders. This chapter deals with the detection of financial statement fraud within an organization; later chapters examine how investors can detect fraud in public financial statements.

Financial statement fraud within an organization is harmful because it falsifies the information used by executives to make important business decisions, and ultimately affects the public financial statements that investors and business owners rely on. It is typically associated with other serious problems, including embezzlement and theft of inventory. Detection of financial statement fraud requires the involvement of staff at every level of an organization. Executives and management should be aware of situations that might be conducive to fraud and of suspicious aberrations in business patterns. It is important that an organization maintain strong internal controls and ongoing surveillance of its accounting practices to detect fraud in its early stages.

STRAIGHT FROM THE HEADLINES

Nicor Inc.: Using fraudulent financial statements to get higher bonuses

On July 18, 2002, Nicor Inc. issued a press release announcing that its financial results for the second quarter and first half of 2002 had been negatively affected by irregularities in accounting at Nicor Energy, a retail energy marketing company established in 1997 as a 50/50 joint venture by Nicor Inc. and Dynegy Inc. The next day, the stock price of Nicor Inc. fell approximately 40 percent. Nicor Energy was subsequently liquidated.

An indictment returned by a federal grand jury charged Kevin Stoffer, the president and CEO responsible for day-to-day operations of Nicor Energy, and Andrew Johnson, director of financial services, responsible for Nicor Energy's accounting, finances, and back office functions, including billing and accounts receivable, with five counts of wire fraud. John Fringer, the vice president of major markets and power services who was responsible for the company's electric power business, and Michael Munson, an attorney, were each charged with four counts of wire fraud. Munson, a solo-practice attorney, allegedly had an incentive to please Nicor's managers because he would receive additional legal work and hoped to be hired as the company's in-house general counsel.

According to the indictment, "Nicor Energy had a bonus and profit sharing plan that made the payment of any bonuses in 2002 directly dependent on the company meeting or exceeding a target profit at the end of 2001. Between March 2001 and July 2002, the defendants allegedly caused the reporting of false financial figures on Nicor Energy's 2001 financial statements, including balance sheets and income statements, and caused false information concerning Nicor Energy's revenue and expenses for 2001 to be provided to representatives of Nicor Energy's parent companies and Nicor Energy's outside auditors. At times during 2001, Stoffer and Johnson allegedly caused Nicor Energy's unbilled revenue figures to be inflated by as much as $6 million."

Among other things, the defendants made expenses for 2001 appear lower by recording part of a large legal settlement as an expense in 2002, though it was concluded in 2001. The indictment also alleges that information from fraudulent financial statements sent to members of the Executive Committee of Nicor Energy was incorporated into financial reports that Nicor Energy's parent companies, Nicor Inc. and Dynegy Inc. Nicor Inc. and Dynegy filed with the SEC. As a result, investors and potential investors in Nicor Inc. and Dynegy Inc. were deprived of accurate financial information regarding these companies and risked substantial losses.

The three company executives pleaded guilty, but the charges against the attorney were dismissed because of a mistrial in 2003. In March 2007, Nicor Inc. and its former controller agreed to pay more than $10 million to settle charges by the SEC that they engaged in improper transactions and made false representations about the company's gas inventory to meet earnings targets. The U.S. Securities and Exchange Commission said the financial fraud lasted from 1999 to 2002 and was done to increase the company's revenues under a performance-based rate plan administered by the Illinois Commerce Commission.

Red flags for financial statement fraud

Detection of financial statement fraud within an organization relies on two major activities: an awareness and investigation of warning signs that fraud might be occurring (red flags), and constant monitoring and surveillance of accounting practices and business transactions.

Fraudulent financial statements are drawn from fraudulent data in company accounts. At some point in the accounting process, someone is tampering with the data. It can occur at any level in an organization: the invoices and bank deposit slips from which data is first entered into the accounting system; manipulation of data already in the accounting system; or at the executive level, where and financial officers elect to use suspect accounting policies and procedures. Among the financial statement fraud cases studied for the ACFE's *2008 Report to the Nation*, 70 percent were perpetrated by executives or employees in the accounting department. These employees have access to accounting systems and the authority to override controls. The following red flags are indicators that financial fraud could be occurring in an organization:

- **Lack of adequate internal controls**

  Without a system of checks and balances in place to detect accounting errors, it is easy for an employee to commit fraud.

- **Organization always seems to be operating in crisis mode**

  When an organization is continually dealing with one crisis after another, regular accounting procedures and internal controls are often put aside, security measures are overlooked, and employees may have unofficial access to accounting records. The crisis itself may be a sign of accounting fraud — for example, there might not be enough cash available for daily operating expenses because someone is overstating revenue, understating expenses, or altering accounts to cover up theft.

- **One person has authority over several or all of the accounting functions**

  The most effective method for preventing theft is separation of duties — the division of responsibility for handling cash and accounting among two or more individuals. When one person is responsible for multiple duties, such as receiving incoming payments, depositing them in the bank, and recording them in the accounts, that person has an opportunity to commit fraud unobserved. In small organizations where one individual is responsible for all bookkeeping functions, an executive or supervisor should review transactions and sign off on bank deposits.

- **Discrepancies in accounts**

  Discrepancies in the accounts may simply be due to errors, or it may be a sign that fraud is occurring; either way, the source of the discrepancy should be found and examined.

- **Poor recordkeeping**

  Poorly kept accounting records make it easy for employees to conceal theft and may even be a deliberate attempt by an employee to conceal irregular activities. Without accurate records, it is difficult to verify financial statements and determine exactly what is going on.

- **Missing or damaged documents**

  Missing or altered bank statements, invoices, receipts, deposit slips, cancelled checks, cash register tapes, and other supporting documents are all signs that an employee may be entering fraudulent information into the accounting system.

- **Unexplained changes in business patterns**

  An unexplained increase or drop in sales, increase in the number of write-offs, change in the timing of bank deposits and other regular transactions, or any change to an established pattern should be investigated.

- **Bank deposits made at irregular intervals**

  Bank deposits made at irregular intervals may be a sign that an employee is involved in a lapping scheme, using cash from recent sales to make up a deficit in the previous bank deposit.

- **Bank reconciliations not performed in timely manner**

  Delays in performing bank reconciliations may be an attempt to mask accounting fraud.

- **Accounts receivable increasing or decreasing out of synchronization with sales figures**

  Accounts receivable should increase or decrease along with the company's sales figures.

- **Employee reluctant to write off accounts receivable**
  An employee who is using accounts receivable to mask a theft may demonstrate reluctance to write off an account.

- **Sales figures increase suddenly from previous periods**
  An employee whose sales figures suddenly increase may be recording fictitious sales in order to get a larger commission.

- **Employee's sales figures increase at end of each period, followed by cancellations and returns at beginning of next period**
  An employee may be recording fictitious sales at the end of one period and canceling them after a commission or bonus has been received.

- **Unrealistic goals or expectations imposed by management**
  There is a balance between inspiring employees to strive for a sales target and demanding they achieve the impossible. A company that imposes unrealistic and unachievable goals creates a situation conducive to financial statement fraud. Employees who feel pressured to meet unrealistic goals may resort to financial statement fraud to create the appearance that they are fulfilling management's expectations.

- **Compensation based on performance**
  Whenever compensation includes bonuses, commissions or stock options, there is motivation for employees to overstate sales or revenue figures.

Techniques for Detecting Financial Statement Fraud

Unlike skimming or bribery and corruption schemes, accounting fraud involves manipulation of records kept in the company's accounting system. Irregularities in the accounting system ultimately appear in the figures on a company's financial statements. Evidence of accounting fraud will eventually emerge when these irregularities are detected, when the organization's financial reports deviate from expected and historical norms, or when a business fails to perform according to estimates based on its previous financial reports. A system for monitoring and double-checking accounting records can be effective in preventing and hastening the discovery of financial statement fraud.

- **Employee background checks**

  Background checks should be run on employees who handle cash and have access to the accounting system. Though the ACFE studies show that only a small percentage of fraud perpetrators have a previous criminal history, you certainly would not want to give responsibility to someone who has been charged in the past with a fraud-related offense or dismissed by a previous employer because of financial misconduct.

- **Internal controls**

  The same system of checks and balances that helps to prevent fraud may also expose it by revealing discrepancies in the accounts and subjecting accounting transactions to a second set of "eyes."

- **Whistleblower hotline**

  As with other types of fraud, a tip from a fellow employee, vendor, or customer is frequently the first clue something is wrong. Every organization should establish a procedure for confidential reporting of tips and complaints, and encourage employees to report irregular activities.

- **Employee red flags**

  As discussed in previous chapters, certain types of employee behavior are associated with fraud. A belligerent or uncooperative accounting employee may have something to hide, and an overbearing and intimidating executive may be trying to discourage employees from asking embarrassing questions. An employee with serious financial difficulties, a gambling problem, or excessive motivation to achieve financial success may turn to fraud as a "solution" to his or her problems.

- **Internal and external audits, surprise audits**

  Internal and external audits are more effective at uncovering financial statement fraud than other types of fraud because they examine financial transactions and evaluate internal controls. During the audit, representative samples of transactions are selected for closer review, and this process may discover irregularities such as missing or altered documentation, or unsupported adjustments to the accounts. Unannounced, surprise audits may catch a fraud perpetrator unprepared, before he or she has time to make the usual adjustments to the accounts to hide the fraud.

- **Manual fraud monitoring**

  Once potential fraud risks in an accounting system have been identified, accounts can be regularly reviewed for signs of fraud. For example, a supervisor or director can regularly review bank statements and bank reconciliations, and match documentation such as signed deposit slips to accounting records. Inventory and sales accounts can be compared to detect theft.

- **Monitoring with anti-fraud software**

  Anti-fraud software can conduct continual fraud monitoring (CFM) by automatically checking each new transaction against a variety of data and flagging any situation that suggests fraud for special attention. The software performs standard evaluations and can also be programmed to watch for specific signs of fraud. Anti-fraud software can also be used to conduct specialized investigations. The software can monitor unlimited amounts of transactions, but its effectiveness is limited if the accounting system is poorly organized and transaction data is not entered in the system. When antifraud software flags certain transactions as suspicious, someone must be prepared to respond and investigate them.

- **Comparative analysis of financial statements**

  Financial statement fraud can sometimes be detected by comparing figures from the most recent financial statement with financial statements from previous periods. An unexplained deviation from historical patterns may indicate that information on a financial statement is being manipulated or falsified. Two traditional types of analysis, percentage (vertical and horizontal) analysis and ratio analysis, will be explained briefly below. Antifraud software can use data from an organization's accounting system to perform these types of analysis and create charts and reports.

- **Review of the accounting system**

  Any time the accounting system is subjected to extra scrutiny, the likelihood of exposing fraudulent activity increases. Most fraud schemes are not carefully orchestrated, but have flaws that will lead to their eventual discovery. The following checklist can be used to conduct a quick review of internal controls and the accounting system for signs of financial statement fraud.

CHECKLIST FOR ACCOUNTING FRAUD

Use this checklist to conduct a review of your accounting system for possible weaknesses or signs of fraud.

Cash Receipts	
✓	How are checks and cash protected and secured?
	Who prepares the deposits? Who takes them to the bank?
	Who posts cash receipts to the accounting system?
	Who supervises the processing of cash receipts?
	Are there missing or altered bank deposit slips?
	Are there large numbers of voided transactions?
	How often are bank deposits prepared? When are they taken to the bank?

Bank Statements	
✓	Are deposits made on a regular basis?
	Are there large, recurring fluctuations in the bank balance? If so, why?
	Are bank reconciliations done in a timely manner?

Accounts Receivable	
✓	Who receives incoming payments?
	Who posts them to the accounting system?
	What is the policy for write-offs?
	Who reviews and approves write-offs?
	Are there any unapproved write-offs or adjustments in accounts receivable?

Bank Statements	
✓	How are vendor records created and updated?
	How are updates to vendor records updated?
	Who prepares checks for payments to vendors?
	Who posts these payments to the accounts?
	Are there multiple vendors with similar names?
	Is there a recurring amount paid to the same vendor?
	Is there a vendor whose invoices have sequential numbers?
	Have payments to one vendor increased significantly? Why?
	Are payments to vendors posted directly to an expense account instead of accounts payable?
	Is there a noticeable pattern of adjustments for goods returned to vendors?

Financial Statement Analysis

Business owners, executives, and lenders rely primarily on analysis of two types of financial statements: balance sheets and income statements. A balance sheet, also known as a statement of financial position, is a snapshot of the organization's financial status at a particular point in time, usually after all the day's financial transactions have been recorded. The balance sheet shows everything the company owns and everything it owes to creditors on the statement date. Some intangible assets that may be very valuable are not reflected on a balance sheet, such as brand recognition, unique intellectual property, and customer goodwill.

The income statement — also called the profit and loss statement, the P&L, the statement of income, or the statement of operations — is a report of the total revenues, gains, cost of goods sold, expenses, losses, and net income for a specified period of time.

Mathematical analysis of balance sheets and income statements, as well as comparison with data from earlier statements, reveals useful information about a company's business and financial activity, such as changes in the relationship between sales, costs, and profits. Unexplained aberrations in business patterns may mean that fraudulent information is being entered into the accounting system or that accounting practices have been altered to produce more favorable results.

Vertical analysis

Vertical analysis expresses each item on a financial statement as a percentage of the total at the bottom of the statement.

Simple example of a vertical analysis

ASSETS	Year 1	Vertical Analysis	Year 2	Vertical Analysis	Year 3	Vertical Analysis
Cash	100,000	42.92%	180,000	54.05%	400,000	84.21%
Current Assets	37,000	15.88%	43,000	12.91%	12,000	2.53%
Accts. Receivable	56,000	24.03%	70,000	21.02%	23,000	4.84%
Inventory	40,000	17.17%	40,000	12.01%	40,000	8.42%
Total	**233,000**	**100.00%**	**333,000**	**100.00%**	**475,000**	**100.00%**

In the example above, the percentages for the first two years are fairly similar, but the percentage of cash for the third year jumps dramatically, while the percentages of current assets and accounts receivable drop significantly. If such a dramatic change is not due to a restructuring of the business model, it indicates either a serious accounting error or possible fraud.

Horizontal analysis

Horizontal analysis presents the change in each item from one year to the next as a percentage of the previous year.

Simple example of a horizontal analysis

ASSETS	Year 1	Year 2	Change from Year 1 to Year 2	Percentage of Change	Year 3	Change from Year 2 to Year 3	Percentage of Change
Cash	100,000	180,000	80,000	80.00%	400,000	220,000	122.22%
Current Assets	37,000	43,000	6,000	16.22%	12,000	-31,000	-72.09%
Accts. Receivable	56,000	70,000	14,000	25.00%	23,000	-47,000	-67.14%
Inventory	40,000	40,000	0	0.00%	40,000	0	0.00%
Total	**233,000**	**333,000**	**100,000**	**42.92%**	**475,000**	**142,000**	**42.64%**

In this example, the change in total assets increases steadily from year to year, but the change for each item differs dramatically. Current assets dropped from a change of 16 percent the second year to a change of –72 percent the third year. The reason for such a drastic drop requires further examination.

Ratio Analysis

Ratio analysis expresses the relationship between the amounts of two different items on a financial statement as a ratio, then compares it either to the average ratio for other businesses in the same industry or to ratios from the company's previous financial statements. Under normal circumstances, a ratio stays fairly constant from one financial statement to the next. Even if the amounts on the financial statement rise and fall, the relationship between the various items should remain the same. A significant change in the ratio from one statement to the next means the amount of one item on the statement has risen or fallen relative to the other item. Significant changes in key ratios should be investigated to see what caused them.

Ratio analysis cannot detect small-scale fraud and is most effective when the amounts on a financial statement reflect large quantities of transactions. On the financial statements of small businesses, which do not have tens of thousands of transactions, one or two large transactions would be enough to cause a change in key ratios.

The key financial ratios that might lead to discovery of fraud are:

Ratio	Formula	What it Measures	What it Means
Current ratio	$\dfrac{\text{Current assets}}{\text{Current liabilities}}$	A company's ability to meet current liabilities using liquid assets.	Embezzlement will cause this ratio to decrease. Concealing liabilities will cause it to rise.
Quick ratio (Acid test ratio)	$\dfrac{\text{Cash} + \text{Temporary investments} + \text{Accounts receivable}}{\text{Current liabilities}}$	A company's ability to meet current liabilities using assets that can quickly be turned into cash.	A decrease in cash, indicating a billing fraud scheme, will cause this ratio to decrease.
Receivable turnover	$\dfrac{\text{Net sales on account}}{\text{Average net receivables}}$	The amount of time between when sales are made on account and payment is collected.	Fictitious sales will cause this ratio to decrease, because payments are never collected from customers.
Collection ratio	$\dfrac{365}{\text{Receivable turnover}}$	The average number of days to collect receivables (payments).	A high ratio means that receivables are not being collected, an indication of fictitious sales, larceny, or skimming.
Inventory turnover	$\dfrac{\text{Cost of goods sold}}{\text{Average inventory}}$	Number of times inventory is sold during an accounting period.	A high ratio indicates efficient purchasing, production, and sales, but an unusually high ratio may indicate that inventory is being stolen.
Average No. of days inventory in stock	$\dfrac{365}{\text{Inventory turnover}}$	Average number of days that inventory is in stock.	Significant changes in this ratio indicate possible inventory theft or purchasing schemes.
Debt to Equity	$\dfrac{\text{Total liabilities}}{\text{Total equity}}$	Compares outstanding debt to owner's investment in the business.	An increase in accounts payable causes this ratio to increase. This could indicate fictitious sales or embezzlement.
Profit margin (Efficiency ratio)	$\dfrac{\text{Net income}}{\text{Net sales}}$	Profits earned per dollar of sales	An abnormally high ratio indicates inflated sales. A low ratio indicates fraudulent disbursements. This ratio should remain constant over time.
Asset turnover	$\dfrac{\text{Net sales}}{\text{Average assets}}$	Amount of sales generated for every dollar of assets	A low ratio indicates that assets are not being used as efficiently, indicating misappropriation or misuse.

Software that helps detect fraud

Manually searching for "red flags" in a company's accounting system by comparing invoices with receipts and records, regularly verifying vendor addresses and information, and looking for suspicious entries in expense accounts would be a full-time job in a small company and practically impossible for a corporation that has millions of transactions each month. Instead, auditors select and examine random statistical samples of transactions and documents — a strategy that can still fail to catch specific instances of fraud. Computers, however, are capable of searching, comparing, and extracting data from millions of records almost instantaneously. Businesses are increasingly using general auditing and specialized fraud detection software to search for and "flag" transactions that should be investigated more closely. Some of these applications can be set up to continually monitor transactions as they occur and call immediate attention to potential fraud situations.

Analytical software is used by auditors to look for anomalies between a company's current business data and patterns established by data from previous years or other mathematical models. It also searches for specific red flags, such as transactions of a specified amount, or multiple transactions of the same amount. Statistical tools, such as Benford's Law, are used to identify unusual or suspicious activity. Benford's Law states that within a particular set of data, digits and digit sequences occur in a predictable pattern, and lower digits (1, 2, 3, 4) occur more frequently at the beginning of numbers than higher digits do. Analytical software counts how many times various digit values appear in a set of data and compares the totals to a result predicted according to Benford's Law. If the two counts vary by more than a small percentage, the data must be examined closely to see why it does not follow statistical averages. In many sets of data, the numbers begin with a "1" about 25 percent more often than they begin with a "9." A series of transactions in which most of the amounts begin with $99 would be suspect and would be flagged for closer examination.

Monitoring applications cross-reference a company's business records such as employees' schedules, hours worked, and salaries; employees' access to computer networks and databases; vendor records; accounts payable; and general ledger entries. They search for possible red flags such as conflicts of interest, timesheets that do not coincide with hours billed, employees and vendors with the same address or phone number, duplicate social security numbers, goods that were shipped but not ordered, and managers' authorizing multiple payments that are just under their spending limit. Monitoring may be automated and continual, or it may be customized and used for specific investigations. Some software products combine monitoring applications with statistical analysis.

To detect possible credit card fraud and identity theft, many large companies use a program called Falcon, created by Fair Isaac Corporation, that is based on neural networks. Neural networks mimic the way the human brain acquires knowledge and detects patterns. A large number of simple processing modules collect and store information while forming connections with each other based on the relative importance assigned to each piece of information. Neural networks attempt to identify a pattern of spending behavior for each customer and relate it to a general pattern of typical spending behavior, such as the spending habits of a "traveling salesman" or a "sedentary shopper." If a customer makes purchases that deviate from his or her typical pattern, an alarm is triggered. For example, a purchase made in Rome, Italy, with a card used to buy gas in Idaho just two hours earlier, is suspicious. You may have received a call from your bank at some time, asking whether you had made a certain purchase: the bank wants to verify that someone else is not using your stolen credit card. A similar system can be used to monitor complex business activities and identify any that do not fit a normal pattern of activity.

Antifraud software ranges from expensive, complex applications customized for a particular company to relatively simple and inexpensive downloads of analytics programs that search a company's data for universal signs of fraud, such as duplicate invoices and changes in key ratios. Many applications include features that provide easily understood reports and allow management to create specialized queries. Some provide step-by-step guidance to investigate possible instances of fraud after they have been detected. Antifraud software has the capability to compare and analyze an unlimited amount of data very quickly, but it must be coupled with human investigative minds that can distinguish between real instances of wrongdoing and incidents that have a legitimate explanation. When the software flags certain transactions as questionable, management must decide what to do with this information. The implementation of antifraud and analytical software includes education and training for everyone involved in using it.

Two factors affect the usefulness and accuracy of antifraud software: the integrity of the data in the business system, and how well the people setting up the software understand the company's business processes and fraud risks. Antifraud software is only as good as the data it analyzes. If a business processes invoices or timesheets manually, that information will not be available to the software. Data must be kept up-to-date, and transactions must be entered into the system in a timely manner. If errors are made when data is being typed into the system, or if data is inconsistent, the software may not read it accurately. For example, if a street name or city name has an abbreviation or spelling error, the software may not be able to match it up with the same address spelled correctly on another invoice. For antifraud software to operate with maximum efficiency, a company must have procedures to enforce accurate entry of data into the system. For example, employees should be trained to enter information in a consistent manner, and electronic forms should have error controls that reject data that is not formatted correctly. The databases should be constructed and connected in a logical system.

The descriptions of various fraud schemes explained how a dishonest employee with permission to access the accounts system may be able to alter data electronically, unless a monitoring process catches him or her acting suspiciously. The people who program the antifraud software to look for specific signs of fraud must have a good understanding of how the company's business processes could be manipulated. If the software is not set up correctly, it may still miss signs of fraud, or it may flag legitimate transactions as fraudulent.

Company	Software Product	Purpose	URL
CaseWare	IDEA	Data analysis	www.caseware.com/products/idea
Approva	BizRights	Automate and monitor controls	www.approva.net/products/bizrightsplatform
Oracle/ LogicalApps	Enterprise Control Management	Monitors computer access and business transactions	www.oracle.com/solutions/corporate_governance
SAS	SAS® Fraud Framework	Monitor customer behavior, detect fraud	www.sas.com
SPSS	Fraud Detection and Prevention	Predictive analytics, data mining	www.spss.com/fraud_detection
ACL Services	ACL	Fraud detection in a business	www.acl.com
Agena	Agena Risk	Risk management	http://agena-risk.com
Arbutus Software	Arbutus Connect	Data analysis	www.arbutussoftware.com
Arbutus Software	Arbutus Query	Data analysis	www.arbutussoftware.com
Bennett Technologies	ESuraksha	Secures Web-based software applications	www.bennettss.com/FraudAwareness.html
APEX Analytix®	FirstStrike® Fraud Detect	Detects vendor and accounts payable fraud	www.apexanalytix.com/fraud-detection-software.aspx
Information Active	ActiveData	Data analysis and fraud detection in Excel	www.informationactive.com/ad
ISGN - Fair Isaac	Falcon Fraud Manager	Detects credit card fraud	www.fico.com
FraudLabs™	FraudLabs™ Fraud Detection Web Service	Detects credit card fraud	www.fraudlabs.com/products.aspx

Alaric	Fractals	Credit card fraud detection	www.alaric.com/fraud_detection.html
MaxMind, Inc.	minFraud	Detects credit card fraud	www.maxmind.com
Carreker International	FraudLink On-Us	Detection of banking fraud	www.carreker.fiserv.com/index.htm
Chi-X® Global Inc./Cicada	Cicada Profiler	Prevents fraud in stock brokerages	www.chi-xcanada.com/index.jsp

Data Mining

Data mining is the process of extracting useful information from documents and financial records, regrouping it and analyzing it to arrive at some kind of conclusion. Any document or financial record that exists in some form online, on a computer, or on a memory device — such as a CD — can be "mined." Many types of scanning devices and conversion software can be used to "read" written or printed documents, such as business cards, canceled checks, and invoices, and store them as electronic data. The analytics software described above conducts highly complex data-mining procedures and combines them with statistical formulas and analytical tools to search for fraudulent transactions. Accountants and auditors frequently use spreadsheet software such as Microsoft Excel™ to do simple data-mining procedures such as searching for duplicate transactions. Try the simple data-mining exercise below to see how you can conduct your own investigations and to get a better understanding of how fraud detection software works.

Data mining with Excel

1. **Import a set of records**, such as a bank statement, a list of accounts receivable, a list of vendors, or a list of all company employees' names and personal information, into Excel or another spreadsheet program.

   Most online bank statements or records from accounting software such as Quicken™ or Microsoft Money™ can be exported as spreadsheets, or as a comma-delineated file that you can import into your spreadsheet.

2. **Look over the data**

Take a look at the appearance of the data in your spreadsheet. Is all the information complete? Are all the fields uniform and consistent? Do the addresses have street address, city, and state in different columns, or are they all in one column? If you see misspellings, inconsistent data, or several bits of information in one column, it is a sign that your company needs to clean up its records and place more emphasis on accuracy. Do any vendors have a post office box instead of a street address? For a list of employees or vendors, is there a telephone number and an e-mail address for each listing? Do these look consistent and accurate? In the future, if you begin to use software to manage these records, send out e-mail announcements, or conduct searches, poorly maintained data will cause problems and inaccuracies.

3. **Use the "Data/Sort" function in Excel to look for duplicate entries**

Select a column such as "Amount," "Street Address," or "E-mail address." Highlight the entire database by clicking the square in the top left-hand corner. Now select "Data" from the menu at the top of the screen, and "Sort." Select the column you want to sort and click "OK." All the entries are now arranged in alphabetical or numerical order for the column you selected. Run your eyes up and down the column and look for the rows that have identical data. This is called "eyeballing" data. You might be surprised to find several transactions for exactly the same amount, two employees with the same street address, or several vendors with the same e-mail address. Now look at the information in the associated columns to see whether the entire record is a duplicate, if the transactions were recorded on different dates, or if the same e-mail address is associated with three different vendor names. You may have found a red flag. There may also be a legitimate error, such as the same vendor entered a second time with a misspelled name; this needs to be corrected. Try sorting and scanning several different columns.

4. **Compare with other sets of data**

    You may now want to import other sets of data, such as lists for previous months or years, and compare them to the list you have just looked at. You can also use other spreadsheet functions to conduct a simple analysis, such as adding up the total invoices for each month and comparing them to the same months in a previous year.

    If you have a working knowledge of Microsoft Access™, you can conduct more complex searches by connecting several sets of data. *The CPA Journal*, a publication of the New York State Society of CPAs, offers an online exercise by Mark W. Lehman and Marcia L. Weidenmier (**www.nysscpa.org/cpajournal/2005/405/essentials/p58.htm**) that teaches how to use Access to detect six red flags of billing schemes.

CASE STUDY: DIGITAL ANALYSIS ENABLES PROACTIVE ANTIFRAUD MONITORING

Grasil, Inc.
PO Box 22376
Lake Buena Vista, FL 32830
www.grasil.com
407.355.3744   Info@Grasil.com

Silvio Cherjovsky, CIA, CFE, president and CEO of Grasil, Inc. and chief technology officer of The Fraud Institute, has served twice as president of the Central Florida Chapter of ACFE. He is a pioneer in digital analysis, the detection of fraud through the mathematical analysis of data. Grasil, Inc. will soon launch an affordable software product that can be used by a manager, entrepreneur, or auditor to quickly detect signs of fraud in any database.

Can you explain how digital analysis works?

Digital analysis is based on three important laws: the Law of Probabilities, Benford's Law, and Zipf's Law. Zipf's Law is not as well-known, but it is very powerful. According to Zipf's Law, within any set of events, the number of times that an event occurs is inversely proportional to its rank in the list of events — the most frequent event will occur a certain percentage of the times, the next most frequent event occurs a certain percentage of that, and so on. Digital analysis takes any set of data, determines the patterns that should occur within the data according to these three laws, then points out any abnormal occurrences.

How is digital analysis different from traditional anti-fraud systems?

Most fraud detection systems look for patterns of fraud that are already known from previous cases. They search for a myriad of fraud indicators such as duplicate numbers, recurring transactions, and abnormal ratios. I believe that traditional antifraud monitoring software does not work in detecting fraud. New methods of committing fraud appear every day, and they can easily pass "under the radar" of traditional methodologies. I teach many CFOs, company managers, auditors, fraud examiners, and accountants in my classes. Many of them do not use antifraud software, even if their company has it, because it is too complicated. They do not know how to set it up. Employees have to go through training to use it, and it takes too much of their time. This Antifraud Monitoring System does not look for historical or industry-related patterns; it simply analyzes a given set of data, any set of data, and points out abnormalities. A CFO or a manager who is thoroughly familiar with his business can look at those abnormalities and understand where the problem lies. Abnormal data does not always indicate fraud, but there should be a reasonable explanation for it.

Can you give some examples?

We have used digital analysis to detect many types of fraud. When they are confronted with the evidence, people always ask, "How did you know?" The customs agents from another country asked me to analyze their records because they believed they were not taking in enough customs duty. The analysis pointed out two particular importers whose customs forms exhibited abnormal data. Those two companies' premises were searched, and investigators found caches of high-end computers hidden behind false walls. The companies had falsified the import documents so that they paid import duties for cheap low-end computers when they were really importing computers worth thousands of dollars each.

A divorce lawyer asked me to analyze his client's husband's tax returns for hidden income. An abnormal amount of $80,000 turned up among his business tax deductions, listed as the cost of a "promotion." Further investigation revealed that he had used that money to buy a luxury car for his mistress. The payroll division of a large national company asked me to analyze its accounts. There were too many amounts ending in "00." After tax-withholding and other deductions are taken out, most paycheck disbursements are not rounded numbers. Closer examination showed that employees who relocated were each claiming the maximum relocation allowance for their salary levels — a round number — instead of itemizing their real relocation costs. One executive had claimed $750,000! We helped a national government discover a kickback scheme by showing that licenses and permits for certain companies were being processed through the system at a much faster rate than licenses and permits for similar businesses.

Digital analysis can reveal abnormal events in any set of data. If your data is stored electronically, it can be analyzed immediately; if you are dealing with paper documents, just enter the details into a spreadsheet and it's ready to go. Inventory figures, social security numbers, serial numbers on receipts, dates, words, addresses, weights, or measures — anything can be digitally analyzed.

What about small companies with only a small amount of data, or companies whose data is incomplete or inaccurate?

Digital analysis finds abnormalities in data sets of any size, whether you are dealing with millions of figures or a few dozen. When a database is poorly maintained, incomplete, or inaccurate, digital analysis will reveal the errors along with any other abnormalities, and the company will be able to see where mistakes are being made and what can be done to improve data collection. Those errors need to be found and corrected.

Please describe your new antifraud software product.

Our product is affordable and easy to use. It interacts directly with Quick-Books™ accounting software. Any entrepreneur or manager whose company uses QuickBooks™ will be able to run a few tests and then use knowledge of his or her business to figure out what is wrong. He or she can take the results to the accountant or CFO and say, "See these transactions? What's going on here? Please explain this." It is an instrument that the CPA working with company files can use to check for wrong data when he or she does a data compilation and audits in a company. The risk tolerance level can be adjusted —a high risk tolerance setting will produce only a few results showing the greatest abnormalities in the database; a low risk tolerance setting will produce many more results. In the future, we plan to make the software compatible with all types of accounting software, and maybe create a product specifically for divorce attorneys. Our system works anywhere because it is nonspecific, invariant, and independent. It is not specific to any industry; it doesn't change based on metrics; and it is independent of any standards that might differ from one locality or country to another. Everyone who has tested it has described it as "elegant."

How will this product affect antifraud investigation?

The majority of frauds are discovered by accident or through tips. Digital analysis allows you to be truly proactive in countering fraud. It turns up warning signs wherever they exist, even in unexpected places. So many times, people manage to deflect suspicions of fraud because they are trusted employees. Numbers don't lie; people do. When the numbers show clear evidence that fraud is being committed, the perpetrator can't deny it.

CHAPTER 10

For Investors:
Detecting Financial Statement
Fraud in Public Financial Statements

The previous chapters discussed how managers and executives who rely on financial statements to make business decisions can detect possible financial statement fraud within an organization, primarily by monitoring the accounting system. Investors use a company's public financial statements to determine whether or not that company is a sound investment. Financial statements affect the stock prices of publicly traded companies and can cause millions of dollars in stock market losses if they carry misleading information. The majority of companies produce accurate public financial statements, but there have been numerous cases in which company executives deliberately misrepresented a business's financial status. How can investors, who do not have access to a company's accounting records, determine whether a financial statement presents an accurate picture of the company's business? This chapter describes how you, as an individual investor, can detect fraud in a company's financial statements.

The figures on the public financial statements issued by companies and organizations are taken from their underlying accounting systems. A careful analysis of these statements and their accompanying documents, combined with market data and financial news commentary, can reveal whether an organization's business status is accurately represented. Companies that trade on the U.S. stock exchanges, known as publicly traded companies, are required to file regular annual and quarterly reports with the SEC, which makes them readily available to investors. Lenders and investors in private companies, donors who support charities and non-profit organizations, and taxpayers who want to know how government agencies are using their money may have to specifically request financial statements.

Financial analysts, brokerage houses, journalists, and risk management professionals subscribe to commercial databases that allow them to identify businesses that exhibit specific warning signs of fraud or financial difficulty. LexisNexis (**www.lexisnexis.com**), a division of Reed Elsevier, maintains a searchable archive of content from newspapers, magazines, legal documents, and other printed sources. Standard & Poor's Compustat (**www. compustat.com**) is a searchable database containing almost 50 years' worth of financial, statistical, and market information on active and inactive companies throughout the world. When you are considering a specific company as an investment, look for articles and commentary on that company to support your own analysis.

Where to Find Financial Statements

Publicly traded companies

Basic financial information such as PE ratios, earnings per share market capitalization, and historical performance for publicly traded companies can be found online at Web sites such as **www.nyse.com**, **www.morningstar.com**, **www.msn.com**, and **www.nytimes.com**. Before you begin looking at a company's financial statements, do some research to get an understanding of its general position in the stock market.

Publicly traded companies are required by Sarbanes-Oxley to file annual financial reports with the SEC and to send annual reports to their shareholders. In addition, they must file forms to report a variety of significant events whenever they occur. All of this information is available to the public through EDGAR, the SEC's Electronic Data Gathering, Analysis, and Retrieval system (**www.sec.gov/edgar.shtml**), which performs automated collection, validation, indexing, acceptance, and forwarding of submissions by companies. EDGAR is intended to increase the efficiency and fairness of the securities market by making time-sensitive information available quickly to the public.

Regular filings

- **Form 10-K**

  Every publicly traded company must file a detailed financial report with the SEC using Form 10-K within 90 days (for companies with a capitalization of $75 million or less), 75 days (for companies with a capitalization between $75 million and $700 million), or 60 days (for companies with a capitalization of more than $700 million) of the close of the company's fiscal year. This report must be audited by an independent auditor.

- **Annual report**

  The annual report is sent out once a year to all of a company's shareholders. It contains a summary of the information on the Form 10-K, including financial statements, accompanying footnotes, a report by a CPA, and a letter from the company president.

- **Proxy statement**

  Each company mails a proxy statement to its shareholders before the annual shareholder's meeting, explaining proposals to be voted on at the meeting. The proxy statement contains information about management compensation, stock options and benefits, related-party transactions, and changes in auditors.

Occasional filings

- **Quarterly report: Form 10-Q**

  Every publicly traded company must file a quarterly report with the SEC using Form 10-Q within 45 days (for companies with a capitalization of $75 million or less) or 40 days (for companies with a capitalization of more than $75 million). This report is less detailed than the Form 10-K and contains a balance sheet, a statement of operations and cash flow, footnotes, and management discussion and analysis. Unlike the annual report on Form 10-K, the quarterly report is not audited. It is intended to provide an ongoing picture of the company's financial status throughout the year.

- **Form 8-K**

  Publicly traded companies are required to file Form 8-K to report a variety of events that shareholders should know about, including acquisition and disposition of assets, a change in auditors, and bankruptcy. A complete list of these events can be found on the SEC Web site (**www.sec.gov/answers/form8k.htm**). The company must file a Form 8-K within four days of the event. Though the information on Form 8-Ks is important to investors, companies are not necessarily required to disclose it to them.

- **Form 144**

  A Form 144 must be filed with the SEC whenever an insider (an executive or affiliate of the company) proposes to sell more than 500 shares of stock or shares worth more than $10,000. If the sale is not completed within three months, an amended notice must be filed.

- **Registration**

  Any public company planning to issue shares of stock in an initial public offering must file a registration statement with the SEC using Form S-1 or Form S-20. The statement must include a prospectus describing the company's financial performance, background, and business plan.

Private companies

The AICPA's 2005 *Private Company Financial Reporting, Task Force Report* estimated that 99.7 percent of businesses incorporated in the U.S. in 2005 were private companies. The majority of privately held companies are owned by their founders and their families and heirs; by small groups of investors; or by their employees. Private companies in the United States are not generally required to publish their financial statements, but will typically provide them upon request to lenders and private investors. Private company financial statements follow GAAP standards. Some private organizations have adopted Sarbanes-Oxley requirements such as audit committees and external audits, either because they plan to become public in the future or because they are using donations or taxpayer dollars and are subject to public scrutiny.

Some financial information on private companies can be obtained from the states where they are registered. By typing the company name in an Internet search engine, you can find news articles and financial commentary that may reveal important information about the company's business.

CASE STUDY: U.S. LIBRARY OF CONGRESS — RESEARCHING PRIVATE COMPANIES

Excerpt from Private Company Research, Business Reference Services, U.S. Library of Congress (www.loc.gov/rr/business/company/private.html)

The U.S. Library of Congress recommends the following resources for researching private companies:

- **Ward's Business Directory of U.S. Private and Public Companies:** Available through many libraries, lists 100,000 U.S. public and private companies; primarily private, small-to-mid-size companies.

- **Dun & Bradstreet Reports (www.dnb.com/us):** A useful source for both current business information and business history. Most companies have D&B reports (generally for credit information). Much of the information in a D&B report is voluntary, so the quantity of information will likely vary from company to company.

- **Hoover's (a D&B Company):** Publishers of *Hoover's Handbook of Private Companies*, provides information about private companies on their Web site (**www.hoovers.com/free**).

- **Company Web pages:** Many private companies publish financial information on their own Web sites. Keep in mind that some companies use their Web sites as catalogs, sales brochures, or advertisements.

- **Local Business Journals:** *The American City Business Journals* (**www.bizjournals.com**) are a good source for local company information. The site links to business news from over 30 cities, including Washington, Seattle, Philadelphia, Birmingham, Baltimore, Albany, Orlando, Nashville, and more. Listings of local and city magazines (**www.bibliomaven.com/citymags.html**) and local business magazines at (**www.bibliomaven.com/businessjournals.html**) can be found at Bibliomaven.com.

- **Secretaries of state:** Companies are required to file with the secretary of state of the state in which they are established. The National Association of Secretaries of State (**http://nass.org/index.php?option=contact_display**) has a directory of state Web pages, or you can search for official state business sites online.

Foreign companies

Foreign companies trading on the U.S. stock exchange are required to file an annual report with the SEC using Form 20-F. These forms are available on the Internet in the EDGAR database. Reporting requirements in foreign countries differ from the United State, and information may not be as easily available to the public. The International Organization of Securities Commissioners lists the URLs of its members on its Web site (**www.iosco. org/lists/display_members.cfm?memID=none&orderBy=country**). Remember, accounting standards may be different, and items on foreign financial reports may not be directly comparable to items on U.S. financial reports. Many foreign companies provide their financial reports on their Web sites. There are numerous directories of foreign companies available through libraries — the Library of Congress offers a list of these on their Business references Service Web site (**www.loc.gov/rr/business/company/ foreign.html**).

Reading Annual Financial Statements

A company's Form 10-K, its annual shareholder's report, and its proxy should all be read as one document because each may disclose slightly different information. A typical Form 10-K contains an audited balance sheet, statement of operations, cash flow statement, footnotes to the financial statements, management discussion and analysis, auditor's report, and liquidity position and capital expenditures. The annual shareholders' report includes a summary of the Form 10-K and a letter from the president of the company. Begin your examination of a company by looking, not at the financial statements, but at the accompanying documents. The footnotes, auditor's report, proxy, and president's letter reveal clues about a company's true financial state and may contain warning signs of possible financial statement fraud.

Auditor's report

Every Form 10-K must be accompanied by a report from an independent external auditor. Most auditors' reports confirm the accuracy of the company's financial statements. If an auditor has reservations about a company's financial stability or the accuracy of its accounting methods, it may issue a "qualified opinion." A qualified opinion is a red flag, particularly if it is a "going concern" qualification. A "going concern" qualification indicates that a company is experiencing serious financial difficulties and may not be able to continue operating its business. If the auditor questions the accuracy of the financial statements, it is a sign that management has chosen to use aggressive accounting methods. *Read about aggressive accounting methods in the section on footnotes to financial statements later in this chapter.*

In an auditor's report, you should look out for:

- **A qualified opinion or the absence of a clear opinion.**

- **Auditor reputation.** The majority of publicly traded companies are audited by one of the "Big 4" international accounting and professional service firms, PricewaterhouseCoopers, Deloitte & Touche, Ernst & Young, and KPMG. Though other competitive auditing firms exist, companies prefer to use one of the Big 4 because their reputations inspire investor confidence. The failure and consequent bailout during 2008 and 2009 of major banks and financial institutions such as Lehman Brothers and AIG raised doubts about Big 4 audits. Critics ask why these auditors allowed their clients to continue questionable and dangerous practices unchallenged and why they did not warn investors of the risk. Investor groups have filed numerous law suits against Big 4 auditors, holding them responsible for massive losses. You can learn more about an auditor's reputation by typing its name into an Internet search engine and reading news articles and financial commentary.

- **Assessment of internal controls.** The auditor is required to provide an assessment of the company's internal controls. If the auditor describes the company as having weak internal controls, be cautious. The auditor is not required to do anything to improve internal control — just to state an opinion regarding their effectiveness. Weak internal controls create conditions that invite fraud.

Proxy statement

The proxy statement contains details that company executives would probably rather not tell you, such as how much they are being paid and the types of stock options and benefits directors and executives receive. It announces any changes in auditors or accounting firms, and also contains information about lawsuits against the company and about other possible financial obligations that are not revealed in other documents. By reading the proxy, you can get a good idea of the company's management style and the "flavor" of the business.

In the proxy statement, you should look out for:

- **Excessive executive salaries and benefits**.

- **Related party transactions**. The transfer of assets from one affiliate to another may be generating fictitious revenue or hiding expenses.

- **Litigation against the company**.

- **Frequent changes of accountants or auditors**. If the proxy statements for several years show frequent changes of auditors or accounting firms, it may mean that company executives have been shopping around for a firm that will accept questionable accounting practices.

Footnotes to the financial statements

The footnotes are the fine print that explains the items on the financial statements. Knowing that many investors will not take time to read the footnotes, companies may hide important details there, couched in almost unintelligible language. Make the effort to decipher their meaning. The information in the footnotes is invaluable for assessing the financial condition of a company and detecting whether its reported earnings are genuine. Footnotes contain details such as the accounting principles being used, pending litigation, long-term purchase commitments or contracts, industry-specific notes, and changes in estimates. They may contain information about the company's subsidiaries or about executive compensation. They also indicate which aspects of a company's performance are healthy and which are not.

In the footnotes, you should look out for:

- **Aggressive accounting policies**. Footnotes may contain evidence of aggressive accounting policies — a sure sign that management is manipulating the accounts to produce a desired effect rather than reporting things as they really are. Stock analysts favor companies with conservative accounting principles, not only because the financial statements are more reliable, but because companies that demonstrate integrity in their accounting methods are likely to be responsible in all other aspects of their business. A company that overinflates its earnings by using aggressive accounting principles is likely to have serious problems from which its business may not be able to recover.

Policy	Conservative	Aggressive
Revenue recognition	Revenue is not recognized until after the sale is complete and goods or services delivered	Revenue is recognized when a sales contract is signed but before goods are delivered and services performed
Depreciation	Depreciation of fixed assets, machinery, and equipment is accelerated (a large amount of depreciation is recorded the first year and diminishes each subsequent year).	Depreciation is recorded as a straight-line item (the same amount is recorded every year) over a longer period of time
Inventory method	LIFO (when prices are rising)	FIFO (when prices are rising)

Amortization of goodwill	Goodwill (intangible assets, such as strong brand recognition or reputation, that give the company a competitive advantage) amortized over a short period	Goodwill amortized over a period of 40 years
Estimate of warranty	High estimate for the cost of repairing products sold under warranty	Low estimate for the cost of repairing products sold under warranty
Estimated bad debts	High estimate for amount of uncollectible debts	Low estimate for amount of uncollectible debts
Treatment of advertising	Recorded as an expense	Capitalized (treated as an asset)
Loss contingencies (Reserves set aside to pay for probable losses that will occur after some anticipated event, such as a law suit)	Accrual recorded as an item on the balance sheet	Only mentioned in a footnote

Aggressive or inappropriate inventory valuation. Several methods are used to calculate the value of inventory held in stock. The two most popular are LIFO (last-in-first-out) and FIFO (first-in-first-out). The price of goods or raw material purchased for inventory fluctuates over time, usually rising as time passes due to inflation. When revenue is calculated, the accountant must subtract the cost of goods sold or materials used in production from the selling price of the goods. LIFO subtracts the cost of the most recently purchased, more expensive inventory first and, when that is accounted for, begins subtracting the cost of older, less expensive inventory. FIFO does the reverse — the cheapest inventory is subtracted first and the newest, most expensive inventory is subtracted last. FIFO is considered an aggressive inventory valuation technique because it often undervalues the rising cost of inventory, producing higher reported profits.

Pending or imminent litigation. This information can also be found in Item 3 on Form 10-K. A lawsuit may have a serious effect on a company's ability to continue operating its business. The company must pay for legal expenses and may be liable for large amounts in penalties and damages, which could be a catastrophic drain on its resources. In addition, the company may lose the right to market a product, or its public reputation may be seriously damaged.

Long-term purchase commitments. A long-term purchase commitment is a contract to continue purchasing goods or services at a fixed price over a period of time. Such a commitment could lock a company into paying more than the market price, making it unable to compete with other companies in the same industry.

Changes in accounting principles. The accounting principles selected by management ultimately affect the profits reported on a company's financial reports. When a company changes accounting principles without a reasonable explanation, it may be attempting to improve the numbers on a weak financial statement. For example, changing from LIFO to FIFO inventory valuation could raise profits substantially that year. Changes in accounting methods must also be considered when comparing items on this year's financial report to amounts from previous years.

Letter from the president

Every annual report is prefaced by a letter from the president to the company shareholders. It is typically optimistic in tone and is intended to portray the company in the best possible light. The letter serves as a vague introduction to the truths contained in the financial statements, and negative realities are expressed in euphemistic terms. Read the letter with a degree of skepticism.

In the letter, you should look out for:

- **The tone and feel of the letter**. The president's letter should be evaluated together with the entire package of financial statements and commentary to get a feel for the real business atmosphere of the company and its expectations for the future.

- **Euphemisms**. Look behind the elaborately crafted phrases for the real meaning of the president's message. The letter was probably written by a public relations expert. If the president says that the company "faces challenges," you can be sure it really does. Watch for references to setbacks and litigation, unmet expectations or forecasts, and future plans such as possible mergers or buy-outs.

- **Contradictions between the president's statements and the facts in the financial statement**. It is a sure sign of trouble if the figures on the balance sheet contradict what the president says in the introductory letter.

Management discussions and analysis

Managers are required to discuss specific issues in the financial statements in the section titled "management discussions and analysis" on Form 10-K. This section should contain the managers' assessment of the company's financial situation, its liquidity, and planned capital expenditures for the next year.

In the management discussion and analysis, you should look out for:

- **Evidence of financial difficulties**. If the company is having financial difficulties, the management discussions should reveal the nature of the difficulties, whether they can be expected to continue, and what management is doing about them.

- **Candor about the company's situation**. Problems, if they exist, should be discussed frankly and not misrepresented.

Form 8-K

Search the EDGAR database (**www.sec.gov/edgar.shtml**) for any Forms 8-K recently filed by the company. These forms contain some information that companies are not required to reveal to the public and may concern events that have occurred since the financial statement was filed.

On Form 8-K, you should look out for:

- **Bankruptcy.**

- **Major acquisitions and dispositions.** Companies are required to report when they sell or acquire businesses or important assets. These activities will have an important influence on the company's business operations, size, and future development. Sometimes an acquisition or sale masks a drop in earnings or the overvaluation of an asset.

- **Changes in auditors.** A company may fire an auditor who disagrees with its accounting practices and change to another auditing firm. Companies are supposed to give the details of any auditing disagreement on Form 8-K. Even if there is no detailed explanation, knowledge of the change may clarify other aspects of the financial statement.

Form 144

The EDGAR database will also reveal whether any executive or affiliate of the company has sold more than 500 shares of company stock. A large sale of stock could indicate financial troubles at the company, an impending resignation, or knowledge of an upcoming negative event.

Financial statements

There are four main types of financial statements: balance sheets, income statements, cash flow statements, and statements of shareholders' equity.

This section describes what kind of information is available on each type of financial statement. *See Chapter 13 for details on how to evaluate this information for signs of financial statement fraud.*

1. Balance sheets

A balance sheet is structured to reflect the accounting equation:

ASSETS = LIABILITIES + SHAREHOLDERS' EQUITY

A company's assets are listed on the left, and liabilities and shareholders' equity are listed on the right. Some companies arrange their balance sheets so assets are listed at the top, followed by liabilities, then shareholders' equity. A balance sheet shows a company's financial status at the end of the accounting period and does not contain information about the flow of money into and out of accounts during the period.

Assets: Assets are classified according to how quickly a company expects to convert them into cash:

- **Current assets**: Assets, such as inventory and short-term investments, which will be converted into cash within one year.

- **Noncurrent assets**: Assets that will take longer than a year to sell, or that a company does not intend to convert into cash.

- **Fixed assets**: Assets used in business operations that are not intended for sale, such as buildings, manufacturing equipment, and trucks.

Liabilities: Liabilities represent money the company must pay out for operating expenses, purchase of goods and raw materials, rent, interest, and repayment of debt and other financial obligations. A liability may be an expense, debt, claim, or potential loss.

- **Current liabilities**: Obligations the company expects to pay off within a year.

- **Long-term liabilities**: Financial obligations with payment due dates that are more than one year away.

Shareholders' equity: Shareholders' equity is the amount the company's shareholders (owners and/or investors) have invested in the company, minus the company's earnings or losses since the company began doing business. Companies sometimes distribute earnings as dividends instead of retaining them. Shareholders' equity is equal to the total assets minus the total liabilities.

2. Income statements

An income statement shows how much revenue the company earned over a financial period and the costs and expenses associated with earning that revenue. An income statement is typically structured with the sales total for the financial period at the top, followed by a list of any additional income (such as interest from investments or money from the sale of an asset) and all the expense and losses incurred during the financial period. The types of income and expenses listed vary from company to company and industry to industry. The total income minus total expenses yields the company's earnings for that financial period, known as "the bottom line." Financial analysts strongly encourage investors to look carefully at the individual line items on an income statement rather than focusing on the bottom line.

Bottom line: The bottom line, literally located at the bottom of the statement, shows how much the company earned or lost over the financial period.

Earnings per share (EPS): EPS is the amount an investor would receive for each share of stock if all the earnings were distributed. All of the earnings are typically not distributed, but reinvested in the business. EPS is calculated by dividing the company's net earnings or losses by the number of shares.

Gross revenue (gross sales): Gross revenue is the total amount realized from the sale of goods or services before any expenses have been deducted. This figure is normally at the top of the income statement.

Returns and allowances: Returns and allowances are amounts that the company does not expect to collect from sales, such as returned merchandise; special discounts and conditions of sales; allowances for uncollectible debt; and the cost of honoring warranties.

Net revenue: Net revenue consists of sales after the returns and allowances have been subtracted from gross sales.

Cost of sales: The cost of sales are the expenses directly associated with producing the goods and services sold during the financial period.

Gross profit (gross margin): Gross profit is the net revenue minus the cost of sales. This is the profit realized from sales before other types of expenses are taken out.

Operating expenses: Operating expenses are expenses associated with running the business, such as the salaries of administrative staff and cost of research, development, telephone service, and marketing.

Depreciation: Depreciation is a deduction to account for wear and tear on machinery and equipment, or the obsolescence of computers, which will eventually have to be replaced. Depreciation typically spreads the cost of these assets over the period of years that they are expected to be in use.

Amortization: Amortization is a deduction, similar to depreciation, to account for the loss in value of an asset over time. A fraction of the asset's estimated value is deducted each year. Amortization can apply to tangible assets and to intangible assets such as brand recognition, goodwill, or a patented design.

Operating profit (income from operations): Operating profit equals gross profit minus operating expenses, depreciation, and amortization.

Interest income and expense: Interest income is the interest earned from investments made by the company. Interest expense is the interest paid by the company on its debts. They may be listed as a single item on the balance sheet, or listed separately.

Nonrecurring income or expenses: Nonrecurring income and expenses result from one-time events, such as the sale of a factory or the payment of a legal settlement. If the name of the item on the balance sheet does not reveal its origin, it is usually accompanied by an explanatory footnote. Some companies include nonrecurring items with regular income and expenses; others list them separately.

Profit before income tax: The operating profit minus interest income and expense and nonrecurring items equals the profit before income tax.

Income tax: Income tax is the amount of income tax paid on the company's earnings.

Net profit or losses: Net profit or losses are the total amount that the company earned or lost during the financial period (the bottom line).

3. Cash flow statements

A cash flow statement shows how much cash has come into and gone out of the business during a financial period, using information from the balance sheet and income statement. Cash flow is very significant because every company needs cash to operate its business and keep growing by purchasing assets. A company that shows a high net profit on its income statement but has very little cash coming in is in trouble.

The bottom line of a cash flow statement shows the net increase or decrease in cash during the financial period. Cash flow statements are typically divided into three sections: operating cash flow, investment cash flow, and financing cash flow.

Operating cash flow (OCF): This section reconciles the net income from the income statement to the actual amount of cash that was received from business operations by removing non-cash expense items, such as depreciation, and accounting for any other cash that was spent on operating expenses or provided by operating assets.

Investment cash flow: This section shows cash spent on or received from investments — including cash coming in from interest or the sale of securities — and cash invested in long-term assets, such as land and equipment, or in investment portfolios.

Financing cash flow: Financing cash flow is all cash received from financing activities, such as bank loans or the issuing of stocks or bonds, and cash spent on paying back bank loans or bonds.

4. Statement of shareholders' equity

A statement of shareholders' equity shows changes in the interest of a company's shareholders over a financial period. This statement provides details of activities in the common and preferred stock accounts (including treasury stock), the retained earnings account, and changes to owners' equity that do not appear in the income statement. The more complex a company's ownership structure becomes, the more significant the shareholders' equity statement becomes. It contains information such as the amount paid out from earnings as dividends, the number of shares of stock, and any changes, such as additional shares of stock issued during the financial period.

Preferred stock: Holders of preferred stock have precedence over holders of common stock when dividends are paid out and will be first in line if the company goes into bankruptcy and its assets are distributed. They typically do not have voting rights, and the dividends paid out are a set amount.

Common stock: When a company distributes earnings as dividends, holders of common stock receive their share after the owners of preferred stock have been paid their dividends. Holders of common stock have voting rights at shareholders' meetings.

Treasury stock: Treasury stock is shares of stock held by the company; essentially, the company has bought back shares of common stock to increase its ownership stake. Treasury stock is excluded from the total amount of shareholders' equity.

Unrealized gains or losses: Changes in the market price of shares since the end of the last financial period. They are unrealized because no money is gained or lost until the stock is sold.

Retained earnings: Earnings that are accumulated or reinvested in the business, rather than distributed as dividends.

Dividends: Money paid out from earnings as compensation to stockholders.

Red Flags for Financial Statement Fraud

Apart from the information revealed in financial statements, certain events and circumstances are red flags for financial statement fraud:

- **A company that has experienced rapid growth is maturing and seeing its business level off**

  Businesses develop in cycles. A new business, particularly one in a new industry, may experience rapid growth at the beginning. Eventually competitors emerge, the market becomes saturated, and growth begins to slow. By this time, however, investors have come to expect continued high rates of growth from the company, and executives, fearful that the price of the company's stock will drop when lower earnings are announced, may manipulate financial statements to create an appearance of continued growth.

- **Top executives resigning or being fired**

  The firing or resignation of a CEO or CFO is often the first external sign that a company is experiencing financial turmoil.

- **A company reports unusually strong performance when other companies in the same industry are experiencing fluctuations or difficulties**

  A company that reports high earnings when other companies in the same industry are reporting difficulties may be manipulating its financial statements to support its stock price.

- **Mergers, acquisitions, and related-party transactions**

  Companies that are selling off portions of their businesses or acquiring new businesses may be masking financial difficulties or generating false revenue. Mergers should be closely examined; financial news media typically contains discussions of pending mergers.

CHAPTER 11

Detecting Seven Types of
Financial Statement Manipulations

The previous chapter described how to look for signs of financial statement fraud in the auditor's report, footnotes, proxy, president's letter, and other documents accompanying the financial report. This chapter will describe how this information, combined with an analysis of the financial statements themselves, can reveal exactly where and how a company's accounts are being manipulated to deceive investors. Financial analysts have a whole glossary of terms for this type of manipulation, including "financial shenanigans," "the financial numbers game," "creative accounting," "aggressive accounting," "income smoothing," and "earnings management." Whatever terminology is used to describe them, these manipulations are bad news for investors and ultimately for the companies involved, as altering the numbers on a financial statement to conceal problems only exaggerates those problems in future statements.

The mathematical analysis techniques described in Chapter 9 for detecting accounting fraud in a company's books are similar to the techniques used to detect fraud in financial statements. It is helpful to have financial statements for two or more consecutive periods, so items can be compared to reveal trends or sudden changes. Create a chart using Microsoft Excel™ or another spreadsheet, and list the items from the balance sheet, income statement, and cash flow statements down the side. Using a column for each consecutive financial period, fill in the amounts for each item across the chart. Now, you will be able to compare the different financial periods and see the relative changes for all the items. The comparison can be done using vertical analysis, in which each item on a statement is listed as a percentage of the total amount, and horizontal analysis, which shows the percentage of change in each item from one financial period to the next. Financial statements can also be compared to the statements of similar companies in the same industry — this type of comparison is often done by journalists and professional analysts who have access to commercial databases.

This chapter provides only a brief overview of basic principles and is intended to act as a guide. Detailed analysis of financial statements takes time and involves considerable research. Excellent books and resources are available if you wish to deepen your knowledge and understanding. Many financial analysts bewail the fact (belatedly) that in many cases of financial statement fraud and subsequent collapse of a company, investors failed to "heed the warning signs." If you are considering purchasing a company's stock, check its financial statements for red flags before committing your investment capital.

"Quality of earnings" is to the degree to which revenue reported in a financial statement is substantially realized or collectible. Poor quality of earnings means there is little or no guarantee the reported revenue really represents money coming into a business. The Center for Financial Research and Analysis (CFRA) (**https://fra.riskmetrics.com/fra/default.aspx**), an independent financial research organization that provides quality-of-earnings research for money management, brokerage, banking, accounting, and insurance firms, has identified 30 techniques used to deceive investors, grouped in seven major categories.

1. Recording Revenue Prematurely or Exaggerating Revenue

Deciding when and how to record revenue is one of the most complex areas of accounting, and the area responsible for the majority of financial report restatements. According to GAAP standards, revenue should be recorded only when it is realized or realizable and in the period in which it is earned. SEC guidelines consider revenue realizable and earned when it meets the following criteria:

- Persuasive evidence of an arrangement exists
- Delivery has occurred or services have been rendered
- The seller's price to the buyer is fixed or determinable
- Collectibility is reasonably assured

Premature revenue

A company may inflate its earnings by recording revenue before it has been earned or realized; for example, recording all the revenue that will be realized from a five-year contract in the financial period when the customer first signs the contract, or recording revenue before the goods have been shipped, or before the customer has accepted the shipment and agreed to pay for it. This practice creates a double problem for the company: Because future revenue is being recorded now, there will be less revenue recorded in future periods, and the inflated revenue reported in the current financial statement will make future earnings appear to grow even more slowly. Revenue is also recorded prematurely when the customer is not obligated to pay for the goods or services delivered, such as a bookstore that reserves the right to return unsold books to the publisher, or when the customer has not secured financing to pay for the purchase.

Clues to premature revenue recognition can be found in the footnotes to the financial statements and by analyzing the cash flow statements relative to the income statements.

Warning signs that revenue is being recorded prematurely include:

- **Seller-provided financing**

  Vendors sometimes offer financing to help customers purchase their products. Though this is an accepted sales technique in some industries, excessive customer debt means that the company is essentially buying its own products.

- **Companies offering extended payment terms**

  A company may offer extended payment plans to motivate its customers to purchase goods and services when they do not yet have the means to pay for them. Extended payment means that the company has not yet been paid for goods or services already delivered or performed. Extended payment terms increase the risk that the company will never receive full payment, and in the meantime, the company carries the cost of providing those goods and services. Revenue generated by offering extended payment plans is not quality revenue.

- **Consignment sales**

  Revenue should not be recorded when consignments are delivered to a middleman. It should be recorded after the goods have been sold and paid for.

- **Sales with a right of return**

  As long as the buyer is allowed to return unsold goods, the sale of those goods is not complete and should not be recorded as revenue.

- **Changes in the ending date of the financial quarter**

  A company may increase revenue by changing the closing date of its financial quarter to include a few more days' worth of sales.

- **Changes to more aggressive revenue recognition policies**

  An announcement in the footnotes of a change to a more aggressive revenue recognition policy is a sign that revenue is weak and that the company may be concealing other problems.

- **Unusual changes in revenue growth from financial period to financial period**

  Dramatic increases or decreases in revenue from one financial period to the next should be investigated. Has the company's business experienced a surge of growth, or is the increase due to a one-time event such as a legal settlement?

- **The amount of "unbilled receivables" grows much faster than the amount of "billed receivables"**

  A company may be recording revenue for products that have been commissioned by a client but not yet shipped. Companies with long-term contracts, such as the manufacture of aircraft or large construction products, use "percentage of completion" (POC) accounting to record revenue for the portion of the project that has been completed during the financial period. Manufacturers use "bill and hold" accounting when customers placed future orders and agree to pay for them in the future when the goods are shipped. A rapid increase in "unbilled receivables" relative to "billed receivables" and sales indicates that POC or bill-and-hold accounting is being used too aggressively, and revenue that should be recorded in future financial periods is being prematurely reported.

- **"Operating cash flow" (OCF) begins to lag further and further behind "net income"**

  This indicates that a company is reporting unrealized revenue from transactions that are not bringing cash into the business.

- **Undeliverable products**

  Sometimes a company lags behind a production deadline, and a product that has already been "sold" cannot be delivered on time. A common example is a software application that is still not working properly when it is supposed to have been delivered. The revenue originally realized from the sale will diminish as the company continues spending money to test, solve problems, and re-test the software long after the contract should have been completed. Information on undeliverable products should be included in footnotes or management discussions and is often found in financial news articles.

Exaggerated revenue

Revenue can be exaggerated or artificially inflated by recording sales to affiliates or partners as revenue, offering a valuable incentive such as stock options as a quid pro quo (in return for) sales, or over-reporting sales by including pass-through amounts owed to other entities as revenue. For example, in 1995, Papa John's recorded an extra $78.7 million of revenue for equipment and pizza supplies that it bought and resold to its franchisees at a 10 percent mark-up. The $78.7 million should not have been reported as revenue because it did not represent income from real sales to customers; only the 10 percent profit could be considered revenue.

Warning signs that revenue is being exaggerated include:

- **Unusual transactions between related parties**

  If partners or affiliates are buying and selling goods and services to each other, it could amount to a trade-off rather than generation of revenue.

- **Sales incentives that are not subtracted from revenue**

  Barter exchanges, stock options, or partnership arrangements offered to a buyer as incentive for making a purchase represent a liability that may not be reported as expenses in the same financial period as revenue from the sale, but they are liabilities that will cost the company money. Such arrangements artificially inflate current revenue, but diminish future revenue.

2. Recording Non-Existent Revenue

In effort to boost revenue, a company may report income from other types of transactions on its financial statement as sales revenue, or report sales arrangements that lack economic substance as revenue.

Sales that lack economic substance

A sales contract in which the customer who receives a shipment of goods is not obligated to keep them or pay for them lacks economic substance because the whole transaction could be reversed at a future date. Companies sometimes hide such arrangements from auditors by modifying the terms of sales contracts with secret "side agreements" or "side letters" that grant customers the right to return unsold goods.

Sales lack economic substance when they are based on reciprocal agreements in which the company commits to buying something from its customer or using its own resources to boost customer sales as part of a sales contract. Part of the revenue from such a sale will be wiped out by fulfilling the reciprocal obligation.

The following are examples of different situations that lack economic substance:

- **A loan disguised as a sale**. Sometimes a loan is disguised as a "sale" by claiming that an asset, such as production rights or a real estate property, has been sold when it is really collateral in a loan agreement. Money that has to be paid back is a liability and should never be recorded as revenue.

- **Money received from a partnership or affiliate.** Funds received from a partnership or affiliate to support a project cannot be considered sales revenue because the company and its affiliates are one entity. Such funds do not represent revenue from a sale to unaffiliated customers.

- **Investment income reported as sales revenue.** Income from the sale of assets or investments, and profits or income from investments, is not sales revenue because it is not generated by the sale of the company's products. Reporting proceeds from a one-time sale of an asset or investment as sales revenue can greatly exaggerate sales revenue for that financial period.

- **Recording rebates as revenue.** Rebates on inventory purchased during an earlier period or refunds on goods returned to a supplier are not sales revenue; they represent an adjustment to the cost of inventory. Retailers sometimes report refunds or vendor credits as sales revenue.

- **Holding back revenue before a merger.** After a merger or takeover has been arranged, the target company may hold back on reporting its sales revenue for a period until after the merger has been completed. When the merger is complete, the deferred income may be reported as sales revenue for the new company.

Warning signs of sales that lack substance include:

- **"Operating cash flow" (OCF) lagging behind "net income"**
An investor may not have any way to find out about secret arrangements and side letters that have been hidden from auditors, but the effect of these arrangements will become evident when the company is collecting less and less cash from its sales. When operating cash flow is not increasing as fast as sales, it may be because fictitious sales that are not bringing in real income.

- **Unusual increases in liabilities**

  The costs of fulfilling the hidden agreements in a sales contract, or of repaying a loan, must eventually appear as liabilities on the balance sheet. A sudden increase in marketing costs or debt obligations, or a one-time purchase of an asset, may indicate sales revenue that is not genuine.

- **References to sales of assets or investments in the footnotes**

  Look carefully to see where income from the sale of assets or investments has been reported on the balance sheet.

- **Decline in sales revenue before a merger**

  If a company that is the target of a merger or acquisition exhibits a slowdown in sales revenue during its last quarter, it may be withholding income so it can be reported as sales revenue for the new company. Examine financial reports for all the companies involved in the merger for four to six quarters before the merger. Look for unusual declines in revenue.

3. Boosting Income with One-Time Gains

Financial commentators emphasize that the line items on a company's balance sheet are more important than the "bottom line" (final total). When a company reports a profit for the financial period, the line items show how the profit was derived and whether a similar performance can be expected in future financial periods. A one-time windfall, such as income from a legal settlement or the sale of a valuable asset, can make the bottom line look very good when the company's business is doing very badly. There are several ways in which a company can realize a large one-time profit:

Selling undervalued assets

A company may list real estate, factories, or equipment in its books at lower than their market prices. Profit realized from the sale of these assets can boost income on the balance sheet. This is an acceptable accounting practice, but it can be used to mask weak business performance. Profit realized from the sale of assets such as real estate that have appreciated in value over time but are still listed in the books at their original cost is called "suppressed profit." A company can also realize a windfall profit by selling off undervalued assets acquired by purchasing another company.

The following are examples of different ways of making a profit using undervalued assets:

- **Reporting investment income as revenue.** GAAP standards require one-time income be listed on financial statements separately from income generated by a company's ongoing business operations. Nonoperating gains, such as interest received from loans to customers or income from fees, should not be included in sales revenue or operating income.

- **Reporting investment income or another one-time gain as a reduction of operating expenses**. Income should be reported separately from operating expenses, but sometimes a one-time gain is used to cancel out certain operating expenses. For example, a company that realizes a gain from its pension plan might use it to cancel out its pension expenses for that year and lower its operating expenses. A one-time gain might also be used to write off future operating expenses so that future revenue figures are higher.

Warning signs that a company is selling undervalued assets include:

- **One-time gains in the income section of the balance sheet**
  Look for one-time gains from the sale of assets or investments, or from other sources such as legal settlements or investment windfalls, in the income section of the balance sheet.

- **Changes in operating expenses from one financial period to another**

  A sudden decrease in regular operating expenses should be examined; if there is no other explanation, it might have been achieved by applying a one-time gain.

- **Overfunded pension plans**

  A good year in the stock market could result in a windfall from an overfunded pension plan.

- **References to sales of large assets in the footnotes**

  If the company reports the sale of a large asset or investment, examine how it has been recorded on the balance sheet.

4. Shifting Current Expenses to an Earlier or Later Period

A company can improve its bottom line on the balance sheet by reducing its operating expenses. Sometimes this is done by shifting operating expenses for the current period to an earlier or later period.

Capitalizing operating costs

Instead of reporting an expense as an operating cost and deducting all of it during the current period, a company may report it as a capital expense (the purchase of an asset that will be depleted over time) and deduct it in installments over a period of several years. In the section on fictitious revenue in Chapter 8 was an example of AOL reporting the cost of the CDs it mailed out to its customers as a capital expense instead of a marketing cost for three years ending in 1993. Operating costs that are often capitalized are marketing costs, repair and maintenance, software development, and the costs associated with setting up a new retail store.

The following are examples of ways a business can capitalize on operating costs:

- **Changing accounting policies to shift expenses to an earlier period**. A company can make expenses evaporate from its income statements by changing the way in which they are calculated to apply to earlier periods.

- **Amortizing expenses over a long period of time**. The cost of a fixed asset is usually expensed in installments over the period of years that the asset is expected to remain in use. A company may reduce its current expenses by amortizing the cost of assets over unreasonably long periods of time. The result is similar to taking out a 30-year car loan — payments will still be due long after the car is in the junkyard.

- **Delaying inventory costs**. Typically the cost of inventory is deducted in the period when the inventory is sold. In cases where inventory is sold over several financial periods, the cost is amortized based on the estimated amount of time it will take to sell all the inventory. Overestimating this length of time will extend payment over a longer period and reduce the amount that must be expensed each year.

- **Keeping obsolete or impaired inventory on the books**. Inventory that can no longer be sold should be written off. Some companies keep damaged or obsolete items on their books as an asset for years rather than write them off as an expense.

- **Failing to write off bad debts**. Debts that cannot be collected should be written off as a business loss within a reasonable period of time.

- **Reducing asset reserves**. Reserves are allowances set aside to account for expected losses, such as the cost of carrying out warranty repairs, writing off of obsolete inventory, and uncollectible accounts. These reserves should grow along with their associated accounts, such as receivables or inventory. A company can increase its profits on the balance sheet by reducing these reserves, but it is simply putting off the true cost of operating its business.

Warning signs that a company is capitalizing on operating costs include:

- **Improper capitalization of operating expenses**
  A company may not reveal exactly what expenses have been capitalized, but look for signs of inappropriate capitalization. Items that should not be capitalized: advertising and marketing costs, store pre-opening costs, repair and maintenance costs, software research and development, and landfill development.

- **Long amortization policies**
  Conservative accounting policies pay off assets within a short, reasonable period of time. Long amortization indicates a company is trying to reduce its expenses on the balance sheet.

- **Changes in accounting policies for expenses**
  Watch for policy changes that shift expenses to an earlier or later period. Watch for changes in accounting policy just before a company makes its IPO, or just before the end of a financial period.

- **A decrease in receivable reserves while gross receivables are increasing**
  Receivable reserves should increase in proportion to gross receivables.

- **Absence of reserves for bad debts**
  Every company should have a reserve for uncollectible debt.

- **Reversals of reserves**
  A company can realize a profit on its balance sheet by simply eliminating a reserve or inappropriately reducing a reserve. The reversal may be legitimate if the need for the reserve no longer exists, but it does not mean that the company's business is making a profit.

5. Failing to Record or Underreporting Liabilities

Sometimes companies attempt to improve their "bottom line" by omitting or underreporting liabilities on their balance sheets. Ways in which companies can accomplish this include:

- **Failing to record the expenses of fulfilling future obligations.** Any probable future financial obligation should be reported as an expense on the balance sheet. A company may report sales revenue from a contract that has not been completed and fail to report the future costs of fulfilling it or report a contract for a future purchase. Expected losses from payments due to litigation or tax disputes should be included, according to GAAP standards, whenever the loss is probable and the amount can be reasonably estimated.

- **Reporting sales revenue when cash is received rather than when a contract is completed.** Revenue is inflated when a company fails to expense the future costs of carrying out the contract in the same period when payment for that contract is received.

- **Unrecorded stock option liabilities.** During the 1990s, many executives were compensated with incentive stock options, giving them the right to purchase company stock at a specific price and during a certain period. If the company does well and the price of its stock appreciates, the employees can exercise their right to purchase stock at the lower price, and the company must take a loss by giving them shares at lower than the market price or spending cash to buy back shares from investors. The potential cost to the company, if these stock options are exercised, is a major expense, yet it is often unmentioned as a liability on the balance sheet.

- **Changing accounting policies to reduce liabilities.** Many liabilities on the balance sheet, such as reserves for bad debt, pension costs, and future cost of litigation, are estimates based on specific accounting principles. These estimated costs can be lowered by changing to more aggressive accounting policies that use different assumptions to calculate the estimates.

- **Recording a false rebate as a reduction of expenses**. Instead of paying the asking price for inventory, a company may arrange with the supplier to pay a higher price and receive the difference as a "rebate." Then, instead of subtracting the rebate amount from the cost of inventory, the company reports the rebate as a reduction of expenses.

Warning signs that a company is failing to record or underreporting liabilities include:

- **References in the footnotes to liabilities that are not recorded in the balance sheet**
  Some liabilities will not affect the company's profits, but any liability that represents a future expense should be included in the balance sheet. A company may report pending litigation in the footnotes for which it is not yet able to estimate a cost.

- **Release of reserves into income**
  Moving reserves into income helps to disguise losses.

- **Long term lease commitments in a company that is downsizing**
  A company that is downsizing may be obligated to pay rent for office space that it no longer needs and that will not contribute to its productivity.

- **Employee compensation that includes stock options**
  The proxy statement reveals details of employee compensation and will give an idea of the extent of liabilities for stock option incentives.

- **Changes in accounting policies**
  Look for changes in accounting policies near the end of a financial period that might alter estimated expenses.

- **References to incomplete contracts and future liabilities in the footnotes and M&D**
  Notes accompanying the financial reports may contain references to uncompleted contracts, pending litigation, and other future liabilities.

6. Shifting Current Revenues to a Later Period

The previous financial statement frauds all involved artificially inflating profits. But another type fraud scheme aims to decrease profits from the current financial period so they can be reported in a later period. Ways in which a company can accomplish this include:

- **Creating reserves and releasing them during a later financial period**. A company that is doing very well may manipulate its accounts to shift some of its profits to future financial periods. While many companies experience growth cycles tied to the launch of new products, seasonal sales, and changes in the economy, Wall Street rewards steady, consistent growth. "Income smoothing" is the practice of deferring income from the current period to future periods when sales revenue is weak. This is typically done by creating unnecessary reserves, or allowances, for possible future losses, or by adding excess amounts to existing reserves for uncollectible debts, obsolete inventory, and warranties. In a later financial period when sales are weaker, these reserves are reversed and reported as income.

- **Holding back revenue just before an acquisition is completed**. The previous section in this chapter on recording nonexistent revenue described how a company being bought by another company might be asked to withhold its revenue. After the acquisition is completed, the buyer will include the withheld revenue in its own sales revenue.

Warning signs that a company is shifting current revenues to a later period include:

- **New reserves that were not listed on previous balance sheets**
  Look closely at new reserves to see whether they are really needed.

- **Large increases to existing reserves**
  Reserves should increase in proportion to the amount of the accounts with which they are associated. For example, a reserve for bad debts should increase along with accounts receivable, and a reserve for warranties should increase along with sales. Reserves that suddenly increase in one quarter may indicate that the company's income is being deliberately underreported for that quarter.

- **A drop in revenue in the last quarter before an acquisition**
  Watch a drop in sales revenue for a company going through an acquisition; there may be corresponding increase in sales revenue for the buyer company.

7. Shifting Future Expenses to the Current Period as a Special Charge

Another way to defer revenue is to make a charge for future expenses but report the payment as a current expense. Revenue in future financial quarters will appear higher because expenses incurred in that quarter will have already been charged. This is done in three ways:

- **Inflating the amount of a special charge.** Special charges are expense items that cover one-time events such as a downsizing, a write-off of bad loans, and re-valuation of overpriced inventory.

These amounts can be inflated by adding future operating expenses to the legitimate charge.

- **Writing off costs from an acquisition.** A company making an acquisition may write off part of the acquisition price as an acquisition charge to reduce operating expenses and boost revenue in the current and future quarters. A large acquisition charge is a sign the company being acquired is in financial difficulties.

- **Paying in advance for future operating expenses.** A company with robust profits may "prepay" operating expenses for future quarters by stocking up on inventory and paying for services in advance.

Warning signs that a company is shifting future expenses to the current period include:

- **Special charges on the balance sheet**
  Examine special charges and compare them to the accounts with which they are related to see if they are excessive.

- **Decreases in depreciation or amortization periods**
  Future operating expenses can be reduced by paying off depreciation more rapidly.

- **Changes in accounting policy that accelerate depreciation**
  By accelerating its payment of depreciation, a company will reduce its future operating costs and increase its profits, at the expense of the current period's profits.

CHAPTER 12

Preventing Fraud in Your Company or Business

Modern businesses are increasingly concerned with fraud prevention. Since sociologists and criminologists began to direct their attention to white-collar crime in the 1950s, the study of fraud has become a science. Today, there are ongoing efforts to quantify and measure fraud, and fraud training has become part of every accountant's education. Professionals such as certified fraud examiners specialize in detecting and preventing fraud and have developed new techniques for uncovering frauds. Computer-based accounting systems and the availability of banking information online have made it possible to automatically monitor millions of transactions for irregularities, creating new possibilities for fraud control. Globalization and the emergence of far-reaching megacorporations together with the establishment of stock markets in many countries has magnified the potential damage fraud can cause and increased the exposure of investors to fraud risk. As more individuals become investors through retirement plans like 401(k)s and IRAs, as well as open online stock trading accounts, more people risk financial loss due to fraudulent financial statements. The requirements for internal controls and fraud risk assessments created by Sarbanes-Oxley have caused executives of publicly traded companies to become more active in trying to control fraud.

Fraud prevention is really fraud deterrence. Fraud can never be truly "prevented" as long as the social and economic conditions that motivate people to commit fraud continue to exist. Even when a company has procedures in place to prevent fraud, dishonest employees will look for ways to circumvent them. There are many things that can be done, however, to discourage employees from attempting fraud, to decrease the opportunity to commit fraud, and to detect fraud earlier when it does occur. These include establishing ethical standards within the organization, letting employees know that fraud will be detected and punished, educating employees to detect fraud, creating an effective reporting mechanism, implementing strong internal controls, and regularly monitoring for fraud. Many fraud perpetrators, when interviewed, have said that they would not have become involved in fraud if deterrents had existed.

Creating an Ethical Environment

The most effective fraud deterrent is a corporate culture that does not tolerate fraud. Creating an ethical culture in the workplace is a process that takes time, investment, and continual education. For an ethical culture to become established, both management and employees must be committed to it and willing to live by it every day.

Ethics policy or code of conduct

Every organization should have a formal ethics policy, not only because it deters fraud, but because it legally supports efforts to enforce ethical conduct in the workplace. Employees who have read and signed a formal ethics policy cannot claim they were unaware their conduct was unacceptable. Recommended codes of conduct for various types of organizations are commercially available from human resources firms such as Personnel Policy Inc. (**http://ppspublishers.com/hr-sample-employee-behavior. htm**), but every organization should tailor its own ethics policy to suit its business and its needs. A good ethics policy is simple, easy to understand, addresses general conduct, and offers a few examples to explain how the code might be applied. It should not contain a myriad of rules to cover specific situations, or threats such as "violators will be prosecuted to the full extent of the law." In a legal trial of a fraud perpetrator, it is the judge and not the company who will decide the sentence. An ethics policy or code of conduct should cover:

- **General conduct at work**: Explain ethical and honest behavior is expected of all employees, and they are expected to act in the best interests of the company.

- **Conflicts of interest**: Employees may not understand what does and does not constitute a conflict of interest, so some simple examples are appropriate.

- **Confidentiality**: Company policy on the sharing of information among employees and departments or with people outside the company.

- **Relationships with vendors and customers**: Company policy regarding doing business with a relative, friend, or personal acquaintance.

- **Gifts**: Policy regarding the types and amounts of gifts that may be accepted or given by employees during the course of doing business.

- **Entertainment**: The types of entertainment activities considered appropriate for vendors and customers, and that will be accepted on expense accounts.

- **Relationships with the media**: Company policy regarding who should communicate with the media about company affairs.

- **Use of the organization's assets for personal purposes**: This section should cover personal use of the Internet while at work, as well as use of copy machines, telephones, and company vehicles.

- **Procedure for reporting unethical behavior**: Employees should be encouraged to report any ethical violation, large or small. This section should explain how and to whom reports should be submitted, and the use of a tip hotline, if one exists.

- **Consequences of unethical behavior**: Discipline options should be clearly communicated and consistently enforced.

An ethics policy will not be effective if it is handed to each new employee and then forgotten. The ethics policy should be reviewed with employees every year, ideally as part of an antifraud education program.

You can find free guidance for crafting a code of conduct at **www.conductcode.com**.

Tone at the top

"Tone at the top" refers to the ethical atmosphere created by the organization's leadership. The attitude of senior management has a trickle-down effect on all employees of an organization. According to a study released in 1987 by the National Commission on Fraudulent Reporting (the Treadway Commission), the tone at the top is a strong influence in creating an environment conducive to fraudulent financial reporting. When employees observe that senior management has little regard for the rules and will do whatever it takes to get results, they act in the same way. An employee who sees his or her boss cheating on expense accounts or deceiving customers is likely to follow suit. Fraud deterrence starts with senior management that adheres to ethical principles and does not place results ahead of all other considerations.

Antifraud Education

Tips from employees are the primary way that frauds are discovered. The likelihood fraud will be reported can be increased by providing antifraud education for all employees on a regular basis. Education should include a review of the code of conduct, descriptions of fraud scenarios, instructions for reporting suspected fraud, and the message that fraud will not be tolerated. Specialized education should be provided for departments such as accounting where specific fraud risks have been identified. Employees should understand how fraud impacts them personally by affecting profits, raises, bonuses, morale, and their own integrity.

Perception of Detection

Another effective deterrent is the perception that employees who are caught engaging in occupational fraud will be caught. If employees are aware of antifraud monitoring and security measures, and if they understand that the purpose of internal controls is to prevent fraud, they will be less likely to attempt it. Surprise audits and surprise inventory counts, open discussion of fraud, and analytical reviews can strengthen the perception that fraud will be detected. During audits and management reviews, the subject of fraud should be discussed in a non-accusatory manner, and participants should be asked to share their knowledge of possible weaknesses in the controls system. Involving management in conversations like these conveys a subtle perception that senior managers are also under surveillance.

Internal Controls

Internal controls are the processes within the organization that ensure the integrity of the accounting system and the security of assets. Some internal controls are costly and time-consuming; cost should be weighed against potential loss from fraud in deciding which controls to implement. Other controls, such as having two different people issue payments and record them in the accounts, are simple and basic, but will not be effective against fraud unless they are stringently enforced. There are three types of fraud-related controls: those intended to prevent fraud, such as strict accounting procedures; those intended to detect fraud, such as employee hotlines and regular reviews of bank statements and canceled checks; and corrective controls, such as prescribed disciplinary measures for perpetrators of fraud.

The ACFE's *2008 Report to the Nation* studied the effect of 15 common antifraud controls on losses due to fraud. Organizations that had one or more of the controls in place at the time of the fraud suffered median losses 66 percent to 29 percent lower than those of organizations that did not have antifraud controls. This indicates that while antifraud controls may not be able to prevent fraud, they contribute to its early detection and reduce loss. The antifraud controls examined in the study were:

- Surprise audits
- Job rotation and/or mandatory vacation
- Employee hotline
- Employee support programs
- Fraud training for managers and executives
- Internal audit department or fraud examiner department
- Fraud training for employees
- An anti-fraud policy
- External audit of the organization's internal controls over financial reporting
- Code of conduct
- Regular management review of internal controls
- External audit of financial statements
- Independent audit committee
- Management certification of financial statements
- Rewards for whistleblowers

Six major components of an internal control system

Auditors and accountants recognize that an effective internal control system has five major components:

- **Safeguards over assets**
  Physical assets should be secured with locks on doors, storage areas, and desks, and access to buildings should be controlled with identification badges. The organization should keep accurate records of the information and assets it owns. Checks, purchase orders, and letterhead stationery should be secured. Access to the accounting system should be restricted, and computers should be password-protected. Electronic data and customer information should be protected from unauthorized access and computer hackers.

- **Segregation of duties**
  Custodial, authorization, and recording functions of the accounting system should be performed by different individuals. The person who authorizes payments, the one who prepares the checks, and the one who records the payments in the accounting system should be three different individuals, so that if one of them does something irregular, the other two will detect it. Small organizations frequently fail to segregate duties, leaving all the accounting functions in the hands of one person — sometimes with tragic consequences.

- **Proper authorization of transactions**
  Every organization should have a procedure for senior management to authorize transactions above a certain amount, either with a digital approval or physical signature. Transactions that are not properly authorized are submitted to management for further review. Authorization controls include monitoring for forged signatures and for

attempts to circumvent the policy by breaking a large amount up into several smaller amounts that do not require authorization.

- **Independent checks on performance**
  Independent checks include surprise audits, cash counts, inventory checks, and bank statement reconciliations carried out by an independent person who is not normally involved in those areas.

- **Anonymous reporting mechanism**
  An anonymous reporting system encourages employees, and sometimes vendors and customers, to report fraud. The system must include an effective means of receiving and processing tips, as well as antifraud education for employees. *See the following section on employee hotlines.*

- **Monitoring activities**
  Monitoring includes physical monitoring, such as the use of surveillance cameras and recording access to restricted areas in logbooks. Passwords and access to computer systems and accounting systems should also be monitored, as well as e-mail usage and Internet access. Increasingly, sophisticated software programs are available to monitor transactions and data electronically for irregularities and indicators of fraud. *See the section on fraud detection software in Chapter 9 for more information.*

Employee Hotlines

The importance of tips from employees and outsiders in uncovering fraud has been emphasized throughout this book. Every organization should have a mechanism for reporting suspicious activity to someone who can investigate it. By assuring the tipster's anonymity, reporting mechanisms can overcome fear of reprisal or reluctance to betray a fellow employee. Many companies provide an employee hotline — a telephone number that anyone can call to anonymously report suspicions of fraud. A hotline can be as simple as a voicemail box that is checked by a company employee, or it can be a telephone number maintained by an independent third party who reports to a designated individual in the company. Employees should be able to report to someone who is not their direct superior. When senior management is suspected of fraud, the report should be made to a member of the audit committee or board of directors. E-mail addresses can also be used as hotlines, but the report will not be completely anonymous, as it can always be traced to the computer where it originated. Studies of hotline usage have shown that anonymity is not always important to tipsters, but it should always be made available. Knowing the position and responsibilities of the person reporting the tip is often helpful in investigating whether the tip is substantial.

A key component of an effective hotline is the proper evaluation and handling of tips. For every legitimate tip, there will be dozens, even hundreds of complaints from disgruntled employees and third parties who have their own motives for using the hotline. Adequate staffing should be made available to screen tips, and a clear procedure should be in place for handling tips that merit further attention. The hotline will not be successful if there is not a follow-up plan for investigating tips when they come in, evaluating them and deciding when to conduct a fraud investigation.

Third-party vendors promise complete employee hotline systems that issue phone numbers, answer the telephone calls, and give reports to company management, but every company should determine what type of hotline works best for its particular circumstances. Using third-party hotlines may present problems if legal action is taken against a fraud perpetrator. The third-party vendor's report may lack important details because it is unfamiliar with the nature of the business; the company may lose attorney-client privileges for a portion of the investigation; and the third-party vendor may respond differently from company executives or an audit committee when asked to present evidence or testimony in court.

As mentioned above, an employee hotline is most effective when it is accompanied by regular antifraud education for employees. Employees must know what to watch out for and how to report it in order to use the hotline. Legal counsel should be involved in evaluating tips to ensure that evidence is protected, and counsel should also be made available for employees who fear they may be implicated in a fraud scheme.

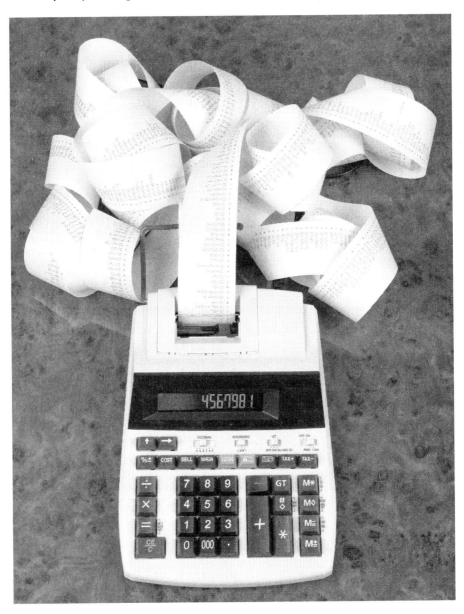

CHAPTER 13

Conducting a Fraud Risk Assessment

A fraud risk assessment is a process that identifies all the possible ways that occupational fraud could be committed in a business and ranks each of them according to the amount of potential damage it could cause. Sarbanes-Oxley requires all publicly traded companies to conduct fraud risk assessments, but it is a good idea for every organization to conduct an annual fraud risk assessment. Many small companies and not-for-profits become victims because their executives do not realize that an opportunity for fraud exists.

A fraud risk assessment at a large corporation can be a time-consuming process involving a significant number of employees and requiring numerous meetings and follow-up sessions. In a small organization, one or more brainstorming sessions with representative employees may be enough to provide executives and business owners with the information they need to implement stronger fraud risk management. Ideally, an auditor or fraud examiner should be present to guide the fraud assessment and provide insight. *See the checklists for various types of fraud in Chapters 5-7, which may be helpful in reviewing an organization's accounting processes.*

Fraud risk assessments help to educate participants about the ways in which fraud is committed and how it can be prevented. They also identify dangerous weaknesses in the organization's processes that need to be corrected. By assigning priorities according to the danger presented by each fraud risk, the assessment helps executives to create an action plan and to decide where and how to allocate resources. Some solutions can be implemented quickly and inexpensively, while others may require considerable investment, such as the hiring of additional staff, purchasing of software or security systems, and training of employees.

Who Should Participate in a Fraud Risk Assessment?

Business owners, executives, and management who are responsible for implementing policies to prevent fraud should definitely participate in a fraud risk assessment, but in the early stages, representatives from every area of a company's operations should be included. Employees who work on the factory floor, in the shipping department, security, human resources, marketing, accounting, payroll, legal, and sales will be most aware of the weaknesses and the potential for fraud in these areas. The picture they present may be far less optimistic than the conceptions of senior management. Ideally, these employees should be included in brainstorming sessions conducted by an auditor or a fraud professional. After receiving some fraud education, employees should be asked to identify areas in which the company could be exposed to criminal activity that could result in financial loss, damage to public reputation, or any other liability, such as lawsuits. Information should be as specific and detailed as possible regarding how fraud schemes might be carried out.

Cookie-cutter fraud risk assessment programs exist, but because each company's business is unique, individualized fraud risk assessments are more successful at identifying specific fraud risks.

Identifying Fraud Risk Factors

Chapter 3 identified three factors that contribute to occupational fraud:

- **Motivation**: Pressures and incentives, both in personal life and at work, that lead an employee to commit fraud.
- **Opportunity**: Circumstances that allow fraud to be committed.
- **Rationalization**: Attitudes and rationalizations that justify a the fraud.

The first step in a fraud risk assessment is to identify these fraud risk factors — the areas of the company's business where motivation, opportunity, or rationalization for fraud exists. Some fraud risk factors are very general, such as a downturn in the economy that affects sales, and some might be specific, such as resentment among employees in a certain department because of insensitive management. The *Appendix to U. S. Auditing Standards AU Section 316, Consideration of Fraud in a Financial Statement Audit* (**www.aicpa.org/download/members/div/auditstd/AU-00316.PDF**) lists a number of common fraud risk factors. Fraud risk factors can be identified by doing research; studying frauds that have been committed in the same industry or previously in the company; reading management reports; and conducting interviews and brainstorming sessions with employees. When employees are presented with a list of fraud risk factors, they will often be stimulated to think of new ones.

After fraud risk factors have been identified, establish detailed scenarios of specific types of fraud that might occur in those circumstances and how they might be carried out. For example, if sales results are slipping, what kind of fictitious revenue scheme might be used to boost sales figures? The more precise and detailed the fraud risk assessment is, the more effectively management will be able to prioritize risks and determine the best courses of action to take.

Initially, the fraud risks should be identified without consideration for the internal controls or security measures already existing in the company. They will be factored in later when the fraud risks are evaluated.

Evaluating Fraud Risk

Once fraud risks have been identified and described in detail, management must measure and prioritize them. Risk assessment is now treated as a science, but many experts agree that it can never be a completely objective process. Fraud risks are identified without consideration for the company's existing fraud controls. In evaluating each fraud risk, management looks at how the company's existing policies already mitigate the risk associated with each fraud scheme.

Each fraud risk should be evaluated by:

- **Type of fraud**: Financial statement fraud, fraudulent disbursement, larceny, and so on.

- **Likelihood**: The likelihood that a fraud will occur, usually expressed with a scale of high, medium, and low probability, or with a numerical scale.

- **Impact**: The magnitude of the impact that the fraud could have on the company, expressed with a scale of high, medium, and low probability, or with a numerical scale.

- **Pervasiveness**: Whether the risk is present throughout the company, or is specific to one department or one individual.

Fraud risk assessments typically use a visual chart to prioritize fraud risks. There are several methods for prioritizing fraud risks using X and Y coordinates on a graph chart.

First, each fraud is rated on a scale of one to ten for the likelihood that it might occur, where one is the lowest probability and ten is the highest. This is the X coordinate. Next, each fraud risk is rated on a scale of one to ten for the seriousness of the impact it could have on the company. This is the Y coordinate.

Each fraud is then plotted on a chart with shaded squares like the one below to create a fraud risk map:

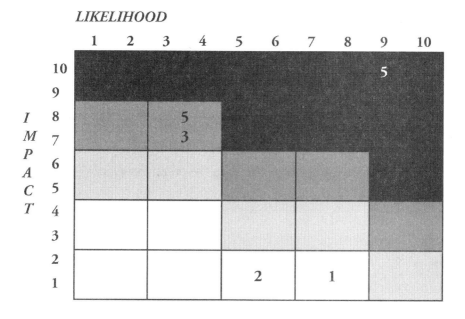

1. *Theft of inventory (likelihood 7, impact 2)*
2. *Theft from the cash register (likelihood 5, impact 1)*
3. *Ghost employees (likelihood 3, impact 7)*
4. *Check tampering (likelihood 9, impact 10)*
5. *Billing fraud (likelihood 4, impact 8)*

Items in the black area represent the greatest risk to the company, and items in the white area present the least risk.

This example is very simple; a real fraud risk assessment could become very complex, and it may be difficult to decide which of two fraud risks from the same section of the grid, like No. 3 and No. 5 above, should be given priority. A geometric, staggered progression method, known as the chessboard method, assigns a monetary value to each fraud risk based on how frequently it is likely to occur and makes it easier to compare the potential danger of each fraud.

Choosing and Implementing Strategies

Once fraud risks have been identified and prioritized, management must decide how to respond to each one. There are four basic ways to respond to a fraud risk:

Avoid the risk

A risk can be avoided altogether by ending the practice associated with it. A simple example would be a freezer from which customers in a convenience store can choose their own popsicles. If the store employees cannot stop people from stealing popsicles from that freezer several times a day, the freezer should be moved behind the counter where only staff can open it and locked. A company may decide to close a line of business that presents a very high risk of fraud or find another way of operating the business. For instance, high potential fraud losses from a poorly supervised, remote location are likely to outweigh the benefits of keeping the location open.

Transfer the risk

A company can protect itself by transferring the risk associated with fraud to someone else. For example, if there is a high potential for fraud loss in the shipping department, packing and shipping can be outsourced to a specialized shipping company that is insured to cover losses. The company can also purchase insurance to cover potential loss from fraud. For example, a business that accepts credit card payments can buy coverage for fraudulent credit card transactions. Many public schools that became victims of accounting fraud have been able to recover their losses because they were insured.

Accept the risk

A company may decide to simply do nothing about a fraud risk with a low probability and a small impact. If the fraud occurs, the company will then determine what action to take.

Control the risk

The most common response to fraud risk is to strengthen internal controls, implement security measures, educate employees, improve morale to reduce risk factors, and hasten the detection of fraud when it does occur. Management must determine weigh costs against potential benefits based on the company's risk tolerance, and choose the methods and practices that fit the company's budget and resources.

CHAPTER 14

Conducting an
Internal Fraud Investigation

E very organization should have a clear plan for dealing with suspected fraud. Many frauds are discovered because of a tip from an employee, vendor, or customer. No tip should be dismissed without a preliminary examination to see if it might be valid. An employee or manager should be designated to receive and evaluate tips and assign the responsibility for investigating each valid tip to the appropriate individual. A good fraud investigation policy identifies specific red flags that warrant attention, the action that should be taken in response to each one, and who should take that action. The appropriate response to some red flags might be to monitor a situation for further evidence for fraud, while other red flags may call for an immediate full-scale fraud investigation. In a large corporation, a fraud investigation policy can involve multiple levels of decision-making; a floor supervisor takes evidence of suspected fraud to a manager and, together, they decide whether to report the situation to senior management.

Deciding When and How to Conduct a Fraud Examination

When a fraud is discovered in an organization, the obvious response would seem to be to conduct a full-scale fraud investigation immediately, determine exactly when and how the fraud was committed, and take legal action against the wrong-doer(s). In reality, many organizations choose not to conduct full-scale investigations and settle instead for disciplinary action and measures to prevent fraud from recurring in the future. Very little of the money stolen by fraudsters is ever recoverable. A company may wish to avoid negative publicity if the case should come to trial. A full-scale fraud investigation can be costly, tie up staff and resources, and disrupt the company's business. Management must weigh the cost of carrying out a full-scale fraud investigation against the benefits that will derive from it.

Fraud investigations are typically initiated by two sets of circumstances: A person in the company has been discovered to be committing fraud or strong evidence of fraud exists, such as abnormal transactions flagged by antifraud monitoring software, but the full nature of the fraud and the perpetrator are still unknown. In either case, the first priority is to stop the fraud by identifying the perpetrator(s) and to learn enough about the fraud scheme to prevent it from happening again. The next priority is to determine the extent of the loss. The organization may then decide whether to take legal action to try to recover lost assets and to bring the perpetrator to trial.

A publicly traded company is likely to carry out a full-scale investigation to comply with Sarbanes-Oxley requirements and because the company is responsible to its investors. Executives of public companies cannot afford to overlook details because they must personally certify financial statements. Government entities funded with tax dollars are equally responsible to the public. If the organization is insured against losses from fraud, a detailed report may be necessary for the insurance claim. When the victim wants to bring legal action, a detailed report will help the prosecutor to build a case against a fraud perpetrator. Otherwise, the victim organization may decide to carry out a simpler investigation to establish the nature of the fraud, identify the perpetrators and estimate losses. Rather than combing through years' worth of documents and records, investigators can establish that fraud occurred by examining a sample from one or two financial periods.

Fraud professionals often comment that the first discovery of a fraud is just the "tip of the iceberg." Subsequent investigation typically uncovers a tangle of related fraud schemes reaching further and deeper, and going back longer, than was first supposed.

Confronting the Fraud Perpetrator

There will probably be only one opportunity to question an employee suspected of fraud. A person who knows he or she is under suspicion will refuse to answer any further questions. Even though it might seem safer to remove a fraud perpetrator from the premises immediately, the fraud investigation will be more successful if that person is not confronted until after sufficient evidence has been collected. Interrogation of a suspect should be carried out by a professional, such as a fraud examiner or auditor, under the guidance of legal counsel. Testimony collected during an interrogation must be handled correctly so it can serve as evidence in future legal proceedings. A fraud professional skilled in interrogative techniques will know how to extract crucial information without damaging the case.

Preparing for a Fraud Investigation

After assessing the extent and nature of the fraud, management must decide what kind of fraud investigation to conduct. Executives and managers typically do not have wide experience with fraud cases and may need professional guidance. Large corporations often have full-time antifraud professionals on their staff or a CPA who can direct an internal investigation. An auditing firm can conduct an investigation unless its previous relationships with the persons being investigated might affect its independence. An antifraud professional has skills and experience that auditors and accountants do not have, including knowledge of the legal ramifications of a fraud investigation. Before calling in an antifraud professional, management should answer these questions:

What is the purpose and goal of this investigation?

- Establish guilt
- Quantify losses
- Discover exactly how the fraud was perpetrated
- Determine the extent and nature of the fraud
- Satisfy regulatory or insurance requirements
- Bring legal action against the perpetrator(s)
- Make adjustments to accounts and corrections to financial statements

How much can the organization spend on this investigation?

What resources will the company devote to the investigation?

- Employees
- Office space and equipment
- Computers and data storage

Who will conduct this investigation?

- CFO or chief accountant
- Internal auditor
- External auditor
- Member of audit committee
- Legal counsel
- Certified fraud examiner
- Law enforcement

If an outside investigator is being brought in, who will act as their liaison?

How long should this investigation last, and when will it end?

What documents will be needed for this investigation; how will they be made available; and where will they be stored?

- Documentary evidence is very important during a fraud examination. Sensitive documents must be protected, and documents must be organized and stored in a way that makes them conveniently accessible to the fraud investigators.

What disciplinary action will be taken against the fraud perpetrator?

Making these decisions in advance will facilitate negotiations with an outside auditor or fraud examiner, who needs to know exactly what the company expects.

Putting Together a Fraud Investigation Team

A fraud investigation begins with the assembly of a team of professionals appropriate to the size of the investigation and the type of fraud. The team can consist of both outside professionals and company employees who can contribute useful information when it is needed and facilitate the search for evidence. Not all members of the team will need to be involved all of the time. Some of the people who might be included in a fraud investigation team are:

- **Legal counsel:** An attorney should determine the overall direction of the investigation because the way in which it is conducted will have legal ramifications. If the investigation ends with criminal or civil prosecution, legal counsel can ensure that the correct procedures are followed to collect and preserve evidence, and ensure that each party's legal rights are protected.

- **Fraud examiner or forensic accountant**: A fraud examiner or forensic accountant should plan and perform the investigation. An outside fraud examiner who is independent of the company will be able to view policies and procedures with fresh eyes and will not be influenced by prior acquaintance with the fraud perpetrator(s). Fraud examiners have experience with many types of fraud and investigative skills that auditors and accountants do not have.

- **Internal and external auditors**: Auditors are familiar with company policies and accounting processes, and will be able to support the fraud examiner in obtaining necessary evidence and examining the accounts for irregularities.

- **Management representative(s)**: One or more members of management should participate in the investigation to represent the interests of the company, communicate the progress of the investigation to upper management, and provide information about company policies. The management representative should be a superior to the person suspected of fraud. If senior management is suspected of fraud, the company's interests can be represented by a member of the audit committee or board of directors.

- **Board of director's representative**: A representative of the board of directors should also participate and be responsible for communicating about the investigation to the rest of the board.

- **Human resources**: The human resource representative will be able to provide background information on employees, work schedules, and details of wages and benefits whenever needed.

- **Corporate security**: A representative from corporate security will be able to contribute knowledge about security controls and procedures in the company and provide access to video from security cameras, logbooks, and other security data. The investigation process can also help to educate corporate security about possible security weaknesses.

- **IT representative**: A representative from the IT department can provide information about computer security measures and passwords and may be able to retrieve evidence from back-up tapes or e-mail.

- **Outside consultants**: Depending on the nature of the fraud and the type of investigation, consultants such as computer forensics experts or private investigators may be called in to help gather evidence.

If local, state, or national law enforcement entities have been notified of the fraud, the investigative team should be cooperative in gathering and protecting evidence but should not be directed by them. Law enforcement entities do not work for the company.

Conducting the Fraud Investigation

The investigation process should take place as discreetly as possible and not interrupt other employees' workflow. The fraud has already damaged the organization financially, and disrupting the work environment will only result in more losses. A fraud investigation can affect employee morale and create an atmosphere of suspicion and instability. The investigative team should work in an area removed from the general observation of employees, and specific staff members should be designated to provide documents and information as needed.

Results of a Fraud Investigation

The result of a fraud investigation is typically a report presented to management, the audit committee, or the client who initiated the investigation. Before writing the report, the investigator should consult the client's legal counsel because the report becomes legal evidence and may affect future litigation. In cases where the report contains information detrimental to the client in some way, the investigation may be terminated before the report is written. A typical fraud investigation report identifies the parties involved, explains the evidence, and gives the investigator's conclusion, accompanied by some of the incriminating documents or exhibits.

Once the report has been issued, management and legal counsel must decide what action to take. If the fraud perpetrator is still employed by the company, management may decide to discipline him or her, terminate employment, or do nothing if the evidence is not conclusive. If the company has business insurance covering fraud or employee theft, the insurance company should be notified as soon as the fraud is suspected. The fraud investigator's report will expedite the settlement of the insurance claim. The company may decide to file a civil suit against the perpetrator, or it may take the report to law enforcement authorities, who make the decision whether to bring criminal charges. If criminal charges have already been filed, the fraud investigator's report will assist in collecting evidence.

Finding a Professional Fraud Investigator

A professional fraud investigator is someone who has received special training and is experienced in investigating fraud. An accounting or auditing firm may have fraud professionals on staff, or you can seek out a company that specializes in fraud investigation. Be sure to ask for references and follow up on them. When negotiating a contact with a fraud investigator, an organization should clearly communicate what it expects to accomplish through the investigation, the amount it is willing to spend on the investigation, the resources it will make available to the investigator, how it will communicate with the investigator, and the circumstances under which the investigation will be terminated.

Certified fraud examiner (CFE) is a certification given by the ACFE. Candidates must have a bachelor's degree and at least two years of experience in a fraud-related field such as accounting and auditing, criminology, loss prevention, fraud investigation, and some areas of law. They receive the CFE certification after passing a CFE exam and being approved by a certification committee and must receive at least 20 hours of continuing professional education every year to maintain it. The ACFE Web site offers a searchable database of its almost 50,000 members worldwide at **http://eweb.acfe. com/eweb/DynamicPage.aspx?Site=ACFE&WebCode=CFEDirectory**.

Forensic accountants are certified public accountants (CPAs) who complete a training course through the National Association of Forensic Accountants (NAFA) and are recertified every year. A forensic accountant is trained to examine accounting records and search for evidence of specific transactions or activities.

Fraud auditors assess an organization's internal controls, identify fraud risks, and make recommendations, but are not necessarily trained to detect fraud that has already occurred.

CONCLUSION

"Numbers don't lie; people do."

A careful study of occupational fraud leads to one conclusion: Human nature is weak and vulnerable in the face of temptation. The case studies in this book illustrate how business owners, managers, and investors are deceived over and over again, and how they are betrayed by the people who seem the most trustworthy. One lesson is clear: Financial matters should be kept separate from personal affairs. An accountant may appear to be extremely capable, a financial advisor may exude charisma, and an investment brochure may be full of promises, but the real truth lies in the numbers. Use common sense. Implement basic internal controls in your business and stick to them. Research your investments carefully and choose stability over seductively high rates of return. Do not make it easy for someone to take advantage of you.

You have many allies against the hundreds of people who are out there trying to steal your money and assets, including government regulators, watchdog organizations, professional associations, journalists, and law enforcement agencies. Use their resources and experience to educate and protect yourself. The more knowledge you acquire, the better you will be equipped to defend yourself and everyone who relies on you against financial predators.

STRAIGHT FROM THE HEADLINES

Lou Pearlman Used Success to Attract Investors

Episode #18 of CNBC's "American Greed" chronicles the rise and fall of Lou Pearlman, known as the founder of boy bands Backstreet Boys and *NSYNC — and the perpetrator of a Ponzi scheme that defrauded investors of $300 million. Pearlman used the reputation of the wildly popular boy bands to woo investors for his companies, Trans Continental Airlines, Inc. and Trans Continental Travel, Inc. Investors interviewed for the episode describe how they were charmed by Pearlman, entertained and driven around in the Backstreet Boys bus, attracting crowds wherever they went. Pearlman gave them fabricated financial statements, reports, and documents listing nonexistent assets, including 40 airplanes. In fact, Trans Continental Airlines owned only one plane. Pearlman also promoted an "Employee Investment Savings Account" (E.I.S.A.) program, which was nothing more than a Ponzi scheme. More than 1,500 investors lost their life savings. Pearlman was arrested in 2007 and sentenced to 25 years in prison in 2008. Many of his victims say that they were blinded by his apparent success as a music mogul into believing that he "knew what he was doing."

APPENDIX A

Useful Resources and Web Sites

Information on Occupational Fraud

ACFE Report to the Nation on Occupational Fraud and Abuse
(**www.acfe.com/documents/2008-rttn.pdf**)
An ongoing study of occupational fraud based on surveys of certified fraud examiners.

Appendix to U. S. Auditing Standards AU Section 316, Consideration of Fraud in a Financial Statement Audit (**www.aicpa.org/download/ members/div/auditstd/AU-00316.PDF**)
A list of common fraud risk factors.

Association of Certified Fraud Examiners (ACFE) (**www.acfe.com**)
The ACFE provides information and articles about occupational fraud, offers educational resources, and administers the certified fraud examiner certification. The ACFE Web site offers a searchable database of its 30,000 members worldwide at (**http://eweb.acfe.com/eweb/DynamicPage.aspx ?Site=ACFE&WebCode=CFEDirectory**)

FBI: White Collar Crime (www.fbi.gov/whitecollarcrime.htm)
Contains news and information and an online crime reporting form.

***Forensic Focus*, McGovern and Greene, CPAs and Forensic Accountants (www.mcgoverngreene.com/forensicfocus/forensic_focus.html)**
A bimonthly magazine covering many fraud topics.

Journal of Accountancy, September 2009 "What's Your Fraud IQ?" (www.journalofaccountancy.com/Issues/2009/Sep/20091565.htm)
Quiz yourself to see how much you have learned about fraud. At the bottom of the page are links to other fraud quizzes.

National Association of Corporate Directors (NACD) (www.nacdonline.org)
NACD has a membership of 10,000 directors and executives from leading public, private, and nonprofit companies; nationally recognized firms who provide professional services for corporate governance needs; and governance experts. It provides education and resources for fraud prevention and risk assessment.

National Association of Forensic Accountants (NAFA) (www.nafanet.com/index.htm)
The National Association of Forensic Accountants (NAFA) provides training and certification to certified public accountants in various fields of forensic accounting and provides availability and a directory of NAFA-certified accountants.

National White Collar Crime Center (www.nw3c.org)
A non-profit membership organization dedicated to supporting law enforcement in the prevention, investigation, and prosecution of economic and high-tech crime. NW3C has been continuously funded through competitive grants for over three decades. NW3C membership consists of law enforcement agencies from all 50 states and four continents.

Red Flags for Fraud, Office of the Comptroller, State of New York (www.osc.state.ny.us/localgov/pubs/red_flags_fraud.pdf)
An overview of the red flags for fraud.

Taxpayers Against Fraud (TAF) THE FEDERAL FALSE CLAIMS ACT, 31 U.S.C. §§ 3729-3733
As amended May 2009 (www.taf.org/federalfca.htm)
Full text of the Federal False Claims Act and education about fraud and government contracts.

The Institute of Fraud Risk Management (TIFRM) (www.tifrm.net/index.aspx)
TIFRM is a professional organization dedicated to combating fraud by offering effective training courses designed to increase awareness and teach risk management strategies to minimize the associated risks.

White-Collar Crime Fighter (www.wccfighter.com/index.html)
A publication offering advice and insights into the detection, prevention, and investigation of all forms of white-collar crime in both the public and private sectors.

Government and Regulatory Agencies

American Management Association (AMA) (www.amanet.org/Default.aspx)
The American Management Association provides resources and educational material for all areas of management, including the establishment of an ethical culture and employee education.

American Institute of Certified Public Accountants (AICPA) (www.aicpa.org)
AICPA is the national, professional organization for all certified public accountants. Its mission is to provide members with the resources, infor-

mation, and leadership that enable them to provide valuable services in the highest professional manner to benefit the public as well as employers and clients.

Corporate Fraud Data Base. Law.com (http://www.law.com/jsp/cc/PubArticleCC.jsp?id=1193821435624)

A database of corporate fraud cases and their outcomes.

Financial Accounting Standards Board (FASB) (www.fasb.org)

Since 1973, the Financial Accounting Standards Board (FASB) has been the designated organization in the private sector for establishing standards of financial accounting. Those standards govern the preparation of financial statements. They are officially recognized as authoritative by the Securities and Exchange Commission (SEC) and the American Institute of Certified Public Accountants (AICPA).

Office of the Comptroller of Currency (OCC) (www.occ.treas.gov/index.htm)

The Office of the Comptroller of the Currency (OCC) is a bureau of the U.S. Department of the Treasury that charters, regulates, and supervises all national banks, and supervises the federal branches and agencies of foreign banks.

Federal Trade Commission (www.ftc.gov)

The FTC works to prevent unfair methods of competition in commerce and polices anticompetitive practices.

Committee of Sponsoring Organizations of the Treadway Commission (www.coso.org)

COSO is a voluntary private-sector organization dedicated to guiding executive management and governance entities toward the establishment of more effective, efficient, and ethical business operations on a global basis.

It sponsors and disseminates frameworks and guidance based on in-depth research, analysis, and best practices.

"Detecting Occupational Fraud: Billing Schemes" Mark W. Lehman and Marcia L. Weidenmier, *The CPA Journal.* **(www.nysscpa.org/cpajournal/2005/405/essentials/p58.htm)**
An article explaining step-by-step how you can use Microsoft Access to detect billing schemes.

Financial Executives International (FEI) (www.financialexecutives.org)
An international association for CFOs and other senior finance executives. FEI provides networking, advocacy, timely updates, and CPE on financial management and reporting; Sarbanes-Oxley Act compliance; and regulatory updates from the SEC, FASB, PCAOB, and IASB.

Federal Accounting Standards Advisory Board (FASAB)
(www.fasab.gov/accepted.html)
FASAB is designated by the AICPA as the body that establishes generally accepted accounting principles (GAAP) for federal reporting entities. As such, the FASAB is responsible for identifying the "GAAP hierarchy" for federal reporting entities.

Government Accountability Office (GAO) (www.gao.gov)
GAO is an independent, nonpartisan agency that works for Congress. Often called the "congressional watchdog," GAO investigates how the federal government spends taxpayer dollars.

International Accounting Standards Board (IASB)
(www.iasb.org/Home.htm)
The independent standard-setting body of the International Accounting Standards Committee Foundation (IASC Foundation). IASB is dedicated to developing a single set of high-quality, understandable, and

international financial reporting standards (IFRS) for general purpose financial statements.

Institute of Internal Auditors (IIA) (www.theiia.org/theiia/about-the-institute)

The IIA is the internal audit profession's global voice, recognized authority, acknowledged leader, chief advocate, and principal educator. Members work in internal auditing, risk management, governance, internal control, information technology audit, education, and security.

Library of Congress Business References Service (www.loc.gov/rr/business/company)

Resources and suggestions for researching companies.

Public Company Accounting Oversight Board (PCAOB) (www.pcaobus.org)

A private-sector nonprofit corporation created by the Sarbanes-Oxley Act to oversee auditors of public companies and protect the interests of the public.

Sarbanes-Oxley Financial and Accounting Information. Sarbanes-Oxley.com. (www.sarbanes-oxley.com)

A complete cross-referenced index of SEC filers, audit firms, offices, CPAs, services, fees, compliance/enforcement actions, and other critical disclosure information.

U.S. Code (http://uscode.house.gov)

A consolidation and codification by subject matter of the general and permanent laws of the United States, prepared and published by the Office of the Law Revision Counsel.

Internet Security

Computer Crime/WWW Issues (www.ou.edu/oupd/inetmenu.htm)
Presentation by the University of Oklahoma University Police Department on identity theft and credit card fraud.

FBI Cyber Investigations (www.fbi.gov/cyberinvest/cyberhome.htm)
Among its missions, FBI Cyber Investigations aims to counteract operations that target U.S. intellectual property and to dismantle national and transnational organized criminal enterprises engaging in Internet fraud.

National Institute of Justice, "Guide for First Responders" (www.nwfia.org/NIJGuideforFirstResponders.pdf)
A guide to safeguarding electronic evidence.

Financial Statement Research

AICPA, "A Framework for Detecting Financial Statement Fraud" (http://fvs.aicpa.org/Resources/Antifraud+Forensic+Accounting/ CPAs+and+Others+Performing+Fraud+Consulting+Services/ Skills+and+Techniques+Required+of+a+Fraud+Consultant/ Fraud+Investigation+Techniques/A+Framework+for+Detecting+Fina ncial+Statement+Fraud.htm)

Compustat (www.compustat.com)
Owned by Standard & Poor's, Compustat

EDGAR (www.sec.gov/edgar.shtml)
The SEC's Electronic Data Gathering, Analysis, and Retrieval system. It gives access to all the financial statements and reports filed by publicly-traded companies in the United States.

Financial Industry Regulatory Authority (FINRA) (www.finra.org/index.htm)

FINRA is the largest independent regulator for all securities firms doing business in the United States. It registers securities firms, writes, and enforces rules and provides education for investors and professionals.

International Organization of Securities Commissioners (www.iosco. org/lists/display_members.cfm?memID=none&orderBy=country)

A source of information on foreign companies.

LexisNexis (www.lexisnexis.com)

A division of Reed Elsevier that maintains a searchable archive of content from newspapers, magazines, legal documents, and other printed sources.

Morningstar (www.morningstar.com)

An independent investment research company whose Web site offers investor education and detailed information about publicly traded companies.

National Information Center (NIC) - Federal Reserve System (www.ffiec.gov/nicpubweb/nicweb/nichome.aspx)

The National Information Center (NIC) Web site provides access to data about banks and other institutions for which the Federal Reserve has a supervisory, regulatory, or research interest, including both domestic and foreign banking organizations operating in the United States.

North American Securities Administrators Association (NASAA) "Fraud Scene Investigator" (www.nasaa.org/Investor_Education/FSI)

Interactive program to educate investors about financial statement fraud.

NYSE Euronext (www.nyse.com)

The New York Stock Exchange provides detailed information on all of its publicly traded companies.

SEC. *Beginner's Guide to Financial Statements.* (**www.sec.gov/investor/pubs/begfinstmtguide.htm**)

A tutorial explaining the basics of financial statements.

Media

Business Week (**www.businessweek.com**)

CNN Money (**www.money.cnn.com**)

Financial Times (**http://news.ft.com/home/us**)

Kiplinger (**www.kiplinger.com**)

The New York Times (**www.nytimes.com/pages/business/index.html**)

Smart Money (**www.smartmoney.com**)

Conducting a Fraud Risk Assessment

MindTools.com, "Risk Analysis and Risk Management" (**www.mindtools.com/pages/article/newTMC_07.htm**)

APPENDIX B

Glossary of Terms

Accounting Period - The time period encompassed by a financial report.

Aging - A system that tracks the number of days an account receivable is overdue — the longer an account is overdue, the more likely it will not be paid.

Aggressive Accounting - The selection of accounting methods that tend to overstate earnings and understate expenses.

Annual Report to Shareholders - The annual financial report that publicly traded companies must send out to shareholders.

American Institute of Certified Public Accountants (AICPA) - The national professional association for all certified public accountants.

AML Compliance - Anti-money-laundering compliance, the regulations that financial institutions are required to follow to reduce the incidence of money-laundering.

Amortize - To pay off in installments.

Association of Certified Fraud Examiners (ACFE) - An association that certifies professional fraud examiners and provides education and resources.

Audit - A professional examination and evaluation of a company's accounting systems.

Audit Committee - A committee composed of independent members of the board of directors that oversees the financial reporting process.

Balance Sheet - A snapshot of the organization's financial status at a particular point in time.

Big 4 - The four major international accounting and professional service firms: PricewaterhouseCoopers, Deloitte & Touche, Ernst & Young, and KPMG.

Bill and Hold - An arrangement in which customers place future orders and agree to be billed and pay for them in the future when the goods are shipped.

Billing Scheme - A scheme in which the perpetrator uses false or altered invoices to induce a company to make fraudulent payments.

Capitalization - The recharacterization of revenue-based expenses as capital expenses.

Cash Disbursement Fraud - A scheme in which legitimate procedures are manipulated to induce a company to make fraudulent disbursements.

Cash Generation Scheme - A scheme in which false invoices or vouchers are used to collect payment for fictitious or overpriced goods or services.

Certified Public Accountant - An accountant who has passed the Uniform Certified Public Accountant Examination and met local and state licensing requirements.

Channel Stuffing - The practice of inducing regular customers or distributors to "stock up" on excess goods or unneeded supplies just before the end of a financial period.

Chargeback Insurance - Insurance that protects a merchant against losses from purchases made with stolen credit cards.

Chart of Accounts - A list of all the accounts used by an organization to record and sort its business transactions.

Check Tampering - The alteration or forgery of checks in order to steal or misdirect funds.

Collateral - Assets used to secure a loan.

Commercial Bribery - Bribery in the context of a corporation or a private company.

Completed Contract Method - A method for recognizing revenue from a long-term contract in which revenue and expenses are not recorded until the contract is complete.

Confidentiality Clause - A legal clause in an employment contract that prevents an employee from disclosing trade secrets or confidential information to competitors.

Continual Fraud Monitoring (CFM) - A computer software application that continually monitors financial transactions for signs of fraud.

Corporate Espionage - The theft and sale of trade secrets, data, or confidential information belonging to a corporation.

Creative Accounting -The use of accounting methods to manipulate the resulting financial statements.

Cressey Triangle - A diagram created by Donald R. Cressey showing the three elements of fraud: motivation, opportunity, and justification.

Current Assets - Cash on hand, prepaid expenses, accounts receivable, and inventory and marketable securities that can be converted to cash in less than a year.

Current Ratio - The ration of a company's current assets to its current liabilities.

Dot-com Bubble - A period in the late 1990s when the stock prices of new Internet-based businesses soared.

Double Endorsement - A check that is signed over by the original payee to another person and then endorsed by that person.

Embezzlement - The theft or misuse of cash entrusted to one's custody or control.

External Audit - A review of a company's financial records conducted by an outside professional auditor.

Eyeballing - Physically looking over a database to see if it is accurate.

Fiduciary - A financial agent who is expected to act with integrity and responsibility on behalf of the entity he or she represents.

Financial Accounting Foundation (FAF) - A nonprofit organization that oversees and funds the FASB.

Financial Accounting Standards Board (FASB) - A public watchdog organization that sets accounting standards.

Financial Numbers Game - A term for the manipulation of financial statements.

Financial Period - The time period encompassed by a financial report.

Financial Shenanigans - A term for financial statement fraud.

Forensic Accountant - An accountant skilled in probing account records to detect how transactions have passed through the accounting system.

Foreign Corrupt Practices Act of 1977 (FCPA) - A law that prohibits U.S. companies from bribing foreign governments or companies.

Forged Endorsement Scheme - A scheme in which endorsements are forged on stolen third-party checks so that they can be cashed.

Fraud Examiner - A professional trained in forensic accounting, criminology, and private investigation.

Fraud Risk Factors - The areas of the company's business where motivation, opportunity, and rationalization for committing fraud exist.

Fraud Triangle - A diagram created by Donald R. Cressey showing the three elements of fraud: motivation, opportunity, and justification.

Future Profits - A method of assigning value to an asset based on the estimated profits the company will earn by possessing it.

Full Disclosure - The obligation to disclose deviations from standard accounting principles, events that could impact future earnings, and legal liabilities on a company's financial statement.

Generally Accepted Accounting Principles (GAAP) - Generally accepted accounting standards for the ways in which earnings, assets, revenues, and expenses can be stated.

Ghost Employee - A fictitious person or non-employee who is added to a company payroll.

Going Concern - The assumption that a business will continue operating indefinitely.

Goodwill - An intangible asset, such as a public reputation or strong brand recognition, that gives a company a competitive advantage.

Gross Domestic Product (GDP) - The market value of all the goods and services produced by a country during a year.

Hedge Fund - An investment fund open to a limited group of wealthy or professional investors that is not subject to the same regulations that restrict funds offered to the public.

Horizontal Analysis - A method of comparing financial statements by calculating the percentage of change from one financial period to the next for each item on the statement.

Illegal Gratuity - A gift given after an employee has acted to ensure that a transaction was favorable to a particular vendor or contractor.

Income Smoothing - The spreading of earnings from one financial period over statements for several financial periods to reduce the appearance of volatility.

Income Statement - A report of a business's total revenues, gains, cost of goods sold, expenses, losses, and net income for a specified period of time.

Independent - A professional who is not affiliated with a company or organization.

Internal Audit - An evaluation by a company's own employees of its financial and business processes.

Internal Controls - The procedures followed by employees in a company to ensure that accounts are accurate.

Invigilation - The creation of a baseline or expected trend report and its comparison with actual sales figures or financial reports to expose possible irregularities.

IT - Information technology, the department responsible for managing computer services at a company.

Kickback - An illegal commission given to an employee for directing a sale or contract to a particular vendor.

KYC Compliance - Know-Your-Customer compliance, regulations requiring financial institutions to verify customer information before approving transactions.

Lapping - A strategy used to conceal theft, in which cash is continually taken from current payments or deposits to make up for an amount stolen from earlier payments or deposits.

Leased Asset - An asset that is rented rather than purchased.

Loan Covenant - The terms of the legal contract that secures a loan.

Long-term Purchase Commitment - A contract to continue purchasing goods or services at a fixed price over a period of time.

Loss Contingency - A reserve set aside to pay for a loss that will probably occur as the result of some future event.

Litigation - The process of bringing a lawsuit to court.

Materiality - The extent to which a piece of information affects business decisions.

Merchant Service Company - A company that processes credit card sales for merchants and sometimes performs other financial services.

Moonlighting - Earning extra income by performing work outside of a regular job.

National Commission on Fraudulent Reporting - An organization established in 1985 to examine the problem of fraudulent financial reporting and make recommendations.

Net Realizable Value - An asset's value based on the price it will sell for at some point in the future, minus the costs of owning, operating, and selling it.

Occupational Fraud - The use of one's occupation to conduct illegal activities for financial gain or personal benefit.

Packet Sniffer - Software program that intercepts and logs transactions passing over digital networks.

Pass-through Scheme - A fraud scheme in which an employee sets up a shell company to sell goods and services to the employer at inflated prices.

Percentage of Completion Method (POC) - A method of revenue recognition for long-term contracts in which a percentage of the revenue and expenses is recognized each financial period until the contract is complete.

Ponzi Scheme - A fraud in which the perpetrators promise unrealistic rates of return and use money from new investors to pay off older investors.

Premature Revenue Recognition - A scheme in which revenue is recorded before sales are completed.

Price to Earnings Ratio (PE) - The price of a share of stock divided by the earnings per share.

Price-Level Adjusted Historical Cost - The representation of an asset's value as what it would currently cost, adjusting for inflation.

Privately Held Company - A company whose shares are held by a small group of investors, often members of a family or company employees.

Pro Forma Financial Statement - A statement prepared in advance of a new business venture or a planned transaction, such as a merger, to show its expected impact on a company's business.

Proxy - A statement out before an annual shareholders' meeting, containing details about management compensation, stock options, and benefits.

Public Company Accounting Oversight Board (PCAOB) - A board established by the Sarbanes-Oxley Act to oversee the audit of publicly traded companies.

Purchase Order - An official document authorizing the purchase of goods or services.

Qualified Opinion - An auditor's statement expressing reservations about a financial report.

Quality of Earnings - The degree to which revenue reported in a fi-

nancial statement is substantially realized or collectible.

Quid Pro Quo - Literally "something for something" — a condition imposed on a transaction in which each partner offers something to the other.

Red Flag - A sign that fraud might be occurring, such as accounting irregularities or aberrant behavior of an employee.

Related Party - A family member or relative, stockholder, or a corporation associated with the ownership of a company.

Related Party Transactions - Transactions between two entities that are controlled by the same company or management.

Replacement Cost - The amount it would cost to replace an asset at current market prices.

Rubber Stamp Supervisor - An inattentive or overly trusting supervisor who does not review documents presented by an employee before approving them.

Sale With Condition - A sale accompanied by a promise that the sale can later be reversed or canceled at the buyer's option.

Sarbanes-Oxley Act of 2002 - An Act passed by Congress to set new standards for the boards of directors and managers of publicly traded companies, and for public accountants.

Security - Policies and practices that protect an organization's assets, including cash, inventory, property, and computer files.

Separation of Duties - The division of responsibilities for handling and accounting for cash among two or more people to prevent theft.

Shell Company - A company that serves as a vehicle for specific business dealings and has no assets of its own.

Shrinkage - The unexplained depletion of inventory.

Side Letter - A document that alters the terms and conditions of an invoice or contract.

Skimming - The practice of stealing cash receipts before they are entered into the accounting system.

Statistical Sampling - The use of statistical data to select sample transactions or documents for closer examination.

Third-Party Check - A check made out to a payee other than the person who is cashing the check.

Trusted Employee - An employee in a position to exercise authority, particularly in financial matters, on behalf of the employer.

Tone at the Top - The corporate culture established by senior managers in a company through their attitudes and actions.

Treadway Commission - National Commission on Fraudulent Reporting.

Uniform Trade Secrets Act (UTSA) - A model law drafted by the National Conference of Commissioners on Uniform State Laws to better define the rights and remedies of common law trade secrets; adopted by many states.

United States Code (U.S. Code) - A consolidation and codification by subject matter of the general and permanent laws of the United States.

Vertical Analysis - A method for comparing financial statements in which each item on the statement is expressed as a percentage of the total.

Volatility - The tendency of stock prices or business earnings to fluctuate over a period of time.

Voucher - A file containing all the documentation for a purchase, including invoices, receipts, and delivery confirmations.

Whistleblower - A person who reports a fraud to management or regulators.

 # BIBLIOGRAPHY

Albrecht, W. Steve, Keith R. Howe, and Marshall B. Romney. *Deterring fraud: the internal auditor's perspective.* Institute of Internal Auditors Research Foundation., p. xiv. Altamonte Springs, Fla. 1984.

Arena, Kelli and Harris, Art. "FBI arrests 8 in fraud scheme targeting McDonald's game." *CNN.com.* August 22, 2001. (**http://archives.cnn. com/2001/LAW/08/21/monopoly.arrests/index.html**)

Associated Press. "Former HANO chief financial officer pleads guilty to embezzlement." *WWLTV.com, Louisiana's News Leader.* September 23, 2009.

Association of Certified Fraud Examiners. *2008 Report to the Nation on Occupational Fraud and Abuse.* (**www.acfe.com/resources/publications. asp?copy=rttn**)

Biegelman, M.T., and Bartow, J.T. *Executive roadmap to fraud prevention and internal control: creating a culture of compliance.* Hoboken, N.J., Wiley. 2006.

Bishop, Toby J.F., and Frank E. Hydoski. *Corporate resiliency: managing the growing risk of fraud and corruption.* Hoboken, N.J.: Wiley. 2009.

Bonafide, Margaret F. "Employees of defense contractor in Red Bank plead guilty in conspiracy to accept kickbacks." *APP.com.* September 28, 2009.

"Bookkeeping." AccountingCoach.com (**www.accountingcoach.com/ online-accounting-course/accounting-bookkeeping.html**)

"Bribery." Lawyershop.com (**www.lawyershop.com/practice-areas/criminal-law/white-collar-crimes/bribery-kickbacks/**)

Broder, James F. *Risk analysis and the security survey.* Boston: Butterworth Heinemann (2000) 24.

Brooke, James. "Salt Lake City Mayor Quits As Olympic Scandal Grows." *New York Times.* January 12, 1999. (**www.nytimes.com/1999/01/12/us/ salt-lake-city-mayor-quits-as-olympic-scandal-grows.html**)

Brown, Laura. "Police Raid French Auto Magazine in Renault Industrial Espionage Investigation." *Edmunds InsideLine.* Edmunds.com. July 16, 2008. (**www.edmunds.com/insideline/do/News/articleId=129188**)

Bullock, DeShaunta. "Embezzlement at a Fresno County School." *ABCLocal. KFSN-TV FRESNO, CA.* May 28, 2009. (**http://abclocal.go.com/ kfsn/story?section=news/local&id=6837384**)

Chew, Robert. "A Madoff Whistle-Blower Tells His Story." *Time Magazine.* February 4, 2009. (**www.time.com/time/business/article/0,8599,1877181,00.html**)

Coenen, Tracy. *Essentials of corporate fraud.* Essentials series. Hoboken, N.J.: John Wiley & Sons.2008.

Coenen, Tracy. *Expert fraud investigation: a step-by-step guide.* Hoboken, N.J., John Wiley & Sons. 2009.

Columbia Regional Business Report. "Two Midlands people receive prison time for embezzlement." Staff Report. *Columbia Regional Business Report.* September 3, 2009. (**www.columbiabusinessreport.com/news/29306/print**)

Corporate Fraud Data Base. Law.com (**www.law.com/jsp/cc/PubArticleCC.jsp?id=1193821435624**)

Corporate Meetings and Incentives. "Starwood Accuses Hilton of Corporate Espionage." Meetingsnet.com. April 17, 2009. (**http://meetingsnet.com/corporatemeetingsincentives/news/0417-starwood-hilton-corporate-espionage/**)

CreditCardAssist. "13 Arrested in Restaurant Skimming Scam." *CreditCardAssist.com.* April 16, 2007. (**www.creditcardassist.com/blog/arrests-made-in-restaurant-skimming-scam/**)

Culshaw, Peter. "Nick Leeson: how the original rogue trader at Barings Bank is thriving in the credit crunch." *Telegraph.co.uk.* January 8, 2009. (**www.telegraph.co.uk/finance/4177449/Nick-Leeson-how-the-original-rogue-trader-at-Barings-Bank-is-thriving-in-the-credit-crunch.html**)

"Data taken, company says." *The Vancouver Sun.* November 27, 2008. (**www.canada.com/vancouversun/news/westcoastnews/story.html?id=055fa12a-2bca-4804-9bef-a44eee60de5f**)

"Daughter says embezzling mom was a gambler." KVOA Tucson. September 10, 2009.

Davis, Trey. "Banks, law firms were pivotal in executing Enron securities fraud." *Press Release.* University of California, Office of the President. April 8, 2002. (**www.ucop.edu/news/enron/art408.htm**)

Davidson, Gary. "Bealls Employee Charged with Grand Theft." *Daytona Beach News-journalonline.com*, August 15, 2009. (**www.volusia.org/sheriff/press/2009PressReleases/August/090124.htm**)

Edmonds, Cindy D., & Edmonds, Thomas P., McNair, Frances M., & Milam, Edward E., & Olds, Philip R., Schneider, Nancy W. . *Fundamental Financial Accounting Concepts.* New York: McGraw-Hill. 2003.

Eggen, Dan. "Democrats Vow To Return Money From Financier: Nemazee, a Top Fundraiser for Party, Is Charged With Fraud Related to Loan." *Washington Post.* August 27, 2009. (**www.washingtonpost.com/wp-dyn/content/article/2009/08/26/AR2009082603498_2.html**)

"Ex-church accountant gets 5 years for embezzling." Fraudbaron.com. April 14, 2009. (**www.blog.fraudbaron.com/2009/04/exchurch-accountant-gets-5-years-for-embezzling.html#more**)

Federal Bureau of Investigation. "White Collar Crime." *Federal Bureau of Investigation Strategic Plan 2004 – 2009.* FBI.gov. (**www.fbi.gov/publications/strategicplan/stategicplantext.htm#whitecollar**) Accessed November 3, 2009.

Financial Accounting Standards Board (FASB). "Facts About FASB." FASB.org. (**www.fasb.org/jsp/FASB/Page/SectionPage&cid=1176154526495#eitf**)

Financial Executives International. *FEI Survey: Average 2007 SOX Compliance Cost $1.7 Million.* Financial Executives International. Florham Park, N.J. (**http://fei.mediaroom.com/index.php?s=43&item=204**)

Gellatly, Mike. "John Harte Jr. pleads guilty in fraud scheme." *Aiken Standard.* September 19, 2009. (**www.aikenstandard.com/ mostcomments/0919-harte**)

Gellatly, Mike. "Lawyers' licenses suspended over embezzlement." *Aiken Standard.* September 25, 2009. (**www.aikenstandard.com/ Local/0925Harte**)

Hancox, Stephen J., Deputy Comptroller, Division of Local Government and School Accountability. *Red Flags for Fraud.* Office of the State Comptroller, State of New York. (**www.osc.state.ny.us/localgov/pubs/ red_flags_fraud.pdf**)

Hays, Tom and Neumeister, Larry. "Madoff's Ponzi Scheme: $50 Billion Figure May Be Fictitious." *Huffington Post.* March 6, 2009. (**www.huffingtonpost.com/2009/03/06/madoffs-ponzi-scheme-50-b_n_172427. html**)

Hill, Lee E., II. "Gary Ernest Williams Sentenced for Embezzling $10 Million from Marian Gardens Tree Farm in Groveland, Florida." *Associated Content.* December 3, 2009. (**www.associatedcontent.com/article/2449200/gary_ernest_williams_sentenced_for.html?cat=17**)

Hinkelman, Michael. "Allentown woman pleads guilty to embezzlement scam" *Philadelphia Daily News.* September 9, 2009. (**www.philly.com/ dailynews/local/20090909_Allentown_woman_pleads_guilty_to_embezzlement_scam.html**)

Keener, Ronald E. "Fast growth and few controls invite employee embezzlement: Pastor shocked by people who said they would not prosecute wrongdoers for theft of monies from their congregations." *Church Executive magazine,* Volume 2008, Issue 5. May, 2008. (**http://churchexecutive.com/article.asp?IndexID=1032**)

Kelley, Ann and Clay, Nolan. "Former Oklahoma CASA Association director sentenced to 35 years." NewsOK.com in the *Tulsa World*, (**www. tulsaworld.com/news/article.aspx?subjectid=12&articleid=20090904 _12_0_OKLAHO586318&rss_lnk=1**), September 4, 2009.

Kerber, Ross. "TJX settles with MasterCard over data breach." *Boston Globe*. April 2, 2008. (**www.boston.com/business/ticker/2008/04/tjx_ settles_wit_1.html**)

"Kickbacks." FreeAdvice.com, accessed October 8, 2009. (**http://criminal-law.freeadvice.com/criminal-law/kickbacks.htm**)

KOCO5 Oklahoma. "Former CASA Director Naukam Pleads Guilty." KOCO.com (**www.koco.com/news/20726889/detail.html**), September 4, 2009.

Lawinski, Jennifer. "Connecticut Town Loses Big in Wake of Madoff's Alleged Ponzi Scheme." *FoxNews.com*. December 17, 2008. (**www.foxnews. com/story/0,2933,468824,00.html**)

Longman, Jere. "OLYMPICS; 2 Officials Quit in Salt Lake City As Olympic Scandal Details Grow." *New York Times*. January 9, 1999. (**www.nytimes.com/1999/01/09/sports/olympics-2-officials-quit-in-salt-lake-city-as-olympic-scandal-details-grow.html?pagewanted=all**)

Lopez, Pablo. "Local briefs: Ex-Fresno Co. worker convicted of ID theft." *The Fresno Bee*. Fresno, California. September 9, 2009. (**www.fresnobee. com/local/crime/story/1718173.html**)

"Manhattan U.S. Attorney Charges Colorado Man as Accomplice of Hassan Nemazee in Bank Fraud Ponzi Scheme." *The Boston Globe*. September 25, 2009. (**http://finance.boston.com/boston/?GUID=10204391&Pag e=MEDIAVIEWER**)

McKenna, Francine. "Which Big 4 Firms Will Audit the Failing Banks?" *SeekingAlpha.com.* (**http://seekingalpha.com/article/96755-which-big-4-firms-will-audit-the-failing-banks**)

Mulford, Charles W., and Eugene E. Comiskey. *The financial numbers game: detecting creative accounting practices.* New York: Wiley. 2002.

"Nicor to pay $10 million to settle SEC probe." ChicagoBusiness. com. March 29, 2007. (**www.chicagobusiness.com/cgi-bin/news. pl?id=24418&seenIt=1**)

Poulsen, Kevin. "Feds Charge 11 in Breaches at TJ Maxx, Office-Max, DSW, Others." Wired.com. August 5, 2008. (**www.wired.com/ threatlevel/2008/08/11-charged-in-m/**)

Reynolds, Karen. "Boy Band Bandit: Lou Pearlman's 500 million Ponzi." CNBC.com. January 8, 2009. (**www.cnbc.com/id/28566355**)

Robertson, Jordan. "Sun may have broken bribery laws outside U.S.." Associated Press in the *San Francisco Chronicle.* May 9, 2009. (**www.sfgate. com/cgi-bin/article.cgi?f=/c/a/2009/05/09/BUMR17HD6V.DTL**)

Rosenberg McKay, Dawn. "*Surfing the Net on Your Boss's Time: Personal Internet Use at Work.*" About.com. (**http://careerplanning.about.com/cs/ bosscoworkers/a/net_at_work.htm**)

Sarbanes-Oxley Financial and Accounting Information. Sarbanes-Oxley. com. (**www.sarbanes-oxley.com**)

Schilit, H.M. *Financial shenanigans: how to detect accounting gimmicks and fraud in financial reports.* New York, McGraw-Hill. 1993.

Securities and Exchange Commission. "About EDGAR." SEC.gov. (**www. sec.gov/edgar/aboutedgar.htm**)

Securities and Exchange Commission. *Beginner's Guide to Financial Statements*. SEC.gov. (**www.sec.gov/investor/pubs/begfinstmtguide.htm**)

Securities and Exchange Commission. *Final Report of the Advisory Committee on Smaller Public Companies to the Securities and Exchange Commission*. SEC.gov. April 23, 2006. (**www.sec.gov/info/smallbus/acspc/acspc-finalreport.pdf**)

Securities and Exchange Commission, "First Amended Complaint, SECURITIES AND EXCHANGE COMMISSION, Plaintiff, v. STANFORD INTERNATIONAL BANK, LTD., STANFORD GROUP COMPANY, STANFORD CAPITAL MANAGEMENT, LLC, R. ALLEN STANFORD, JAMES M. DAVIS, and LAURA PENDERGEST-HOLT, Case No.: 3:09-cv-0298-N" F. (**www.sec.gov/litigation/complaints/2009/stanford-first-amended-022709.pdf**)

Securities and Exchange Commission. *Insider Trading: Information on Bounties. Modified January 6, 2006*. U.S. Securities and Exchange Commission. SEC.gov. (**www.sec.gov/divisions/enforce/insider.htm**)

Securities and Exchange Commission. "Securities and Exchange Commission v. Samuel D. Waksal." LITIGATION RELEASE NO. 18026. 02-CIV-4407 (NB)(S.D.N.Y.) Washington, D.C. March 11, 2003. (**www.sec.gov/litigation/litreleases/lr18026.htm**)

Securities and Exchange Commission. *Staff Accounting Bulletin No. 104: Revenue Recognition, corrected copy*. SEC.gov. Dec. 17, 2003. (**www.sec.gov/interps/account.shtml**)

Securities and Exchange Commission. "The Coca-Cola Company Settles Antifraud And Periodic Reporting Charges Relating To Its Failure To Disclose Japanese Gallon Pushing." *Press Release 2005-58*. Securities and Exchange Commission. 2005-58. Washington, D.C., April 18, 2005. (**www.sec.gov/news/press/2005-58.htm**)

Securities and Exchange Commission. "United States Of America Before The Securities And Exchange Commission. Securities Exchange Act of 1934, Release No. 42781 / May 15,2000. Accounting and Auditing Enforcement, Release No. 1257 / May 15, 2000. Administrative Proceeding, File No. 3-10203." (**www.sec.gov/litigation/admin/34-42781.htm**)

"Sentenced in embezzlement." *The Emporia Gazette.* September 9, 2009. (**www.emporiagazette.com/news/2009/sep/09/sentenced_embezzlement/**)

Smith, Kim. "Tucson Museum of Arts worker arraigned in $973,000 theft." **Arizona Daily Star**. Tucson, Arizona. May 4, 2009. (**www.museum-security.org/?p=2133**)

Smith, Martin. "The Madoff Affair." *FRONTLINE.* May 9, 2009. (**www.pbs.org/wgbh/pages/frontline/madoff/view/**)

Speer, Lawrence J. "Magazine raided in Renault espionage case." *Automotive News.* July 16, 2008. (**www.autonews.com/article/20080716/COPY01/960676731/1018**)

Spirgel, Larry and Grover, Gavin B. Sarbanes-Oxley "Hotline" Procedures: Who Should Be Doing the Listening?. Morrison & Foerster LLP. 2003. Findlaw.com (**http://library.findlaw.com/2003/May/27/132768.html**)

"Stanford bank in Antigua seized," BBC.com. February 21, 2009. (**http://news.bbc.co.uk/2/hi/business/7902667.stm**)

"Starwood sues Hilton Hotels over alleged corporate espionage." *Hotel Check-in. USA Today.* April 16, 2009. (**http://content.usatoday.com/communities/hotelcheckin/post/2009/04/65574153/1**)

"Statement of Shareholders' Equity." FinancialEducation.com. (**http://financial-education.com/2007/03/15/statement-of-shareholders-equity/**)

Sullivan, Bob. "40 million credit cards exposed: Payment processor blamed in mishap." *msnbc.com.* June 20, 2005. (**www.msnbc.msn.com/ id/8260050/**)

The American Institute of Certified Public Accountants. *Private Company Financial Reporting, Task Force Report.* AICPA.org. February 28, 2005. (**www.aicpa.org/members/div/acctstd/pvtco_fincl_reprt/download/ Report_Draft_Final.pdf**)

Urban, Mike. "Reading School District withholds diplomas as it investigates grade-changing scheme at high school." *Reading Eagle.* June 4, 2009. (**http://readingeagle.com/article.aspx?id=141523**)

U.S. Census Bureau. "Single-Parent Households Showed Little Variation Since 1994," *Census Bureau Reports, U.S. Census Bureau News.* March 27, 2007. (**www.census.gov/Press-Release/www/releases/archives/families_ households/009842.html**)

United States Attorney's Office, District of South Carolina. "Two Lawyers Indicted, One Pleads Guilty to Money Laundering, Mail Fraud Conspiracy." September 18, 2009. (**http://columbia.fbi.gov/dojpressrel/2009/ co091809a.htm**)

United States Attorney's Office, Southern District of New York. "Manhattan U.S. Attorney Charges Chairman And Chief Executive Officer of Nemazee Capital With Bank Fraud." *Press Release.* August 25, 2009. (**www.usdoj. gov/usao/nys/pressreleases/August09/nemazeehassancomplaintpr.pdf**)

U.S. Department of Justice. "Former Accounting Supervisor of Local Company Indicted for Embezzling Millions from Employer." Federal Bureau of Investigation Houston. *Press Release.* September 2, 2009. (**http:// houston.fbi.gov/dojpressrel/pressrel09/ho090209.htm**)

U.S. Department of Justice. *The Foreign Corrupt Practices Act of 1977* (FCPA). (**www.justice.gov/criminal/fraud/fcpa/**)

U.S. Department of Justice, United States Attorney John C. Richter, Western District of Oklahoma. "Former Apache Tribal Secretary-Treasurer/Tax Commissioner Convicted Of Embezzling From Tribe; Evidence Showed Over $107,000 of Tribal Tax Funds Diverted." *Press release.* December 12, 2008. (**http://oklahomacity.fbi.gov/dojpressrel/pressrel08/oc121208.htm**)

U.S. Department of Justice Press Release. United States Attorney, Northern District of Illinois. "THREE FORMER NICOR ENERGY EXECUTIVES AND OUTSIDE LAWYER INDICTED IN ALLEGED CORPORATE FRAUD SCHEME." 2003. (**www.fbi.gov/dojpressrel/pressrel03/nicor121003.htm**)

U.S. Department of Justice. "United States Of America V. Vivian K. Williams." In The United States District Court For The Eastern District Of Pennsylvania. (**www.usdoj.gov/usao/pae/News/Pr/2009/jul/williamsinfo.pdf**)

U.S. Library of Congress. *Private Company Research, Business Reference Services.* (**www.loc.gov/rr/business/company/private.html**)

Watson, Brian P. "Fraud Detection Software: Shutting the Door on Scam Artists." *Baseline.* June 7, 2006. (**www.baselinemag.com/c/a/Projects-Security/Fraud-Detection-Software-Shutting-the-Door-on-Scam-Artists**)

WAVY-TV10."VB woman pleads guilty to embezzlement." *WAVY.com.* September 4, 2009. (**www.wavy.com/dpp/news/crime/local_wavy_norfolk_vb_woman_pleads_guilty_20090904**)

Wells, Joseph T. *Corporate fraud handbook: prevention and detection.* Hoboken, N.J.: John Wiley & Sons. 2007.

Witosky, Tom. "Des Moines woman accused of embezzling $5.9 million from Aviva." *Des Moines Register.* Des Moines, Iowa. September 30, 2009.

"Woman Indicted In Aviva Embezzlement Case." KCCI.com. October 23, 2009. (**www.kcci.com/news/21403259/detail.html**)

Yancey, Kim. "Embezzlement suspect jailed: Former city employee turns herself in." by *Los Banos Enterprise.* California. August 28, 2009. (**www. losbanosenterprise.com/114/story/45948.html**)

 # AUTHOR BIOGRAPHY

Martha Maeda is an economic historian who writes on politics, ethics, finance, and modern philosophy. After graduating from Northwestern University, she lived and worked in Australia, Japan, Latin America, and several African countries before settling in the United States. She has a particular interest in micro-economics and the effects of globalization on the lives and businesses of people all over the world.

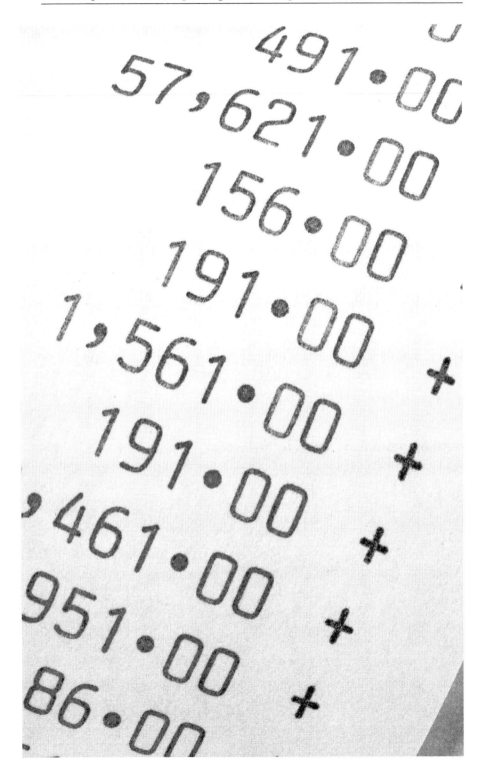

INDEX

Ponzi Scheme, 315, 323-324, 176, 194-195, 298, 9, 14

Price rigging, 139

Proxy statement, 231, 237, 265

Public Company Accounting Oversight Board, 304, 316, 197

Pyramid Scheme, 14

R

Ratio analysis, 78, 91, 213, 217

Rubber-stamp supervisors, 116

S

Sarbanes-Oxley Act, 303-304, 316-317, 26, 54, 183, 197-198, 200-203

Shell company, 315, 317, 96-97, 100-101, 124, 143

Skimming, 317, 321, 62, 66-69, 71-72, 75-78, 80, 83, 90-91, 101, 210, 218

Surprise audit, 86

T

Tax evasion, 27, 41, 47

U

U.S. Government Accountability Office, 141

Understated expenses, 187

Understated sales, 69

V

Vertical analysis, 318, 252, 215

Voucher, 318, 96, 129

W

Whistleblower, 318, 196, 199, 201-202, 211

White-collar crime, 301, 269, 32, 44, 141, 165, 202